P9-CLS-201

COUNTRY GIRL

Also by Edna O'Brien

FICTION

The Country Girls
The Lonely Girl
Girls in Their Married Bliss
August Is a Wicked Month
Casualties of Peace
The Love Object and Other Stories
A Pagan Place
Zee and Co.
Night
A Scandalous Woman and Other Stories
A Rose in the Heart
Returning
A Fanatic Heart
The High Road
Lantern Slides
House of Splendid Isolation
Down by the River
Wild Decembers
In the Forest
The Light of the Evening
Saints and Sinners

NONFICTION

Mother Ireland
James Joyce (biography)
Byron in Love

DRAMA

A Pagan Place
Virginia (The Life of Virginia Woolf)
Family Butchers
Triptych
Haunted

COUNTRY GIRL

A MEMOIR

EDNA O'BRIEN

Little, Brown and Company
NEW YORK BOSTON LONDON

Little, Brown and Company
Hachette Book Group
237 Park Avenue, New York, NY 10017
littlebrown.com

First North American Edition: April 2013
Originally published in Great Britain by Faber and Faber Limited, October 2012

Little, Brown and Company is a division of Hachette Book Group, Inc. The Little, Brown name and logo are trademarks of Hachette Book Group, Inc.

Library of Congress Cataloging-in-Publication Data
O'Brien, Edna.
Country girl : a memoir / Edna O'Brien.—First North American edition.
pages cm
ISBN 978-0-316-12270-2
1. O'Brien, Edna. 2. Women authors, Irish—20th century—Biography.
I. Title.
PR6065.B7Z46 2013
823'.914—dc23
[B] 2012047510

10 9 8 7 6 5 4 3 2 1

RRD-C

Printed in the United States of America

For my warrior sons,
Carlo and Sasha Gébler

It was when I got here I really realized—I'm here.

—TYSON GAY, AMERICAN SPRINTER,
ON THE EVE OF THE LONDON 2012 OLYMPICS

Contents

PART THREE

PART FOUR

COUNTRY GIRL

Prologue

I was in a National Health clinic in London, and an amiable girl with a mass of brown hair and a foreign accent had tested me for deafness. "You are quite well, but with regard to your hearing, you are broken piano." She looked to see if this had any disquieting effect upon me and then reeled off the hazards of old age. Finally, she wrote down the day and the date on which I could come and collect my two hearing aids, which I dutifully did, though I have failed to befriend them. They slipped like little ball bearings into the cavity of my ears, and retrieving them was hazardous. In fact, they are back in the brown envelope in which they came.

At home the garden was waiting, the second flowering of the roses, washed pink and blowsy but beautiful, and the massed leaves on the three fig trees were a ripple as birds darted in and out, chasing each other, half in courtship and half in combat.

"Broken piano" in all its connotations kept saying itself to me, and yet I thought of life's many bounties—to have known the extremities of joy and sorrow, love, crossed love and unrequited love, success and failure, fame and slaughter, to have read in the newspapers that as a writer I was past my sell-by date, and moreover a "bargain basement Molly Bloom," yet, regardless, to go on writing and reading, to be lucky enough to be able to immerse myself in those two intensities that have buttressed my whole life.

I got out a cookery book from Ballymaloe House in County Cork, where I'd stayed a couple of times and partook of delicacies such as nettle soup, carrageen moss soufflé, lemon posset with rose-scented geranium, and gooseberry frangipane with baby banoffees. It was where I had seen for the first time and been astonished by Jack Yeats's paintings, thick palettes of curdled blues that spoke to me then as deeply of Ireland as any poem or fragment of prose could do. I looked up the recipe for soda bread and did something that I had not done in thirty-odd years. I made bread. Broken piano or not, I felt very alive, as the smell of the baking bread filled the air. It was an old smell, the begetter of many a memory, and so on that day in August, in my seventy-eighth year, I sat down to begin the memoir which I swore I would never write.

PART ONE

Ghosts

The two dreams could not be more contrasting. In one I am walking up the avenue, toward Drewsboro, the house I was born in, and it is a veritable temple. The gold light on the windowpanes, rivering, the rooms flooded in a warm pink light for a feasting within, and along the paling wire, torches of flame, furling, unfurling. As I slide the hasp of the gate and walk toward the hall door, I see the line of men in livery, soldiers, the tips of their spears red-hot through and through, as if they have just been pulled out of fire. These are hard men that bar the way.

In the second dream, I am in the house in the blue room where I was born. Doors and windows all locked, and even the space under the door, where motes of dust used to sidle, is sealed with some sort of wadding. The furniture is as it was—a double wardrobe of walnut with matching dressing table and washstand. There is the slop bucket in green, with a plaited basket button. I am there, alone, incarcerated. All the others have died. I am there to answer for my crimes. It makes no difference that my interrogators are all dead.

It seems to me that I saw things before I actually saw them; they were always there, the way I believe that the words are always there, coursing through us. I think, for instance, that I recognized the blue walls of the blue room, walls weeping quietly away from endless damp and no fire, even though there was a fire grate, ridiculously small compared with the size of the room, in which the lid of a chocolate box had been laid as an ornament. And Our Lady? She was not the sallow creature in paintings that I would come to see on different walls, but a buxom Our Lady of Limerick, with a host of infants around her ankles, as though she had just given birth to them. Her accouchement was far happier than that of my mother, who would talk of it down the years: her labor, her long labor, the night in December and the black frost that was usual for that time of year, the midwife late and the hullabaloo, which turned out to be needless, on being told that I had club feet because I came into the world the wrong way. The child before me had died in infancy, but I always believed that she wasn't dead, she was in one of the bedrooms, in a cupboard, or a nightdress case, and after I learned to walk, I would never go up there alone, not even in daylight.

My father and his brother, Jack, were downstairs drinking, and on being told the good news they staggered up, bringing strips of goose which they had just cooked, it being the Christmas season. In my mother's telling of it, the goose was half-cooked, pink and tough. Jack gave a rendering of "Red River Valley":

> Come and sit by my side, if you love me
> Do not hasten to bid me adieu
> Just remember the Red River Valley
> And the cowboy who loved you so true.

I was an ugly child, so ugly that when Ger McNamara, the son of the couple who lived in our gate lodge and a captain in the Irish army, came to congratulate her, my mother said I was too unsightly to be shown and therefore kept me hidden under the red herringbone quilt.

Such is the ragbag of anecdote, hearsay, allegory, and consternation that filled the canvas of my early life, at once beautiful and frightening, tender and savage.

My mother, Lena, Boston, 1920.

Drewsboro was a large two-storey house, with bay windows, and could be approached by two avenues, an old and a new. The goldish sandstone of which it was built was from the burnt ruin of a "Big House" that had belonged to the English and that had been burnt in the Troubles, during the 1920s. My mother, as a young girl, would be invited to the annual garden party held each year for the local peasantry, where they were served iced buns and homemade lemonade with wasps swarming the buffet table.

Drewsboro owed something to the stylish houses my mother had seen in America. There were ornamental piers on the gateway, bay windows, and a tiled porch that was called a vestibule opening into a tiled hallway. No other house around there had bay windows or a vestibule. The lawn had many trees, not planted in succession as in a demesne, but each tree in its own massive empire, leaves stirring and drowsing in summer and in winter, the boughs groaning and creaking, as if they were about to expire.

By the time I was born we were no longer rich. True, we had the large house and the two avenues, but the thousand acres or more that my father had inherited had been sold off in bits, or given away in fits of generosity, or bartered to pay debts. My father had inherited a fortune from rich uncles who, when they were ordained as priests, emigrated to New England and served in the parish of Lowell, outside Boston. There, they combined spiritual and secular powers by patenting a medicine called Father John's, which was reputed to be a cure for everything and sold by the gallon.

Not far from our house was the ruin of the old house, also called Drewsboro, which like many big houses had been burned in order that the English militia, the Black and Tans, could not occupy them as a barracks. My father took part in that burning and would describe the high spirits with which he and other gallants doused rags in petrol, then went all around with the petrol cans, soaking walls and woodwork. Scores of matches were struck, and the subsequent bonfire, seen for miles around, was another notch of victory over the invader.

Long before, Lord and Lady Drew had lived there, and the story went that the ghost of Lady Drew, in her shift, roamed our fields at night, wailing the loss of her acres, a woman dispossessed.

My great-grandmother, who was widowed, acquired that house from the Drews, the money having come from the priests in Lowell. She was a haughty woman, who was driven in her pony and trap each Sunday to view her lands and her herds and then onward to glimpse the red deer as they rushed from their brakes into the heart of the wood, where oak, ash, and beech had grown into one another. By the time I was growing up, that wood had become the preserve of foxes, stoats, badgers, and pine martens who warred in the night as our dogs, too frightened to go in there, barked hysterically from the outskirts.

Though she lived alone, she would dress each evening for dinner, always in black, with a white lace ruff, and she drank toddies from a silver-topped horn cup that bore the questionable motto of the O'Briens—"Might Before Right." She was waited upon by a factotum named Dan Egan, and there was a verse about him, as indeed there were verses about many local people:

Dan Egan's in Drewsboro
The Wattles at the Gate
Manny Parker's in the Avenue
And the Nigger's walking straight.

The Nigger had a strawberry face that wasn't black but dark puce, with berries hanging from it. He worked in a slate quarry. Manny Parker was a hermit who claimed to be a botanist, roamed our fields, and sometimes slept in a tent in our bog so that he could study the habits of birds and insects who, like himself, eschewed chimney corners and barn and church porches. The Wattles were so named because a daughter had gone to Australia and used the word frequently in her letters home. A postcard of hers that opened out concertina-wise, showing reefs and blue islands, was displayed on their front window.

I preferred the outdoors, fields that ran into other fields, storm and sleet, showers and sun showers; then, as if by enchantment, primroses and cowslips sprang up next to the tall thistles and fresh cowpats that were elegantly called "pancakes." Time flew out there, but indoors was different, being often fraught.

My mother's family was different from my father's, poor people evicted from the wealthier environs of County Kildare who trudged across the central plain, met the mountains, and, in a godforsaken place, built a cabin on a bit of stone land. It was about five miles from Drewsboro, and I sometimes attribute my two conflicting selves to my contrasting grandparents, the one a lady, the other a peasant. Quite recently this was brought home to me when I was approached by an Irish newspaper to have my DNA tested, along with other people with historic family names. I balked at the procedure, but the journalist assured me that when I received the kit, he would tell me exactly what to do and what it entailed, which indeed he did. The swab was returned, and in due course I was told that, according to their findings, I share DNA with the last tsarina of Russia, Marie Antoinette, and Susan Sarandon. Asked what I felt about the royal lineage, I flinched at the unfortunate fate of the first two, and my efforts to reach Susan Sarandon proved futile.

The ruins of the big house held a fascination for me. Along with the weasels, there were the signs of its former life: torn tongues of dark green wallpaper embossed with acorns hung in the reception room, and in the kitchen there was a set of gongs with thick crusts of verdigris, the green and silver brilliancies of bygone days. On a high mound of rubble was an elderberry tree that birds must have seeded, and my mother and I would pick the berries to make wine, which had to be hidden from my father, who might be tempted by it and after a mere sip go on the batter. It was reserved for visitors, who, apart from tinkers and Mad Mabel, were few and far between. The rungs of a staircase dangled down into what had once been a ballroom, feeding the various fantasies that I contrived, of balls, carriages along the back avenue, and footmen rushing out with lit sods of turf to help the visitors down. There would be pipers in the forecourt and tables with jugs of mulled wine, and feasting as in the sagas of old. My great-grandmother I pictured in black taffeta with an ermine coatee and a corsage, maybe violets or some other woodland flower. My mother, hearing these ravings, would smile, but then frown, desperate as she was to keep everything together and possibly sensing that the prodigal blood of the O'Briens reigned uppermost in me, rather than the blood of her own people, the Clearys, who clung steadfastly to their little mountain holding.

Once, when I got home from school, a bailiff was sitting in our kitchen, drinking tea. He was an affable man, and before long he spoke to me, asked about school and what I had learned that day. Then he asked me to recite a poem. I recited "Fontenoy," a heroic ballad of Irish earls and chieftains, banished and serving in foreign brigades all over Europe, missing their native soil. It was very rousing and patriotic as, even on the brink of battle, they thirsted, they starved, for their native County Clare.

My mother called me into the pantry and put her finger to her upper lip to signify that I must tell no one of the disgrace we were in. My father had gone out, presumably to borrow money, and it was near dark when he returned and conferred with the bailiff, who then left. Disaster was postponed. Then ructions. Horses. Horses, the waste they were, strutting around the fields eating all before them, having to be sent to stud farm to be covered, eating up still more money and losing races, as my mother saw it, out of pure spite. There was one, Shannon Rose, which she singled out for particular odium, saying that the filly could come first, if she wanted to, but chose to come third, the difference between the two prize monies being exorbitant. It ended with my father going up to bed, which was far preferable to his going out, where he would be tempted, in anger and frustration, to drink.

Horses always loomed in my mind as dangers, creatures that led to argument and pending destitution, their eyes so moist and shining in contrast to their movements, which were jerky and unpredictable as they whinnied their way from one field to the next. I would see them in the fields and then again in my mind's eye—that great unleashing of energy, when they exploded as one into a mad gallop, their flying tails arched up, moving with such daring, such speed, showered in the dust they had raised and in their exhilaration seeming to float.

Two summers ago a plaque was unveiled in my honor on one of the piers that led to the old avenue. Unlike the time when I was considered something of a Jezebel because of my books, now from the altar the priest spoke of the honor that it was to have me back and encouraged people to attend the ceremony. There was a small crowd, children cycling in and out, bursting with laughter, as I made a short speech on the influence Drewsboro had on my writing. "A font of inspiration" was the phrase I used, at which children laughed even more.

It was a warm summer evening, and afterward my nephew Michael and I picked our steps over the high grass and crawled under loops of barbed wire to visit the house. It was going back to nature: trees and briars and bushes had moved in like an army to overtake it. Ivy and saplings climbed up to where the cut stone met the plaster, along with shoots and briars and ferns that wove their way, to get a grip, establishing their ownership of the place, as none of the living had succeeded in doing. Even the wild cats had gone. Some red, ribbony roses that my mother had planted threaded their way through the fallen hedging, and, picking a few as a keepsake for me, Michael cut himself, the red spurt of blood as vivid and alive as the stored memories. This the house my mother strove to keep together, this the house she swore she would never give to her thankless son, this the house with our unfinished stories and our unfinished quarrels with one another.

My mother and father, Lena and Michael O'Brien, in Drewsboro, 1970s.

My mother's death was sudden. I had gone to see her in the Mater Hospital in Dublin, where she had been admitted with shingles. With a nun, Sister R., who had become her friend, she smeared a brown ointment over them; it was one she had got from a faith healer, and they both believed that it would cure her. She was due to be discharged in a week, but calling me over to the side of the bed, she said that we would have to go down home, just for the day. I was to fix it with the matron and the registrar, and hire a car to bring us there and back. It was like this. Long ago, when they were in danger of losing the place completely, my father, after one of his drinking sprees and in contrition, had signed the place over to her, as she would be a better manager of things. Two years before and after much insistence, my brother, John, had asked her to make a will, saying he and his wife would accompany her to the solicitors. She made the will, giving him Drewsboro, believing in her heart that at a later date she could make another. What she wanted now was to go down home in secret and make the second will, giving me the house and the surrounding lawn. I said there was no hurry, it could all be done in the fullness of time and openly, when she was recovered.

To this day, no matter how I try to reconstruct it, I cannot arrive at the exact moment of my mother's death, although I know the circumstances of it. It was in March 1977. I was in the airplane returning from New York, and, when I got home, the telephone was ringing; it was my sister, giving me the news. Later, from Sister R., I learned of the several comings and goings of that last flurried day. My mother was going home. A driver was coming to collect her. Since breakfast she had been ready, dressed for travel, sitting on her bed with a walking frame and a walking stick, which the nun had given her on the quiet, to take with her as a gift for her husband. In the days leading up to her going home she had been indiscreet, telling various nurses how proud she was of her intention of changing her will. One nurse, who boasted about being a friend of my brother's, rang him urgently at his practice in Monasterevin to tell him of the crooked plan his mother was hatching. He arrived in an utter fury. Unluckily Sister R., signed up that day for a course at the university, was not present for the ugly confrontation, but as she told me in a letter, when she did return at lunchtime and popped in to say "Hello," she found that between mother and son there was a ghastly tension.

"A pity you couldn't have come sooner," my mother had said to her, barely able to hold back her tears, and the nun, not wishing to interfere in family grief, excused herself. My brother, it seems, left some time after, and still dressed for travel, my mother waited for the driver from home, who was already a few hours late.

Sister R.'s letter was handed to me in the chapel by the undertaker, after the coffin was brought in and laid down on its trestle, and it was there that I read it. She described her hurried visit at lunchtime and how later she learned that my mother had not yet left and so went to see her, only to find that she was in the lavatory and could be heard calling plaintively. She was brought out, and, as she got paler and began to tremble, the cardiac arrest team was called and she was wheeled, bed and all, into the operating theater. When I read Sister R.'s words "I had to let go of her," I realized what a deep friendship had sprung up between them in so short a time. It seems that briefly, as they waited to put in a pacemaker, my mother rallied, sat up, and, in one last desperate attempt at greatness, she asked those around her not to cry, for "death shall be no more." I never felt closer to my mother than when I heard those words that had come from her lips, she who had found literature to be inimical had nevertheless uttered those words as a farewell.

It was after her funeral that the local solicitor came to our house in order for the will to be read aloud. We were a small group, my father crying, saying repeatedly we had lost the best friend in the world, my sister with her husband, my other sister absent because of living in South Africa, my children and myself. On the opposite side of the fireplace, in which no fire blazed and into which my father had thrown hundreds of cigarette butts in the twelve days of her absence, stood my brother and his wife. I could feel the hover of my mother's ghost as the door of the china cabinet swung open when anyone walked by it. I could hear her voice, lamenting the little teacups with the motifs of violets that got cracked, but were kept, to put sugar-loaf in. The will was short. She had left Drewsboro and the adjoining lands to her son and, should he predecease her, to his wife. Each of the three daughters got mementos, china, silver, and glass. There was a silence, then my brother, in high theatricality, put an arm around his wife's waist and said, "My darling, now we all know who Mam really loved."

I thought his words so smug, so hollow, and pictured my mother in her last hours, sitting on the bed, alone and stranded, shaking from the quarrel he had brought upon her, and I realized that she did have some intimation of her sudden death the day she begged of me to go down to Clare with her so that she could change her will, because as I was leaving she clung to my hand and said, "I hope I get out of here alive."

Yet my brother and his wife never lived there, choosing instead to go to their own bungalow in Mount Shannon about five miles hence, which he had bought for his retirement. Some fear or phobia had so possessed them that they did not spend one night in Drewsboro, merely left a radio on, padlocked the bedroom doors, threw dust sheets on the good sofa, and had barbed wire and electric fences erected to keep us out. Now they were dead, and as Michael told me, rumors abounded, such as that there was going to be a nursing home or a five-star hotel, or the house would be razed to the ground as a site for a hundred bungalows.

But in the lambent light of that August evening, with the sun going down, a bit of creeper crimsoning and latticed along an upstairs window, the whole place seemed to hold, and would forever hold, for me, regardless of bungalows or a five-star hotel, the essence of itself, the thing that gave it the sacred and abiding name of Home.

Abdullah

The field that led up to the house was called the lawn, but that was a misnomer. Horses and cattle sometimes grazed there, and as a result the ground was torn and tussocky, which in winter they called *poached.* It was high summer, no end of ragwort and dandelions and thistles as high as myself, being about three at that time, and the animals shifted to elsewhere.

Feeling adventurous as well as curious, I decided to walk as far as the lower gate and through the rungs look at the outside world, by which I was fascinated. Unbeknownst to my mother, I had put on my best blue dress, the one that had come from America and that boasted the Stars and Stripes in the folds of the box pleating.

We had three dogs at that time. Two chummed together and went off all day hunting foxes and rabbits, and came back in the evenings smelling of fresh blood. The third was short-haired, the color of smoke, a sulky animal, a cross between a Kerry blue and breeds with unmatching eyes. He belonged to my uncle, who for some reason had left him with us. His name was Abdullah, and he passed his days lying in hiding down near the lower gate, so as to be able to jump up and assault any vehicle or person that approached. The postman and callers were in dread of him.

I had forgotten that he might be there, and seeing me, he crawled along the ground, snarling, snarling, and then jumped up, and what perhaps had been intended as some wild sport soon became vicious. He was jumping up and down, frothing and snapping at my knees, when I made a run back to the house, which was the worst thing I could have done. This gave vent to his rage. He was prone to fits, for which he used to be given powders and then locked up, and obviously a fresh fit had come upon him. He was literally going mad, tearing at the dress, spitting bits of it out, but was still tethered to me as I ran and ran, fearing that not an ounce of breath was left in my windpipe. At the wicket gate, I eluded him for a few seconds, but quickly he found a way through a hole that he had long made in the hedge and was in the kitchen almost as soon as I was. I had jumped up on a chair for safety and from that leaped onto the table, where he followed, and presently I keeled over under his weight and felt the bite, his teeth like nails boring into my neck, and the scoop of flesh that he was trying to bite off. It was probably no more than a minute, an eternity of a minute, when someone, not my mother or father and not our workman Carnero, but a total stranger, happened to pass by the window and, seeing Abdullah in a terrific lather, thought he had climbed up to get at the hunk of bread. He rushed in, pulled Abdullah to the floor, kicked him several times, then by the short hairs dragged him from the kitchen, down over the flag and into the pump house, where Abdullah hurled himself against the galvanized door and let out rending whines.

Everything so quiet then. Only the steam from a kettle, its sound sidling through the air, until they came, saw the gash in the neck, the toothmarks, the blood, the blue dress in flitters, asking repeatedly how such a thing could have happened. Peakie, the man who had saved me, was being congratulated on the fact that he had heard screams as he passed by with a bag of turf.

The wound did not heal, and soon a swelling the size of an egg cup ballooned out and had to be pierced with a needle each morning for the pus to be discharged. The fear was that it had reinfected an earlier tubercular gland; on hearing TB, which is how they referred to it, I thought I was preparing for death. A girl in my older sister's class had died of it, just wasted away. I was given little biscuits called Irish Diamonds that were covered with icing, some round, some triangular, and some shaped like a starburst.

The smell I principally remember is that of iodoform gauze, two patches of it, held down with plaster, in the belief that by hiding it, the wound would go away. Yet before long there were two smells, the nice smell of the gauze and the putrid smell of paste. A lady doctor, whom my father was on saluting terms with, was asked to look at it: she wrinkled her nose several times, her nose which was covered with an unbecoming orange powder, and went, "Hm, hm, hm," to my mother, saying it called for the knife.

Two mornings later she returned. I can still see her Baby Ford motorcar and her in a fur coat and felt hat with a huge pearled hat pin that had dents in it. Her doctor's bag of brown leather was most imposing. It was squat at the bottom, the leather tucked in and narrowing along the sides to reach the bright, brazen, brass hasp. She unlocked it in an instant, and my father, peering in, said, "All the tools of the trade, Dr. McCann."

He had been smoking, but anticipating the task ahead, he quenched his unfinished cigarette and restored it to the Gold Flake package. My sisters were ordered to go out on the flag and do their step dancing and hum loudly. I knew without knowing that something awful was about to happen. Carnero came in, sheepish-looking, and a man painting the chimney pots followed, his white overalls spattered with red paint. In a saucepan of boiling water instruments were being sterilized and my mother was telling me that if I was a good girl, there would be a reward. Then the moment has come, and the three men grasp my head in different places and tilt it to one side.

Their strengths are massive. I thought of pigs having their throats slit up in the yard and the roars they let out and resolved that I too would roar, except for the fact that a big paw had muzzled me. The slash of the knife as it tore at the flesh and into the flesh was utter, different from that of the dog's teeth, and I believed that my head was coming off. In the delirium and ridiculously, I started to recite "Humpty Dumpty," who had had a great fall and whom all the King's Horses and all the King's Men could not put together again. The last bout of screaming was apparently so loud that it was heard down on the road, yet to me it seemed feeble, imprisoned in the pouch of hands that smelled of tobacco.

Then oblivion, a no-time, and gradually coming back to life and hearing the single words as through a fog—"Creature—it's all right now"—while the doctor with her sewing needle and thickish thread had begun to stitch the wound. My mother was thanking her profusely, whereas I could hardly believe that my head was still attached to me, since I thought that, like John the Baptist's, it would by now be on a platter. The big bandage was a shield between them and me, all of them and me. The reward was a slice of orange cake with lemon curd, but I would not eat it and I would not speak.

"She'll never forgive us," I heard Carnero say, and saw my mother clout him, telling him to go off to the fields and not talk such balderdash.

I was allowed to finger my sister's rosary beads, which were kept in a little silver reliquary that I coveted. They were blue and glassy, and I remember the feel of each one and how I squeezed it.

Ever after, in fearful times, I had to hold on to something, anything, to defer annihilation.

The Dining Room

The dining room was Heaven. I named it so. There was an arbutus table, its deep, red-brown hues so striking, a table that could, by the addition of a spare leaf, seat twenty, though I had never seen anyone sit at it. There was as well a bamboo whatnot on which a wise white owl presided, dust congealing in the folds of its breast feathers. My mother had a craze for overmantel mirrors, and a gorgeous one in a gilt frame hung above the fireplace, except it was hung so high that one had to stand on the curb of the tiled surround and crane to see oneself.

I still recall the rapture as a child, gazing, gazing at a great amphora of artificial tea roses in yellow and red, far more beautiful than the dog roses on the briars or the devil's pokers in the garden outside, which, because of the way they smoldered, somehow looked spiteful. In that same room, filled with ornaments, were the busts of two plaster-of-Paris ladies, whom my mother named Iris and Gala, and whose cheeks she lovingly rouged. On the sideboard were a few pieces of silver and a jam dish of cloudy, yellow Vaseline glass, with a spoon that hung from the handle that bore the image of the Pope, in scarlet mantle and small, tasseled skullcap. To lick that spoon was a guarantee of a partial indulgence, which meant a few hours less in Purgatory in the next world.

I used to sit there, admiring the room and its pale yellow walls and the two paintings depicting waves that were descending violently on a range of gray-black cliffs, somewhere in England. It was there, on top of the china cabinet, that I kept dolls which a Protestant woman, a friend of my mother's, had sent to me each Christmas. First was the Princess, whom I called Rosaleen, a sleeping doll, cheeks vivid as if colored with fresh cochineal, and eyelashes that by a mere tilt of the head would exquisitely flutter. The doll the following year was male, a little Dutch drummer boy in red and fawn, a velvet pajama suit and a drummer's orange hat. He too came in an oblong box, snug inside folds of tissue paper, and one day I did what I dimly knew to be a profane thing. I took the little drummer boy and laid him over the Princess in her blue taffeta dress, with its apron of net, put the lid back on, and left them to their mischiefs.

On another occasion, a neighbor's daughter called Eily sat in one of the high straight-backed chairs in our dining room, her eyes dark and shiny as ink, her face lovely and trustful, waiting for a sweetheart to come while my mother came and went on tiptoe, watching for the figure that must appear beyond the glass paneling of the hall door, which was without knocker or doorbell. Only two days before Eily and my mother had walked three miles to the doctor in the next town-land, since she was, as she put it, suffering from heartburn. I went with them. It was on the Lake Road, a hot day, waves and wavelets dancing on the water and a little breeze that came in wafts, except that there was no curing my mother's deep suspicions. She kept asking if *it* was possible. The word "pregnancy" was not uttered, partly because of my being there and partly because it was too terrible for it to be said. Eily would grasp my mother's hand in umbrage and then, in an orgy of lamentation, would ask how could my mother think such a thing, and then both women would cry. I was too afraid to glance at her stomach, in case some stirrings would reveal the truth. Again and again my mother repeated her key question, and by the time we got to the doctor's surgery, Eily had clamped her hands over her ears, deaf to everything.

The visit to the doctor did not go as they had hoped and no cure was forthcoming.

Next evening, her sweetheart arrived and the couple were left to confer alone. Later my mother announced wedding plans in June to my father, who was oblivious to all this furor. Telling the girl's parents was a quite different matter, and it is probable that the full truth was withheld. All they knew was that Eily was marrying and that the groom was coming to pay a visit.

Their good room led off the kitchen and was full of oats, which naturally had to be cleared out, and some pieces of furniture had to be procured. My mother helped by giving a wooden garden seat which she had varnished and then decorated, running a sharp nail, zigzag-wise, over the wet varnish to create a mottled effect. Eily's mother had somehow found a small side table that was covered with a red chenille cloth. There was a new sheepskin rug that smelled of the butcher's and was still shedding its hairs. The fire was in two minds about taking off, as there had never been a fire in that grate before. The groom arrived, wearing a leather raincoat and leather gauntlet gloves, which he removed and tossed aside, with some grandeur. He was given the best chair. Eily sat on the window ledge, not looking at him or at anyone and twirling the ends of her wavy, auburn hair. My mother and Eily's mother shared the wooden seat, and my father, who was standing, smoked and looked out at rain pouring from a gully into a rain barrel that overflowed onto a flat field beyond.

The first faux pas happened when Eily's father came in, his wet cap dripping onto the point of his nose; suddenly alarmed at the altered state of the room and the elegance of it, he turned to my father and said, "Am I in my own house at all, mister?" He called all other men mister because, having had no education, he reckoned that others were scholars and deserving of his respect. Then he shook the groom's hand and called him mister.

The conversation turned to the crops: some corn already lodged in the fields from so much rain and whether it would not have been better to have used it for pasture.

I shall never forget the giddy elation in Eily's expression when she jumped up, stood in front of the fire, and thanked everyone profusely for being so good to her. Her father, who loved her and who must have suddenly guessed the implications of what she had just said, ran out of the room, for fear of crying. The tea and porter cake came next.

The couple moved away soon after that, to the opposite end of the county, where the wedding was held, and many years later I saw Eily in Grafton Street in Dublin, much older, her eyes scared, those eyes the color of dark slate and that many had envied. She was talking to herself in a mad, high-pitched voice and scolding people whom she imagined to be staring at her.

Also in that dining room, my mother and I once narrowly escaped death. My father had gone in there with a bottle of whiskey and a revolver that had belonged to my mother's brother, Captain Michael. It was on top of a wardrobe, with a leather holster and bullets. In there, he vowed havoc and slaughter on all of us and on families along the road who had refused him drink, and eventually the sergeant was called and went in to reason with him. After a while, when they had obviously been arguing fiercely, the sergeant came out and said the only person he would give the gun to was my mother, and I went in with her to be her protector.

My father kept swinging the loaded revolver, jauntily, as if it were a toy. My mother asked in a pacifying voice, what did he want? What was it he wanted? He wanted money. "Give it to me. Give it to me," he kept saying. He did not believe that she did not have any, and he put the revolver down on the bamboo whatnot and crossed and stood before us. Then he searched inside her bodice, where she sometimes kept money and where I, and no doubt he, had sometimes seen the jut of an orange-tinted ten-shilling note. She was shaking like a leaf. Then he searched in good cups in the china cabinet, and finding only the delicate handles that were broken off and kept in the hope of their being glued back one day, he became even more enraged. We saw him go back to the bamboo table and pick up the revolver. My mother asked him to put it down, in the name of Jesus, to put it down. That merely egged him on. The shot was the loudest I'd ever heard, not like gunshot from down in the woods, when men hunted rabbits and hares. Crouched down next to her, I thought that we were dead and found it strange to be smothered in burning smoke. The bullet missed us and passed into the frame of the door, where white paint was crumbling and falling off in little shards. Carnero and the sergeant were there in the room, speaking in savage bursts, as though they were about to attack him, and my father had grown peculiarly quiet, almost contrite, as he was being led out.

He would not have been locked in the barracks that night, as it would be too disgraceful to our family, which was once prosperous. He would have been brought in a car, or a hackney car, to a Cistercian monastery in Roscrea, because he was a friend of the abbot's. There monks cared for him as he went through the ordeal of delirium tremens, which I knew little about, and then he would be given broth and semolina pudding and asked to make a resolution, to take the pledge and to never touch a drink again.

Those lulls while he was away were the happiest times in our house, my mother and I baking, cleaning windows inside and out, and once, as I remember, mastering the intricate recipe for queen of puddings, which, when it came out of the oven with its crest of lightly burnt meringue, seemed to levitate from the oblong Pyrex dish.

Visitors

Important visitors were few, except for Yanks who came in the summer and talked with a twang and brought us necklaces and bone bracelets as gifts. Afterward, when they had gone, my mother hankered for her times in America and the style she had had and the flavored ices.

At night we could guess the visitor by the particular clang of the gate. For a while, it was a new guard who had struck up a friendship with my father and called without any reason, knowing that he would be given tea and cake. The other was a bachelor who was writing a history of the parish, which he called a "*histoire*." He lived with his two brothers, who were also bachelors, and they had one good overcoat between them. It meant that on Sundays they had to go to different Masses, one having to travel to the next parish, since there were only two Masses in ours. Reading snatches of his *histoire* aloud to us, he would take the opportunity to touch my mother's knee, over her thick lisle stocking, and refer to her as "Mrs. O.," reiterating what a lady she was. He would also be given tea and fruitcake and then, weary from the *histoire* (my father would have gone up to bed), she would cough and move around, this being the hint for him to leave. When male visitors left, she did two things: she plumped the cushions and smelled the leather seat of the chair, to see if they had farted, and if they had, the removable seat would be lifted out and put on the windowsill to air all night.

We dreaded tinkers, strapping women in plaid shawls, beating their tin cans on front and back door, insisting that we needed our pots mended and demanding milk, along with money. As I had not yet started school, I was given the task of watching out for them when my mother was occupied up in the yard. On many unfortunate occasions they had already come into the kitchen, hussies with their insolent manners demanding things. But one day I was quick enough to spot them as they came in at the lower gate and I yelled for her; we both hid in the shoe closet, which smelled of old shoes and had mice, but it was the only hiding place that did not have a window. We could hear them going all around the house, their threats, their pleadings, since they suspected we were in there, and as they left, they heaped curses on us and swore that we would regret the day.

That evening, when my mother went to search for her good tan shoes, which she had washed and put to dry on the pier of the gate, they were not to be found. The further we looked, the louder her laments became. She described the shoe cream she had specially bought with which to polish them, she pictured the little worms of shoe cream in the punched holes along the toe cap and instep, she imagined outings that she would now never make in them. She dreaded having to admit that most likely the tinkers had swiped them. It was with reluctance that she told the sergeant, never believing he would take the matter further, except that he did. The shoes were found in the bottom of a pram, covered with ticking and a pillow, in the flea hotel where some of the female members of the tinker families lodged. Others were in caravans over in an empty, haunted field, where they drank and had singsongs and later beat each other up. A summons was served on two women, who had identical names, and to her shame my mother had to appear in the local courthouse, where she was jeered and laughed at by warring tribes of tinkers, especially when she walked up to a stand and identified the shoes as being hers. When the sentence of a fine of fifteen shillings was passed, there was uproar;

the judge, banging the table, said a month in jail would do all of them a world of good. The shoes were never the same after that.

The visitor we most dreaded, after tinkers, was Mad Mabel. She moved with such swiftness: she would appear suddenly, as out of nowhere, tall and fluent and wild-eyed, wielding an ash plant, shouting and hitting out at all before her. She would be in our kitchen scolding our mother for her untidiness and her dirt. The ash plant would bounce off the ledge of the dresser as she took particular exception to the ornamental plates arranged along three shelves, one plate eased into the neighboring plate to make room for the half dozen on each shelf. They had colored paintings of pears and apples and pomegranates, and my mother quaked at the thought of one getting broken. Mabel would then smell the flitches of salted bacon that were hanging up on nails near the cupboard, smell them and say they were rotten. She insisted that we had stolen potatoes and duck eggs from their yard and all must be returned by nightfall. It would be not too long after those fearful visits that we would learn of her being carted off to the lunatic asylum and how she had not wanted to go, had run around the farmyard holding a pitchfork, vowing to do herself in, until eventually a father or an uncle or an older brother had had to seize her and tie her with rope and drag her to the waiting horse and cart. She would not be seen or heard of for many months, and then she would return home and we would see her at Mass, so very quiet, peculiar-looking and mumbling to herself.

One day I was getting clothes off the line, which was on a hill not far from our back door, when she surprised me. Her shadow and her gabbling preceded her, a tall streelish figure with a stick, raving, raving. She asked me to say her name, and when I said, "Mabel, Mabel," she burst out laughing, sensing that I was frightened, and went off on a spiel. *Mabel gone. No more Mabel. Mabel dead. Blood blood blood. Ha ha ha. Mabel no more.*

"I'll get you a drink of lemonade," I said, anything to escape her. She refused it, did not want charity, moreover she had important business to do. Then she pulled my mother's stockinette bloomers off the line with such force that the clothes-pegs came off with them, and she left, slashing the air with her stick, saying again she had business to do, to burn down the barracks and the sergeant and all the buggers in it. It was the first time that I came face to face with madness and feared it and was fascinated by it.

Each summer a father and son came from Dublin. They were wealthy cousins of my mother's, and she cherished the distant hope of a little legacy. The preparations were myriad; the house was scoured from top to bottom and new recipes were pored over. She discussed menus with them almost as soon as they arrived, and there were the usual jokes about their "avoirdupois," except I did not know what it meant. They always brought either a tin of Roses assorted sweets or a box of chocolates, which was put on the sideboard. Much was made of their gift, too much. They ate so well that after their big feed in the middle of the day, when they went out in the fields for a "constitutional," they flopped down in a cornfield or a hayfield and dozed, yet they were always ready and peckish for the evening meal, which was usually cold meats with piccalilli and sausage rolls, a delicacy she was proud of.

The legacy was never mentioned, though she drew hope from the fact that the father had mentioned how he had given her name and address to his solicitor. We also hoped that they might leave me a ten-shilling note on departure. I could see its coloring, a golden, prosperous pink, with a picture of a lady wearing a veil. No sooner would their car have disappeared outside the second gate than we ransacked their bedroom, put our hands into pillow slips and bolster cases, turned over the mattress, searched under ornaments and statues, but found nothing. My mother would shed a few tears because, with all the largesse, we now owed money in three shops, and reverting to one of her two faithful platitudes, she would recite, "Money talks, but tell me why all it says is just Goodbye."

Once a year, just before Christmas, there would be a card party in our house. They were held in different houses, and the eventual prize was a goose, which families took it in turn to provide. It was there I had my first glimpse of feuding over politics. Card tables and card chairs were set down in the kitchen, and in the pantry, covered with a slightly dampened piece of muslin, would be the two-tiered plates of sandwiches, with a choice of ham, mutton, or egg. There would also be dainties on a different plate. A fad of my mother's at that time was doughnuts, so the smell of hot oil and warm sugar permeated the kitchen. The game was Forty-five and at first everything was jovial. Partners were decided and people sat at the different tables, their consignments of change set down beside them. It may have been that someone cheated, or reneged, or that a player had mistakenly played against their own partner, but inevitably a row erupted, fists hitting the green baize tops, cards scattered all over, and in the slanging match that followed political memories, so raw and so real, were resumed. It was the old story of Ireland partitioned, the six counties cut off from the motherland and raging argument as to who was to blame. Some were for de Valera and others for Michael Collins, the "long fella" and the "big fella," the pith of the argument being that de Valera had sent Michael Collins to England to negotiate a treaty, knowing that he would come back having had to accede to the detested partition that the English demanded.

Raging grievances against the foe were now mixed with raging grievances against each other, and calm, or the semblance of it, was only gradually restored by one or two reasonable people resorting to clichés about the terrible dark times that Ireland had been through, and sure, wasn't the country only just trying to get back on her feet? The card game was resumed, but somehow the sparkle would have gone out of the evening.

It was borne in on me at that very young age that I came from fierce people and that the wounds of history were as raw and vivid as the pictures on the packs of cards that had been flung down. The North was an area on a map, and yet the way they harangued, losing their reason and hurling accusations at each other, I felt it would one day darken our lives.

Classroom

The classroom had to be swept each morning, the wooden floor sprinkled with water to keep down the dust that rose in little swirls. From the holes in the floor one could hear mice trotting underneath, and sometimes a snout or a brown tail would peep through and girls went berserk, pulling their legs up under their clothes and huddling. The smell of dust was always there, but in summer it would be mixed with the smell of flowers that were in jam jars along the windowsill. Girls that brought flowers were "pets" of the teacher, and the flower smell that lasted longest was that of stocks, which had a perfume even when withered.

On my very first day at school, the teacher picked me up in her arms; the brooch she was wearing was identical to one my mother had, a nest of flowers in a leaf-shaped silver recess. Hers had strawberries and my mother's were violets. She asked me in Irish if I was happy to be at school, and if I would shine and win a scholarship, and proudly she spoke the answer for me in Irish. There was a box for black babies in Africa, and as a surprise she allowed me to put a penny in the slot; the china skull of the black baby, with its braided hair, nodded a thank you. A letter from a leper colony in Uganda, yellow from turf smoke, in which the school had been thanked for monies sent was nailed to the wall. Next to it, on parchment more yellowed, were the reproachful words of the Englishman Sir John Davies, the King's Deputy, written in the 1600s:

For if themselves [the mere Irish] were suffered to possess the whole country as their septs have done for so many hundreds of years past, they would never, to the end of the world, build houses, make townships or villages or manure or improve the land as it ought to be. Therefore it stands neither with Christian belief nor conscience to suffer so good and fruitful a country to lie waste like a wilderness, when His Majesty may lawfully dispose of it to such persons as will make a civil plantation thereupon.

Irish history was the subject she most liked to teach. She strode through the classroom, in and out between the desks, where we sat in pairs, the small white pots of watered ink in an enamel inkwell, and a dent in the wooden slope to hold pen and pencil. With hyperbole she spanned centuries, invoking sieges and battles—Slievemurry, Gorey, and Athenry—bemoaning the seven-hundred-year conquest, the cruelty of the Invader, the Saxon sheriff. She reeled off the names of heroes whose heads were impaled on the gates of Dublin Castle, and yet, and yet, Malachi retained his collar of gold. Hitting with her ruler the cloth map on the wall, she fixed on the name of Kinsale, the six-year siege which marked the end of the cream of Irish soldiery, the great earls, O'Neill, O'Donnell, having to flee their own land, where they soon died of heartbreak, their auxiliaries going to fight as mercenaries in foreign brigades. She would then recite, her eyes filling with tears:

And all Valladolid knew
And out to Simancas all knew
Where they buried Red Hugh.

She spanned centuries, jumping back to the age of mythic men whose lives constituted battle and banquet, whose women were all beautiful, with pale, sea-green eyes, cheeks with the hue of the foxglove, and perched on their shoulders ravens with the gift of prophecy. Cú Chulainn, who took the name of his hound, was the hero she most liked to dwell on, he who had vanquished all the rival tribes and scions of Ireland until the fatal day when the gods deserted him and, as the bird Morrigan had foretold, his bowels spilled out onto the cushions of his chariot. Alone and bleeding, he stooped and drank from a stream, then staggered to a lake into which his blood flowed, and he watched as an otter drank. Rather than die defeated, he strapped himself by his torn tunic to a pillar stone, because he knew from the Olla and the bards that "a great name outlasts a man."

It was a mere trot from Cú Chulainn to Pope Pius XI, who before his death had told Cardinal MacRory, Primate of all Ireland, that the Irish people were God's pure air. "They were everywhere and like the air, giving life and vigor to the Catholic faith." His death was so full of pageantry; we heard, in her lachrymose tones, how doctors, monsignors, and his private sacristan stood aghast at his passing, as the scarlet veil was raised from his face and Cardinal Pacelli, his chamberlain, took a small silver hammer and struck him three times on his forehead, calling him by his Christian name, "Achille, Achille, Achille." When he did not answer, they sank to their knees in lamentation and recited *De Profundis;* then the sad news was immediately dispatched to Il Duce, Benito Mussolini, who in turn informed Victor Emmanuel, King of Italy.

Often, after these great sallies, she would sit, quiet and lank, staring into space, and thinking. Thinking what? Of her own fate, or Ireland's fate? She lived alone in a rookery of a house about half a mile from the school. And one Saturday, before an exam, we had an extra class there. From upstairs she brought down a cake box, in which there were the remains of a rich fruitcake and a lot of broken bits of icing. It reminded me of cakes that brides kept after their wedding, in wait for the christening of their first child, but that could not be true of her, as she was a spinster.

When the school bell rang for lunch, we would go out into the yard to eat our lunches, and one of the girls who was her "pet" would stay behind to make her a jam omelette. I wanted to be one of her pets; I strove in every way, especially with my compositions, except that, pointedly, she slighted me.

The day the inspector came, I thought that I had excelled myself. He wore a tweed jacket with crinkled leather buttons the color of conkers and matching tweed plus-fours. He looked at her syllabus and her logbook, then glancing around, he asked if one of the pupils might like to recite a poem or some catechism. Since I devoured things by heart, she told me to stand up and repeat the miracle of the loaves and fishes from Saint Luke's Gospel. Not content with speaking it, I added a little flourish of my own, saying that after everyone had been fed, Jesus ordered his Disciples to gather up the remaining loaves and fishes that lay strewn on the shores of Galilee. The inspector asked me if I took a great interest in Jesus, to which I replied that I was disappointed that he had been so curt with his mother at the Feast of Cana, when, worried about the scarcity of wine, he said, "It is not my business or thine." There were titters in the classroom, and he strolled around smiling, looked over some girls' shoulders at their copybooks, took a pencil that was in the rim of his tiny diary, made a note, then left us, and, as we later learned, had a long lunch in the pub that boasted the name of a hotel. Far from bestowing praise because of the glowing report he sent back, the teacher had a "set" on me and was determined to punish me. She requested that I bring my china doll Rosaleen for the Nativity play at Christmas, in which I was not given a part. It was galling to see Rosaleen, in her ivory satin dress that was strewn with violets, being passed clumsily from hand to hand, and worse when one of the Three Wise Men almost dropped her. After the performance, when I went to reclaim her, my teacher said she could not be given back, as a photographer was expected to come and take a photograph of the crib, along with Mary, Joseph, and animals that had been fashioned out of straw. In the meantime, the doll was kept in her house, and on the way home from school I could see her through the sitting-room window, propped on a sideboard, her stumpy legs splayed out and her two china hands, as I believed, imploring me to kidnap her. My heart was bursting with anger. Eventually, my mother wrote, saying how attached I was to the doll, but the letter was not referred to and not acknowledged.

Another day she sent me to the town for tuppence-worth of chops. I noticed that father and son smiled when they heard the humble request. I stood between the big haunches of meat that hung from the ceiling, their skins white and larded, with amber flypapers flapping in and out between them. From a gauze-fronted safe the son pulled out some scraps of meat that might have been for dogs and wrapped them in a double fold of white paper, then cleaned his hands in his half-apron, which was of black oilcloth.

Hilarity reigned in the classroom. It was tuppence-worth of chalk I had been sent for. I was an amadán. She made me stand in front of the fireguard, holding the open sheets of blood-spattered paper for everyone to behold, and afterward, when I sat down, girls sympathized with me, except for the few who threw bits of crumbled rubber and toffee papers in my direction.

My brother and sisters, being older, had gone away to boarding school, so walking home alone was full of hazards. There might be tinkers, or some wild man, hiding behind a wall who with a twirl of the finger would spit the words "I want to do pooley in you." Once I arrived home to find that my mother was not there; I could tell by seeing the second gate swinging open, hens on the flag, starving and pecking at bits of lime, our back door not locked—all proof that she had fled to her mother's after a frightful row. It meant my having to stay with the

Mac family in the gate lodge, an older couple who smelt of wintergreen oil, the husband scratching his head and asking his wife how long they would have the nuisance of me. Her hair was snow white and as wavy as the waves of a sea, and seeing that I was sniffling and sad, she would let me sit up that bit late to say the rosary with them. I slept in the attic room, reached by a ladder, and through the skylight window I looked for sky, for stars, and begged for my mother to come home, which she always did, vowing that we would be a happy family from then onward, as my father had taken the pledge. As a celebration, she would make an orange cake, and when it was almost baked, she would take it out of the oven and allow me to plunge a knitting needle into it, which I could then lick—the taste of the warm, orangy dough so delicious.

Our hens began to lay well, as we knew from the jubilant yodel they let out after they had laid, and then it was up to the yard to gather the eggs from under them, in their dank, clammy nests, their eyes with a shine of beads. She cleaned the eggs with a damp cloth and a bit of bread soda, and brought them in her basket to a new shopkeeper in the town. She had credit there, her name being the very first to be entered in his big, important ledger, which looked like a dictionary. I was allowed to get a two-pound pot of blackcurrant jam. It was where the footpath ran out, jumping down onto the road itself, that I dropped it. There it was, a spew, purple and black, pieces of glass everywhere, the tiny blackcurrants like goat droppings. A woman from the nearby garage came out, to sympathize, and then brought a worn goose wing and a bit of cardboard to sweep it up.

It so happened that I had become smitten with film stars, whose photographs came in cigarette packets which I collected from all the men who smoked. Women did not smoke. The photographs were so bewitching that I would make up little dramas about them, and my two chosen stars were Clark Gable and Dorothy Lamour. I twined them in a romantic situation, swearing love, et cetera, when foolishly Dorothy mentioned her suspicions regarding Greer Garson, who lived nearby, also in a shaded mansion. Clark was fuming. Did she not trust him? So things got heated and Clark left in a huff, announcing that he was going to the ocean. Greer then seized her moment to walk across the lawn, seemingly to console her friend, but in truth to persecute her. This playlet got to be known, and one day when I was coming from school a man called Tim called me into his shop and then into a small office where a second man sat on a high stool. A bottle of whiskey lay on the slant of the brown wooden desk, and the two men were skittish. They asked me to put my play on, which I did, interposing the dialogue with the pictures on the cigarette cards, the performance lasting about five minutes. As a reward, I was given a threepenny bit. It felt warm in the palm of my hand, and it had the image of a hound on it. I handed it back to Tim, so he could take it off our bill, and for a minute the two men looked away, not knowing what to make of it, and I tied the threepenny bit into my handkerchief so as not to lose it.

Years later, when I had, as they put it, "gone up in the world," my mother asked me to go and see my old schoolteacher, who had been ailing for some time. Her room had that mustiness that all sickrooms have, as the window was kept shut, along with the smell of medicines and orangeade. Her skin was very yellow, as if she had jaundice, her body skeletonlike, except for the little bowl of her belly under the sheet, and the only trace of her highly strung temperament was the way she fidgeted at the fringing of the cotton quilt on her bed. She barely spoke for some time, then, with her voice whistling through her windpipe and gripping my hand, she asked was she not the first to detect the writing spark in me, was it not she who had first ignited the fire? Then a quick dart of light passed over her eyes, as though she were hearing the sound of Cú Chulainn and his men charging up the quiet street.

Carnero

Our farmhand was nicknamed Carnero. He was roguish, lackadaisical, and disinclined to wash. He ate like a glutton. My mother had to carve the bacon or the chicken in the pantry, otherwise he would grab slices of it when her back was turned. He buttered his bread on both sides, muttering under his breath in defiance, "Let's larrup it on, let's larrup it on." He was about eighteen. On Saturday nights, in his pelt, when he washed in the rain barrel for Sunday Mass, he would sing some of his favourite songs. One was "Oh, Miss Nicholas, don't be so ridiculous, I don't like it in the daytime, Nighttime's the right time. So, Miss Nicholas, don't be so ridiculous..." He wasn't particularly religious. Very few of the men were. They would stand at the back of the chapel and nudge one another when the priest drank the wine from the chalice, whispering about him being a toper. By contrast, most of the women prayed fervently, their eyes raised to the whitewashed ceiling, the better for God to hear their pitiful supplications.

Carnero went to the pub each night, or rather, one of the several pubs, depending on the welcome. Remarkably for a small one-horse town, there were twenty-seven public houses, three grocery shops, one drapery, one chemist, no cinema, and no library. Carnero struck oil when an elderly publican skidded on the cobbles in his own yard and needed help lifting the hooped wooden barrels of porter. Carnero got to be his adjutant and in return had free drink, but to ingratiate himself even more, he stole wood and timber from us and had a blazing fire in that bar that lured customers away from other premises.

Every Saturday night he would bring me a bar of chocolate, dark chocolate with a white filling, or milk chocolate with raisins and almonds, along with Peggy's Leg, which was sweet, cinnamon-colored, and sticky. Since I was fasting a lot to save our family from various disasters, I kept these things in an attaché case, which I would open from time to time, as might a shopkeeper, resolving not to eat them. The taste and texture of the Turkish delight surpassed all, and even thinking about it often made me break my resolve. I would open the suitcase and eat two whole bars in a gulp. My other indulgence was, with my bare hand, to scoop some of the trifle that my mother had put to set in a glass bowl on the vestibule floor and then, to hide my crime, flatten the surface with the back of a soup spoon to make it smooth again.

On Saturdays in summer I would be sent to the bog with Carnero's lunch, which consisted of thick slices of soda bread that was buttered, with sugar sprinkled on because of his sweet tooth. The tea, already milked, would be in a bottle. I loved that journey. Mad Mabel never set foot there, and there were no men or hobos lurking to try and get one behind a wall for a kiss, which they called a "birdy," as they fumbled with one's coat and skirt. Already, in my daft ambition to be a writer, I was studying nature so that I could submit pieces to the local weekly newspaper. There was an anonymous scribe, of whom I was jealous, who wrote articles about storms and seabirds and shelving sea cliffs. That was in the western part of the county on the Atlantic Ocean. We were inland, and I thought Drewsboro the loveliest, leafiest place in the whole world. On either side of the track there were grassy banks full of wildflowers and burdock and flowering weed, bees buzzing and disporting themselves in and out of those honeyed enclaves, and the smell of the nettles so hot. Birds swooped in random gusts, and butterflies, velvet-brown, maroon, and tortoiseshell, their ravishing colors never clashing, never gaudy, moved in the higher strata, like pieces of flying silk.

When I got to the entrance to the bog, Carnero would be beckoning to me to hurry on, because he had "hungry grass." The bog itself (another venue for my future composition) was a vista of colors that stretched miles and miles to the next parish, where we could see the slate blue of the church spire. The cut turf was still black, but the sides of the turf banks were a blacker black that oozed bog water, and the heather, blasted by winter winds, bloomed purple and purple-brown. A tall fringing of soft-green sedge circled the lake where waterbirds nested and let out occasional shrieks of alarm. On the brackish water a few yellow irises, sun-shot and golden, left one in no mistake but that it was high summer. He didn't like the tepid tea, so, pulling heather by the roots and using a few birch branches, he started up a fire to heat it in a billy can. The smell of the fire in the open air was so clean and the thin smoke drifted up in sputters. I had a surprise for him. "What, what?" I kept stringing it along. It concerned Sacko, who was both his friend and his rival. I had brought a newspaper, wrapped around the bottle of tea, in which Sacko's rash adventures were graphically relayed. Carnero lay back, rolling his tongue repeatedly over his unwashed, yellow teeth. He was agog. At that time I was too young to notice that Carnero could neither read nor write.

Only the week before, we were in stitches reading of a Mrs. Considine, up in West Clare, who took a swing at a Mrs. Berg for the larceny of two pounds of sugar, four penny buns, and two candles. The witness, who had been wheeling Mrs. Considine's bicycle, identified himself in the court as having kept apart "from the scenery," but did allow that both women had scratches on their faces and also blood and loose teeth. Still another woman had been charged with a theft of a piece of mutton, worth one shilling and sixpence. Her excuse was that she had laid her own parcels on the counter and, since the butcher was very busy, had erroneously picked up the piece of mutton. "So the mutton got off the counter and walked in under your shawl?" said the district judge, who was known for his asperity, at which she pleaded poor sight and old age. She was fined ten shillings and sixpence for her chicanery.

But the one I was about to read out was nearer home, occurred in the very shop where my mother bought jam and raspberry and custard biscuits when she was flush. It concerned Sacko, known as the "Nocturnal Thief." He was a rover who would come and go, and after long absences would return sporting a silk handkerchief or a silver monogrammed cigarette case, saying he had been given them in return for his services to a lord or an admiral over in England. Everyone knew about the break-in at Eamonn's shop and the eggs that had been stolen and how Sacko had been a suspect, but never was it so splendidly told as in the article that I read out to Carnero.

Eamonn the shopkeeper, asleep on the first floor, heard breaking noise underneath and came down to find the two panes of glass had been removed from a back window, a lamp had been overturned, a number of eggs and also two goose eggs were missing out of the cardboard crate. Eamonn the shopkeeper, though worried, went back to bed. In the morning, with the help of the local guard, they applied some detective work and came to the conclusion that the rude intruder was probably a person five feet six inches in height and weighing no more than twelve stone, so as to be able to pass through the window space. Sacko the suspect, when questioned, presented himself as a blameless neighbourly man and charted his movements from midnight 'til four a.m. He had taken a walk all around the village, he had stopped at the parish pump for a slug of water, he had an engaging discussion with the nightwatchman about the prospects of an oncoming war and being a Samaritan, he had driven four stray calves that were wandering around the road into the shopkeeper's yard, for safety. After that, he had walked a mile out of the town, to a place where a farmer had allowed him to doss, whenever he was stuck for a bed. However, his story had a "lacuna." The cast made of his footprints matched the footprint in the backyard and, moreover, he was the only person around known to suck raw eggs. The plaintiff surpassed himself, telling the judge how he had spent the night, worn out from walking, he had gone to the shed, procured an old stick, which he rested crosswise in a corner, and sat upright with his hands folded, praying to God as he had always done in the trenches.

"Trenches, my backside," Carnero said, but his interest was fully whetted.

Sacko went on to tell the judge that he had never in his life done any injury to anyone and had taken the eggs only since his rheumatism was awful bad from a life of a vagrant, sleeping in stables.

"Anything else exciting?" the judge put to him.

"Yes...I am a versatile man and skilled in musical accomplishments...I am a ventriloquist and a conjuror, gifts that I am sure our local superintendent does not possess...and hence tries to blacken me."

"They are gifts I am happy to do without," the superintendent said, jumping up, red in the face, furious at being mocked by a lying hooligan. But the judge, who himself liked a drink, was lenient that day, or else had enjoyed the repartee, so that Sacko got off on the grounds that the break-in was not serious, and what were a few missing eggs to a prosperous person known as Eamonn the shopkeeper.

"Christ, there's no stopping him now," Carnero said, staring at the photograph of Sacko in an ill-fitting blazer with brass buttons and steel-rimmed glasses that he had worn for effect.

Although the next item that I read out did not interest Carnero, he listened, anything to loll and keep idle. Did it, I asked him, outshine my own more pallid pieces, about bogs and bees and butterflies?

On the west coast of Ireland between Clare and Kerry lies the mouth of the Shannon with Loop Head Peninsula on the Clare side aggressively spearing twenty miles out into the ageless and relentless foe, the Atlantic. Elemental wars of wind and water have vanquished all its supporting land fortifications to north and south and the great Shannon flood, allied with the ocean, has attacked the rear or landward end and all but isled it. Greyly and ever narrowingly the Peninsula lances out with its beetling cliffs, flanks to the Peninsula at Killala, whereon it carries a lighthouse from which, like the grand old warrior it is, it flashes the chivalrous warning, "Beware! I break the ocean, I wreck ships."

It was time to go back home. If on the return journey I saw the same lucky butterfly, then the composition I was intending to write would soar. It had rested on a rock, and was opening and shutting its wings repeatedly, wings like jewels, deep violet with a dusting of marcasite, and it kept doing the same thing, the opening and the shutting of the wings, like a coquette, drunk maybe from the nectar it had just tasted on berries, or perhaps to entice another of its kind.

Then one wet night, as we sat by the fire, our dogs began to bark like mad, and we were surprised that any visitors would set out on such a night. We waited and waited, yet nobody knocked. Eventually my mother went out to the back kitchen, where a letter had been slipped under the door. It was that dreaded thing, an anonymous letter. She read the first lines aloud. Carnero was to be seen in our woods, with the doctor's maid, each night after he left the public house. The subsequent lines were so shaming that my mother called my father out onto the step and shut the door so that I would not overhear. When they came back in, she said, in a dire whisper, that Carnero would have to be given his walking papers. If that happened, we were truly sunk. He ran the place. He milked, he foddered, he plowed, he harrowed, he killed a pig twice a year, and on summer Sundays wrung the necks of cockerels for Sunday's dinner, which consisted of boiled chicken and a white sauce with parsley.

Piecing together the contents of the anonymous letter and Carnero's terrible tryst, I went wild with jealousy and feared for his soul, having no regard for hers. The only punishment I could wreak was to refuse to accept the bars of chocolate and, moreover, not speak to him. I can't remember how long this sulk lasted, except that we learned that the maid, having been locked in a box room by the doctor's wife, was later summarily dismissed.

Then one day, years later, the unthinkable happened. Carnero gave notice that he was leaving. He was going to England, where his cousins had fixed him up in a job with the railway company. One minute, as my father irately put it, he was going to Cambridge, and the next minute it was Oxford, and there was much sarcasm as to which university he would be attending. But as the day of his departure got nearer, the reality of it hit us. My mother began to panic and no longer listed his failings, his lack of hygiene, his emptying his po pot, which was a tin can, through the window at night onto a bit of flag that was permanently slimy as a consequence, his buttering his bread on both sides when her back was turned, his having not one, but two boiled eggs for his breakfast.

I got in from school and saw my mother sitting at the kitchen table crying. She rarely sat, and for the most part fought tears back stoically. But there she was, wringing her hands and pointing to the downstairs room where he slept and where he was presumably packing. She could not understand why it was taking him so long. We listened at the door, and now and then she knocked, but there was no answer. We went back to the kitchen, asking each other, by our woebegone expressions, how in God's name we were going to manage without him, as we waited for him to appear with a brown suitcase and extra things, perhaps, in a flour bag. She was already asking who would milk (my father never milked), and she herself had not done so since she was a young girl on a mountain farm forty years ago. Hazards untold befell us. She suddenly remembered that she had put some bread to bake in a pot oven, in the boil house up in the yard, and she ran to retrieve it.

I took the irrevocable step. Without knocking, I barged into his room. It was one of the few times that I saw him look vexed, and his first instinct was to raise his arms and his hands to ward me off. He knew why I had come. His things were on the bed: his good navy suit, two pairs of overalls, shirts, brown hobnailed boots with the dung dried on them, and junk—bicycle parts, copper piping, wet batteries and dry batteries, and other paraphernalia—which he had intended to sell to a scrap merchant in Limerick.

The little window was wide open, but the smell in the room was still fusty. I do not recall any words spoken. What I did was to kneel down and grasp him by his ankles, imploring him not to leave. He stood there like a statue, never once trying to break free. I clung to him, tighter and tighter, until the moment he rolled down his sleeves and looked at me with what I can only call utter defeat.

My mother was exultant and cooked him the chop that was

meant for my father's tea. We ate in silence, my mother and I at one end of the table, having bread and jam, and Carnero tucking into the chop, which had a plump red kidney attached to it. The tension was unbearable. I knew that I had done something awful. I had killed love, before I even knew the enormity of what love meant.

Summer Holiday

I go into the kitchen in my grandmother's house and I walk around it, unsure. It was dark even in daytime. There was a very low window that admitted little light, a remainder from times past, when fewer windows meant less rent to the English landlords, except that I did not know that then, aged eight or nine.

I used to walk around that kitchen to get to know it and not feel so lonely in it. Away from the hearth and the open fire, on which pots and a kettle hung on the iron swing gate, there was a table, never completely laid or unlaid, saucers put to dry on the upside-down cups for the next round of tea. There was muslin over the milk jug to keep off flies and gnats, and the country butter was overyellow, its strong smell whiffing out from under the glass dome with which it was covered.

Next to a wall was a settle bed that was a trunk when closed, where a workman had slept in past times and would have had to wait until all the others had gone upstairs to bed. Men sat on it at my grandfather's wake, smoking clay pipes as they passed a whiskey bottle around, talking in low tones. Death was upstairs. My grandfather's white face seemed all the whiter because the starched white sheet was drawn up to his chin, and the gray-white mustache looked unnatural on a dead face. The raised veins on the back of his hands were an alphabet that branched together, and there were scabs and brown moles on the crinkles of the skin. Someone had threaded a rosary between the lifeless fingers. Two tall candles were burning on a low table that was covered with a white linen cloth, and the smell in the room was of melting wax and disinfectant, since the linoleum floor had been scrubbed by the woman who laid him out.

On the nearby dresser there was Delft and pans of milk off which the cream would be skimmed. My aunt did it daintily, with the tips of her fingers, and the cream, which would have been delicious on blackberries, was kept to be churned to make the next consignment of strong-smelling butter, most of which she brought to the shop in the town in exchange for groceries. Full of idleness and not knowing how long my incarceration might be, I pined for home. To avoid the kitchen with its smells and my grandmother moaning, I passed the days in the little plantation, where my aunt had sown red dahlias that contrasted so happily with the dark, funereal yew trees.

Late in the evening my aunt would be out of doors milking, feeding calves that she made pets of, and yelling, "Chook, chook, chook," to hens that were unwilling to go into their cramped coop. I would sit with my grandmother in the encroaching dark. She had a necessary thriftiness and knew the hours of light that any one candle could give and was slow to put the taper to it. It was then the crickets began to screech like mad. They lived in holes in the mortar surrounding the fireplace, but with candlelight and the devilment in them they would fly out in swarms. They always landed on a wet towel or a wet tea towel that was hung up to dry, landing there to suck up the moisture. They lived on that. In the dog-eared almanac, in a drawer, there was an article about crickets which said that their screeches came not from their throats but from the brisk attrition of their wings. Neither of us knew what "attrition" meant. My grandmother would rave on about the hardships she had endured and what proud patriots I was descended from. One, nicknamed "Da Stick," had fought in an insurrection, was injured, and long afterward fitted with a wooden leg. I never knew which insurrection it was, as there were so many down the years, all, as I knew from school, botched, both through lack of weapons and the treachery of informers, brothers or cousins informing on their own. Her son Michael had been chief of the 3rd Brigade in East Clare, a fearless soldier on the run from the British army, with a price on his head. He had kept a diary, which she would pull out from a nook in the wall as if it were the Book of Psalms. She read aloud, her voice trembly:

Started ploughing, had one scrape done after dinner, when I sighted lorry of Tans turning Lyon's Cross. Just in the centre of the field in full view. To run would be foolish. Kept on ploughing going towards them 'til I reached headland. They were then one hundred yards away, but in shade of some trees. I cleared fence and retreated to Allen's wood and sat there peacefully watching them searching for me. Slept that night at John Mack's, at 3 a.m. heard lorries, hid in bed, then sent Billy Mack to warn Turner. Billy returned to say they had Turner's house surrounded and it looked bad. Retreated across Bo River to Griffins and waited the urgent news.

By then my grandmother had always succumbed to tears and would get me to decipher the next page and the next, as the ink of many years had faded to a dunnish brown. I craved only one thing, which was a spoon of golden syrup that slid so easily down the throat.

One night long after my grandmother had gone to bed, my aunt Delia, otherwise a gentle woman, decided to play a prank on me. She had a visitor who was also called Delia, and they kept saying, "Fancy, two Delias in the same humble parish." The other Delia had been to America, and that's where the word "fancy" came from, as did the word "darn" instead of "damn." The other Delia was forever boasting of the harmony with her dear dead husband, how they sat of an evening by their friendly fire, giving each other necessary encouragement and saying, "Whatever the darn crops do, you and I will relax." Yet they were known to fight bitterly, and often he left the house at night and was missing for days.

So, as I sat there, my eyes glued, listening to their every word, my aunt suddenly said that my mother was not my real mother. Those were her words. My real mother, as she said, was in Australia. I went shivery and then stone-cold. They went on laughing and embellishing their story. I said my mother was my mother. They said I was too young to recall when the swap-over had happened. They built it up, relishing the fun of it and the fact that I was getting more and more agitated, standing, as I remember, and hitting out with little fists, little useless fists, as this Australian mother began to materialize. Peg was her name, she had brown hair and a heartlessness, evidenced by her giving me away. She lived on a sheep farm out in some remote place, and occasionally sent a five-shilling money order toward my keep. One day I would be sent to her and separated from the mother that I loved so much that I used to promise to die at the very instant she did. The place to which I had to go in my mind, admitting to having no mother, was awful, summoning terrors, great and small. Things in the kitchen began to go blurry, as did they, and in a violent frenzy I ran out to escape them, intending to run the five miles home on dark roads at any cost, to find my mother and hear the sweet, reassuring phrase from her lips, "I am your mother, you are my child." They caught me at the first wicket gate by the sleeve of my cardigan, and I was brought back and put to sit on a rocking chair, half lying down. A towel was put on my chest and over my mouth, to stifle what must have been my roaring. I kept saying, "I want to go home, I want to go home."

Next morning my aunt had to cycle to the crossroads and wait for the mail van as word was sent to my mother to send Carnero to come and fetch me home. No reason was given. The man who drove the mail van was implored to break his journey between post offices and to go up to our house specially with the note. I had already packed my few belongings in a small suitcase and spent the day at the plantation, because my grandmother, upon being told that I had homesickness, started grumbling, saying how spoiled I was and how thankless I was, considering the treats they had given me, jelly and blancmange of a Sunday. The day wore on and on.

Birds for miles around were making their evening excursions, swooping down into the rain barrel where midges had swarmed, and the crows were already roosting in the trees for the night. In the dusk I still waited, and so certain was I that Carnero would come, I kept hearing the scrape of the lych gate on the slate pier where it was hung. I could picture him laying his bicycle down on the ground and taking a shortcut over the high grass, cursing the fact that the dew would ruin the Sunday shoes he had just polished.

Then I was called in for supper. My aunt, feeling remorse, had cut up a slice of shop bread in little pieces and poured liberally from the tin of golden syrup, to coax me. My grandmother railed on about all the suffering and penances she had had to endure and was praying aloud that the Lord would come for her soon. My aunt and I both regretted the coolness with one another, because prior to that we had become firm friends. Each night after my grandmother had gone up to bed, we would sit and chat. First she talked of her dead husband, her partner, the man whose likeness was in a locket that she wore next to her chest and with whom she had conferred from time to time. He had dark eyes and dark hair.

Her one solace was the romance novels that she could get her hands on. Unlike my mother, she loved reading, and by a miracle a retired schoolteacher in County Kerry had sent her a copy of *War and Peace* only a few months before. It was in three small volumes with tiny print, and the paper was so flimsy one had to haw on it to separate the pages. She had shown it to me during my vacation and asked me to print out the names of the Russian characters with their patronymics, so that she would be more familiar with them on her second reading, which would be in the winter nights to come. I came to know a Prince Andrei who wished to be unmarried; Marya Dmitrievna, who puffed heavily when dancing; a beautiful Natasha; Pierre, who picked up the wrong hat in the salon of Anna Pavlovna; and an old contrary prince at Bald Hills who tormented his poor daughter, Mary, and yet on his deathbed told her to put on her white dress, which he liked seeing her in. I had copied these snippets into a notebook, which also contained the yield got from the miller for their corn down the years and the varying price of animal foodstuffs.

Sitting at that table, I wanted, as I am sure my aunt wanted, a truce, but neither of us was willing to take the first step. Then it happened. A shadow passed by the low window, and before I could think, was it or was it not him, Carnero was in the kitchen, in his good navy suit, saying he was gasping with a thirst. My aunt gave him a nip of whiskey in a small beaker that had come with a tonic bottle. He was holding a cushion to put on the bar of the bicycle on which he would bring me home, and already the gloom and persecutions of the holiday were fading. My aunt gave me a very clean new shilling and made me swear that I would never tell the nonsense about Peg, far away in Australia.

All the way Carnero and I chatted, he giving me the various news since I had left and saying there had been no terrible ructions. Sometimes we had to dismount on the steep hills, as he was a quite hefty man and also had the extra weight of me to contend with. We were sitting on a little low stone bridge, the river just beneath, chugging along at a merry musical pace. It was called Bo River, the very place beyond which my dead uncle had retreated when he was on the run. A herd of cows were lying down in the field, close to one another, wheezing the soft wheezes that they made at night. In the hazed blue of oncoming night, mountain and sky had melted into one another and looked substanceless. Feeling happy and content, Carnero lit a cigarette, and in that wild and spontaneous way of his started to sing:

As I went out to the fair of Athy
I saw an aul petticoat hangin' to dry
I took off my drawers and hung them thereby
To keep that aul petticoat war-um.

Books

The first book that I recall holding in my hand was a cloth book with pictures and a rhyme:

> Hey diddle diddle
> The cat and the fiddle,
> The cow jumped over the moon,
> The little dog laughed
> To see such sport,
> And the dish ran away with the spoon.

The letters, tall and painted, were like the painted pillars of a house that would never tumble.

Sitting on my mother's lap, smelling her smell, feeling the itch from the wool of her cardigan, the particular heave of her chest, I studied every feature of her face, which was so beautiful to me, except for the forehead, a map of wrinkles, and on that map I wrote my first words, in praise of her.

Our house was full of prayer books and religious treasuries with soft, dimpled leather covers and gold edging to the pages that glittered when the sun broke through the tiny window in the pantry where they were stacked. There were ribbons of various colors so that one could open a page at random and read the Seven Dolors of the Blessed Virgins, prayers to Saint Peter of Antioch, Saint Bernardine of Siena, Saint Aelrod, Saint Cloud, Saint Colomba, and Saints Colman of Cloyne, of Dromore, of Kilmacduagh and, most wrenchingly of all, the prayers specially addressed to the stigmata of Saint Francis, that he may crucify the flesh from its vices.

These same prayer books are now on my bookshelves in London, and sometimes I take one down and realize how thoroughly they informed my thinking and even my dreams, as my mother and I, huddled close together in bed, recited the words over and over again:

> May nothing in our minds excite
> Vain dreams and phantoms of the night;
> Keep off our enemies, that so
> Our bodies no uncleanness know.

There were morning prayers, evening prayers, vespers, supplications, contritions, psalms, and versicals. There were exhortations about pride, vanity, filthy pleasures, the deformity of our sins being so very great they could not be fully comprehended by human understanding. The flames of Hell seemed as real as the turf burning in the fire. Sometimes, if a sod fell out, my mother would catch it with her bare hand to test her strength for the future and possible flames of eternity. Hell was far more real to us than Heaven. Heaven was golden and vaporish.

I would go alone to the chapel and "contritely say twenty Paters, Aves, and Glorias and contritely kiss the Crucifix." Next it was a meditation, preceding the Stations of the Cross, the dwelling on the Five Holy Wounds, the wound of the left foot, the right foot, the left hand, the right hand, and the sacred side which the Roman soldiers had pierced with their swords, causing blood and water to gush forth. Everything about it was so immediate, as if the image on each gory Station had come alive, and I could almost touch the Crown of Thorns, or the purple garment that was rent, or the towel with which Veronica wiped the face of Jesus, and hear the taunts the soldiers threw at him as they spat in his face. I could almost taste the vinegar and gall that was on the sponge from which he was made to drink.

For home reading we had the Irish *Messenger*, an organ of the Apostleship of Prayer that came once a month and cost threepence.

On the rich, matte, dark red cover there was a picture of the Sacred Heart, arms outstretched, for sinners to crawl under the folds of the copious, dipping sleeves. Years later, my friend Luke Dodd told me that his mother and his aunts availed of this rich matte cover by wetting it with their fingers, as effective as any rouge.

The avowed aim of the magazine was to promote happiness in the home, repel the influx of "hot rhythm dance bands," and avert the advance of communism, which had enslaved Russia, a country forty times the size of Ireland lost to "that red ruin."

There were also tips on how to make a baby's matinee coat with picot edging and how to cast on stitches on numbers nine, ten, and eleven knitting needles for that beautiful Fair Isle cardigan. In one column called "Your Question Answered" all sorts of worries were aired. One reader in great perplexity asked whether the frying of bread in dripping on a Friday constituted a sin, since meat was forbidden, and another wondered if it was indulgent to kiss too frequently the cross that she wore around her neck. The "thanksgiving" columns brimmed with gratitude: *Bleeding from nose stopped, Success of school in needlework examination, Removal of dangerous trees near house, Gangrene averted, Safe delivery of parcel, Good weather for hockey match, Father takes pledge, Money won in sweepstake.*

One could read of the adventures of Irish nuns and priests who roamed the world to reach unfortunate heathens desirous of baptism. There were pictures of nuns on rickshaws being ferried across the Han River in Hanyang and walking along a gangplank, with a skyline of Shanghai in the background. These were daughters of Erin, because "wherever a human need had declared itself, an Irish nun was there to meet it."

Priests, like Christ to the centurions, traveled in blizzards or simmering heat to breach the backwoods of America, the Australian bush, the African veldt, the leper asylums, the cities of China, the Kachin Hills of Burma, the pottery village of Bhamo—places where natives had never seen a white man before, let alone a bearded priest arriving on a donkey or a bullock cart.

The preparations to celebrate Mass in these mission stations had the thrall and improvisation of traveling theater. A portable confessional would have been set up for penitents who longed for conversion, while the altar for Mass was a wooden press, above which hung a dark cloth suspended on a bamboo pole. Two little Hanyang altar boys in their white surplices completed the perfect picture, which was in some abandoned garden, among ancient ruins, overhanging temples, and pagodas, which were infinitely more beautiful than the wooden press, but our God, which was not their God, did not dwell in overhanging ornamental temples. Having celebrated Mass, the priest, using chopsticks, would eat a small bowl of rice, and then set out on his donkey or his bullock cart to spread the holy pasturage in the next distant outpost.

The *Messenger* also carried romantic stories, which were serialized and which invariably hinged on a crisis of conscience. Take young Blanche, "a personable matron of twenty-two," to whom Aunt Louisa had willed the Honeysuckle Cottage in County Wicklow on condition that she would never marry. Blanche gives up her lowly job as secretary to a solicitor, moves to Wicklow, tends her rosebushes, her apple trees, occasionally inviting a few friends from Dublin to visit her on summer Sundays. She is the happiest Blanche alive, until one day a wandering artist knocks on her door, a man with flashing eyes, poor but proud, and fatally persuasive. "Oh, love, what an unreasoning creature it grew to be." Unable to sleep, her hair slipping out of its curling pins, Blanche paces and paces, dreading the bitter fate of life alone, because yield she mustn't, as apart from Aunt Louisa's stricture about wedlock, the wandering artist is not a Roman Catholic, whereas Blanche is endowed with an intense spiritual nature and the religious sentiment of her race. At the end of each episode, there would be the heading for the next thrilling installment—"Her Wild Blood" or "A Blighted Evening"—but I never got to the chapter "When the Curtain Fell," as that edition never reached us, probably because of shortage of money. Threepence seems so little, but there were times when we did not have it. I recall with scalding shame having to ask at the gate lodge for a penny for my dancing class and therefore hating the dancing teacher, with her beautiful black suede court shoes and her calves so sleek and shapely in her navy silk stockings.

One Sunday I came upon a book in a trunk in a neighbor's attic room. How it got there, I will never know. It was a secondhand book which had been presented to a Mary McDonald as a reward for regular attendance and industry, from the Edinburgh School Board, in 1907. The cover was also a rich dark red, like the *Messenger*, but instead of the Sacred Heart a piquant young woman held her arms out, and in the folds of her red cloak were two blank pages, suggesting the drama of her wayward life. It was called *East Lynne.* It was tastefully illustrated, depicting happy families, father in coattails and mother in long gown with leg-of-mutton sleeves, the blond child the very epitome of happiness. There were 548 pages of it, crammed with love, intrigue, faithlessness, cotton handkerchiefs soaked in eau-de-cologne, distressing dreams, secrets in sachets, and a deathbed scene in which an errant mother, who has returned disguised as a governess to her own children, equivocates whether she should disclose to her little dying son, Willy, her ghastly secret. This errant mother, the Lady Isabel, of fair damask cheek and luxurious falling hair, was daughter of a profligate earl, who died leaving her destitute and therefore in need of marriage. Mr. Carlyle, who lived in West Lynne, though reticent and mindful of the age difference, loses his heart to her, and Isabel, while not being wholeheartedly in love, esteems him and hopes that love will ripen with the years. As she walks up the aisle of the little country church, in a thin black gauze dress because of being in mourning for her father, she little knows the sickening jealousy of Barbara Hare, who had set her cap at Mr. Carlyle. Two women then cast a shadow on that otherwise happy union: Barbara, with poison in her heart, and the imperiously willed Miss Corny, sister of Mr. Carlyle, who takes up residence with them and begrudges Isabel her happiness and her lovely black dresses, beaded with jet. The couple settle into married life, stroll in the grounds in the evenings, and Isabel sits at the piano and sweetly sings verses from *The Bohemian Girl,* as, unable to restrain himself, Mr. Carlyle then holds the dear face to him, "taking from it impassioned kisses." Yet shadows loom. Isabel overhears servants talking of Barbara Hare and her former friendship with Mr. Carlyle, and jealousy, like an incubus, takes hold of the young bride. Yes, years pass. There are full moons and half moons, three children are born, and yet Isabel cannot cure herself of the affliction now gnawing at her heart. She falls ill, goes into decline, whereupon a change of air is recommended, and so, alone in Boulogne-sur-Mer, she re-encounters the dashing Captain Levinson, whom she was once madly in love with. As she sits on the sands to enjoy the sea air each morning, Captain Levinson accompanies her, pretending to serve as the anxious brother in the absence of Mr. Carlyle. Soon she is affected by the intoxicating breezes of his attentions, and the symptoms of clandestine happiness are taking root. Her heart beats with rapture, the skies are bluer, the waving trees have an emerald brightness, and she finds herself increasingly reluctant to separate herself from this dangerous foe. One morning, "taking terrible possession of her arm," he tells her that if ever two human beings were formed to love one another, it is they. She flees Boulogne and his dangerous sophistries; she puts the sea between them, only to find that he follows, ingratiates himself with her husband, and one midnight—it had to be midnight—a chaise and four is tearing through the English countryside, leaving a household in disarray, servants fainting, motherless children, a baffled husband reading a farewell letter, the handwriting swimming before his eyes, and the inevitable fact that Isabel had *flown*. Here the author, Mrs. Henry Wood, painted the frightful colors and blackness of guilt, addressing her readers, presumably all female:

> *Lady, wife, mother, should you ever be tempted to abandon your home so will you awake . . . whatever trials may be the lot of your married life, though they may magnify themselves to your crushed spirit as beyond your endurance of woman to bear, resolve to bear them, bear unto death rather than forfeit your fair name and your good conscience, for be assured that the alternative, if you rush unto it, will be far worse than death.*

Isabel is soon plunged into an abyss of horror; the faithless Captain Levinson is in Paris oftener than not, while she languishes, shivering with cold, hunger, and loneliness in a barn in Grenoble. Completely abandoned, she suffers a railway accident in which she is not only disfigured but lamed in one leg. It serves as a blessing and allows her to come back in disguise to East Lynne as governess to her own children, having assumed the name Madame Vine. Clad completely in black, black crepe swathing throat and chin, thick spectacles, and a pronounced French accent, she has to endure the caresses between Mr. Carlyle and his new wife, Barbara Hare, caresses that were once hers. A solitary candle beams its cold rays in a sickroom where her little boy is dying, while down on her knees, her face buried in the counterpane, a corner of it stuffed in her mouth, the disconsolate mother weeps and weeps, and her former husband, restrained and heroic, remains ignorant of her true identity.

Conveniently, his new wife, Barbara, is thirty miles away at a watering place, and no sooner has the funeral taken place than Isabel herself is struck down, just as her little boy was, and rapidly, helplessly, she deteriorates. Shall she tell him of that which she had never meant to? Throwing out her poor, hot hands, she reveals all and begs his forgiveness. After much deliberation, Mr. Carlyle raises his noble form, pushes her hair from her brow, wipes the death dew from her forehead, and "suffered his lips to rest upon hers."

That same death dew and foolish intoxication I would find again in the pages of Tolstoy, as Anna Karenina, with her black gown, her rounded arms, her bracelets, her string of pearls, her unruly curls, her veiled eyes, also succumbed to the diabolical and enchanting lures of illicit love. But whereas Anna's story stayed with me all my life, poor Isabel's faded. The pent-up scenarios, the cheap thrills, and the manipulation of emotions palled. Anna, at the railway station, about to throw herself under a train, both to punish Vronsky and to escape the malice of others, gets down close to the tracks, looks at the bolts, the chains, the tall iron wheels of the first carriage that is moving up, in order to measure the point midway between the front and back wheels of the second carriage, so as to gauge her exact moment to jump. Poor Isabel, by comparison, is whisked off in a chaise and four in full operatic moonlight.

Nevertheless, some of the cloying tendencies of Mrs. Henry Wood stayed with me on my first foray into fiction, aged about eight. It was written on a jotter, and called *Gypsy.* Isolde, the young heroine, dreamed of escape, incarcerated as she was, and often beaten by a cruel and intemperate father, and without the harmonious influence of a mother, who had been killed off. Her charmer arrives in the person of a Gypsy with a gold earring and red bandanna, who recklessly scours the countryside in a caravan and on horseback. Sighting her one day in the fields, he is struck by her beauty, her ringlets, her pensive expression, and her youth. It needs only dusk, when she is driving cattle in to be milked, for him to abduct her, sit her sidesaddle on his steed, a winding sheet over her head and face, and whisk her to his bastion in the remote mountains. Arriving, she meets a world of strangers, women with flashing but unloving eyes who take her aside and give her a new name, a Romany name, so that she is no longer the Isolde she was. Then she is dressed, groomed, and prepared for her nuptial night, in which I did not rule out the possibility of fatality. By midnight horses are heard. A posse of men have arrived on horseback, led by her father, a volley of gunfire is let off as the two sides engage in battle. Fortunately, I did not have to describe the battle, as the palpitating heroine, from whose point of view the story was told, is bundled into the back of the caravan and hidden under a heavy roll of carpet. All I needed to say was that they fought with the fierceness of Apaches (whatever that meant), that she was rescued by her own, and returned home to her old life of drudgery and submission.

I put my story in a green trunk, where my mother kept oats for her hens, and either it was eventually thrown out or mice nibbled the paper to bits.

After these fictions came the lure of drama. Twice a year traveling players came to the town, and in the town hall, on a stage lit with a few paraffin lamps, we were treated to the vagaries of *East Lynne, Murder in the Old Red Barn,* and *Dracula.* The sight of a very large safety pin being drawn across the tender throat of the young heroine in *Dracula* was too terrible to behold, and also riveting. As living theater it was matchless.

Girls and women cried or choked back their tears, while men pretended to make fun of it, and yet, walking home under the stars, we could talk of nothing else.

The actor who played Dracula was in digs with his wife, in a room above a public house. I decided that I would ask if I could join their company. The domestic situation was depressing. There was one child in a pram, which Dracula wheeled back and forth across the floor, while his wife, with a young baby under her arm, was stirring a saucepan of something on a primus stove. Her complexion without all the pancake makeup was a little ruddy. As for him, all that remained of his luring stage presence was his silverish sidelocks. They were surprised at my having been let up at all, and Dracula asked what I had come for. "I'd like to run away with you," I said, at which the wife laughed and Dracula showed some commiseration. He asked nicely why I wanted to run away with them. I said I had written a play called *Dracula's Daughter* and I wanted to see it on a stage. This whetted his interest so much that he said to come back another day and we could read it together. His wife, in full theatrical blaze, picked up the hot saucepan, aimed it at me, and in a beautiful, actressy voice said, "Scram."

I would go out to the fields to write. The words ran away with me. I would write imaginary stories, stories set in our bog and our kitchen garden, but it was not enough, because I wanted to get inside them, in the same way as I was trying to get back into the maw of my mother. Everything about her intrigued me: her body, her being, her pink corset, her fads, and the obsessions to which she was prone. One was about a little silver spoon from a set of six that she had had since her honeymoon. They were kept in a velvet-lined case, the velvet faded and milky, and they were once loaned to the vocational school when dignitaries were coming for a function. However, when the case was returned, there was one spoon missing, and my mother got on her bicycle and went in high dudgeon to the school. There was a thorough search, in drawers, in cupboards, under tables, in the pantry, in two bins, and in the turf shed. Inquiries were sent all over the village, but somehow my mother knew in her bones that she would never see that spoon again, and she never forgave it. She was convinced that she knew who had taken it, a shopkeeper who was jealous of our semi-grandeur, and ever after there was a coolness between them.

When, much later, I wrote about my mother, that preoccupation with her had intensified so that she permeated all worlds—*Her mother was the cupboard with all the things in it, the tabernacle with God in it, the lake with the legends in it, the sea with the oysters and the corpses, a realm into which she longed to vanish forever.*

Brides of Christ

We were in all three hundred women in that convent, a limestone bastion housing choir nuns, lay nuns, boarders, and orphans, the sinful issue of unmarried mothers. We, the boarders, were little recruits for Heaven, where we would learn to be immune to passions, to mortify ourselves in every way, and to put up with our chilblains.

The prevailing smells were of wax floor polish and cabbage, but in the chapel it was the smell of burning incense, so exotic, and afterward that smell lingered on in the wreaths of smoke that clouded the air.

Not long after I had arrived there, crossing the courtyard, I was halted in my tracks by the sound of whistling, and it seemed to me the sweetest and most melodious sound imaginable. I felt that it was a young boy on his way home from work, and I had the deepest longing not to be in that courtyard but to be out there, walking, walking under the stars. Although we were on the edge of the town, we might as well have been in Timbuktu. Our dormitories were on two floors, one for the junior girls and one for the seniors. Seniors had a private cubicle with a curtain at the end, but for us it was a question of washing by a basin at the side of the bed, girls splashing themselves from ewers of freezing water and trying not to let their dressing gowns slip off. My dressing gown had belonged to my mother. It was fawn and hairy, and my name tag was sewn on the back of the collar. You could tell the girls whose parents were rich by their dressing gowns, which were either quilted or satin, in pink and rose colors. My mother had stitched name tags on all my uniform and, as she said, stitched her heart into each one. She cried for a week after I left, and not once did she break her fast. I fasted also, because the food was awful: meat that was stringy in a pool of brown gravy, the faithful cabbage, and, for evening tea, bread that was already spread with a mixture of butter and dripping. It was wartime and butter was rationed. In those first weeks, a girl whose bed backed onto mine had apples that she'd hidden in her clothes cupboard, and when the lights went out, she would eat them. Depending on her mood, she would or would not offer me some. But before long I learned from a senior that the best way to quell hunger was to put a blob of Vicks VapoRub on the tongue, which induced a slight nausea, though when I fell in love, I was not hungry at all.

The nuns, all sixty or seventy of them, wore voluminous black habits with stiff white gimp that framed their faces and chiseled them. Nuns who had taken their final vows wore a wedding band on the ring finger, which signified that they were the Bride of Christ, and lay nuns, who were different from choir nuns, also had those wedding bands, but they wore aprons and did the menial work. Three hundred women with their humors and their tempers and their yearnings and their doubts and their several menstruations. My religious fervor would soar and falter during those years into which I crammed so much knowledge and information that I would in time forget.

They were dour years, in which I came to love Latin, the words so right in my mouth, as if it were the mother tongue—*amo, amas, amat, amamus, amatis, amant;* years in which I failed by a few marks to win a scholarship, the scholarship that my parents so fervently hoped I would win, as the annual fee of forty pounds was a tremendous strain on their resources; years during which I would fall in love with a nun in a manner no different, no less rapturous, from the successive loves which I would conceive for men down the years.

Three times a week we were allowed a walk outside the gates, though not through the town itself, since we might be subjected to worldly or profane temptations. The town, Loughrea, which took its name from the lake, had a population of several hundred souls and, as we were told, was cutting its industrial teeth by mining for zinc and silver some eight miles distant. We walked in pairs and were supposed not to speak, though the tossing of our lunches into the lake inevitably led to hilarity. After the first week, disgusted by the stringy meat and the strips of cabbage, I, like every girl, put my lunch in a bit of paper and tucked it inside my gym frock, to dump in the lake. The gravy leaked into the chest and left a wet, warm patch there. I remember the walks as being windy, and when the lake was frozen, a man in dungarees went in with a sledgehammer and broke the thick shelves of ice in order to let the pairs of swans move about, as they did imperceptibly, breaching the dark pockets of freed water.

The convent had its rules, its friendships, its penances, and its hilarities. Once, by mistake, a girl flushed a ten-shilling note down the lavatory and was in utter despair. It happened to be the same period as when parcels were arriving for Halloween, and when the Head Nun gave her nightly homily, referring to the parcels piling up in the parlor, she said that there seemed to be a great flush of money about. Hearing the word "flush" sent the girls into peals of laughter. We all laughed, including the girl who had lost her ten-shilling note. So perplexed was our nun by this skittishness, and our refusal to say what it was about, that she too began to laugh, and it was the only time it ever occurred to me that she might have a human trait.

The nun I was poised to fall in love with was different. She was younger, her cheeks extremely pale, ivory-colored, with sometimes the merest tincture of wine-red on her cheekbones when in frustration she became inflamed if we failed to grasp the geometry theorem that she had just written on the blackboard.

I would watch for her. I would wait for her. I would rush to her assistance when she came down steps with a load of books and copybooks, often, too often, beaten to it by other strapping girls who were also smitten with her. Yet one evening, when I passed her unexpectedly in the recreation hall, she gave me what I can only call the intimation of a smile—but it *was* an encouragement. In the chapel I saw where she knelt, the slope of her long back an escarpment, her collarbones the pillars of the Parthenon, these newfangled comparisons I had gleaned from a book I had found in the glass bookcase that was opened on Sundays when, for one hour, we were allowed to read for recreation. There were devout books, the lives of saints, the sermons of Cardinal Newman, and the wholesome novels of Canon P. Sheehan describing the dull lives of families in County Tipperary. The book I picked out by accident was an encyclopædia of gods and goddesses, full of strange and unlikely occurrences. Dionysus, god of wine and moisture, visiting King Dion in Aetolia fell in love with Carya, whose jealous sisters were about to betray her to their father, when Dionysus struck them with madness and turned them into rocks. Male gods disguised themselves in such cunning ways, appearing as the North Wind or bedraggled cuckoos or in the fleeces of ewes to ravish nymphs and goddesses, whereupon miraculous conceptions ensued that were, however, unlike that of the Virgin Mary, who had conceived by the Holy Ghost. These long-ago gods, with their cunning and their debaucheries, were so different from our stern God who lived above in the tabernacle where one day I would have to stand as a punishment.

To my astonishment, when the Halloween parcels were handed out, I received one. It was a cone-shaped glass bowl filled with delicacies, covered with red transparent paper that came to a crown at the top and was tied with a white satin bow. It had been sent directly from a shop, and on a white card was printed a woman's name and her compliments. I remembered my mother and I visiting her just outside Galway city, in Salthill, and how smartly dressed she was in a fitted suit as she sat watching us eat, not touching a pick of the food that had been prepared for us. She told us something that nearly caused my mother to faint. For her operation, which she called an "op," and which I suspected concerned women's ailments, her husband had been allowed into the operating theater for a moment beforehand, where he saw her naked. She took pride in telling this. Why she had sent me a parcel I would never know, but my popularity soared as I handed out slices of chocolate cake each evening and gave girls in the dormitory monkey nuts and hazelnuts to crack on.

The air was damp, and that, along with cold nights, as we shivered under one blanket and a cotton eiderdown, meant that girls got chilblains, sore throats, and coughs; some were confined to the big lonely dormitory and given a cup of senna for a cure.

One evening at Benediction the coughing got out of hand. At the very moment when the priest, his hands covered in a white veil, held up the monstrance that contained the Blessed Sacrament and a choir nun was pouring her ecstasy into *Stabat Mater,* a bout of multiple coughs eclipsed all else. It was sacrilege. Afterward the Head Nun asked for those who had been culpable to put their hands up, and my hand went up automatically, but I was alone. For punishment I was told that I would have to stand in the chapel the following day when the other girls went out for their walk.

Standing by the rails that led to the altar, I feared that my nun might come in to say a hurried prayer, and seeing me, she would wonder what my most heinous sin could be. The chapel, without lit candles and other girls, felt lonely, and the smell from the chrysanthemums that were on the altar steps also had a sad smell of clay.

But it was worth everything, the standing, the humiliation, and my smarting at the injustice of the fact that other girls had not owned up. At evening rosary, I noticed that my prayer book had been put back the wrong way. Girls kept prayer books in cubby holes at the back of the chapel, and the nun must have discovered mine with the name "Drewsboro" on the flyleaf. There was a holy picture on yellow parchment. From a golden-hazed sky, watery rays of light, needle-thin, poured down onto a host of angels who were also suspended in a kind of ethereal light. So holy was it that it could serve as a little portable altar. But it was the words written on the back that made me gasp: *O Lord, rebuke me not in thy wrath, neither chasten me in thy hot displeasure.* What did it mean? It didn't matter what it meant. It would carry me through lessons and theorems and soggy meat and cabbage, because now, and in secret, I had been drawn into the wild heart of things.

For the Christmas entertainments a trunk was flung down for us to pick our costumes. Fancy dresses, capes, shawls, all smelling of camphor, for us to rifle. As I was going to recite Mark Antony's baleful speech over Caesar's body, I chose a velvet toga that was much too big and a roped curtain cord to hold it up. When my nun arrived, I was already rehearsing, feverishly—

"Friends, Romans, countrymen, lend me your ears"—and she drew me aside and said to take the speech a little less impulsively, to live the lines and enter into the pity of them, of imperial Caesar, whose wife had warned him not to go out that morning, having seen that he would be slaughtered. She helped me into the clogs that were too big for me and, from a dampish sponge, smeared white matte pancake makeup all over my face. For the performance she stood in the wings praying, and I was conscious of her being there. Afterward she beckoned, and I followed her to the reception parlor, which was exclusive to the Head Nun, yet she risked it. She had a surprise for me, which she hauled from her big, deep pocket. It was a quarter-pound box of chocolates with pictures of blue kingfishers on the paper wrapping. How had she come by it? I thought it must have been a gift to her, and instead of handing it over to the Reverend Mother, in rampant disobedience she had hidden it for me.

That first Christmas at home I was chillier with my mother, who could not understand the change in me. I would not eat the cakes or the trifle that she foisted on me, and I went out each evening to neighbors' houses to sit with them, while my mother longed for me to sit with her. There was a widow whose new house was halfway between the two villages, pebble-dashed, with flower beds in front. It smelled of mortar and fresh paint. In her small kitchen, our knees close up to the enamel stove, we sat, her breakfast things already laid at the far end of the table, a cup and saucer, a porridge bowl, and a linen napkin in a bone ring. She would fill me in on all the latest news, which was unvarying, publicans that were in trouble with guards for after-hours drinking, neighbors in bitter land disputes, and husbands and wives who threatened to kill one another. After a decent interval, she would say, "What about a little toddy?" and disappear, swiftly coming back with the sherry bottle under her arm and two glasses, a small liqueur glass for me and a larger cut-glass one for herself. The sherry was a dark, rich amber color, and there were soft lemon biscuits to break and dip into it and suck from. After a few drinks, she got either skittish or maudlin, missing the husband that had drowned, still cut up because spiteful people had said that it wasn't an accident and that he had done it on purpose, to get away from her. She would then, in a bathos of tears, recite a poem called "People Will Talk."

I did not shed a tear going back after the holidays, knowing that my nun was there waiting for me, and the very first moment that we bumped into one another, I knew by certain signs that, if anything, her affections had deepened.

The County Home, run by the same order, was a mile outside the town, overlooking the lake, and a cousin of my father's, a nursing sister, was matron there. The grounds were full of old people, old men and old women, dribbling and pottering and tending to the rockery. It was not nearly as regimental as the convent, as they were nursing nuns and had a bit more pity. I had brought a Christmas cake from my mother to my father's cousin and so was allowed to deliver it to her. A tiny woman who did not reach my shoulder, she had a birdlike flutter, all excitement, as she laid down the tea tray, rushing in and out, calling to her charges, saying they were stone deaf, giving orders that they could not hear and going herself to get the cup and saucer and the teapot and the large slice of sponge cake with the raspberry jam filling that was on a plate covered with a white doily. She was the soul of affection and far more outspoken than other nuns. She said that had she known how hard religious life was to be and the trials and severities that awaited her, she would never have entered at all.

I did not stay long, because I had a plan. It meant taking a longer route around the lake and to the far end of the town, so as not to be spied upon. A statue of Stoney Brennan, with his bulbous head, whom the English had hanged for having stolen a turnip, was in a recess in the wall, and possibly in honor of Christmas, someone had streaked his cheeks with cardinal-red paint and stuck a cigarette butt in his mouth. The other sign of Christmas was the long strips of tinsel in the pharmacy window, idly whirling.

The sense of elation was almost unbearable: to be out on the street, breathing, as I believed, the wicked air, harboring a hectic love for my nun, and on the point of buying her the gift that would be a godsend to her on cold, frosty nights. In the window of the draper's shop, there was a mannequin of a lady, a Miss Moderna, in a black crepe dress, cut on the bias, and I would have given anything to have been slender enough to fit into it. The shop smelled of every kind of cloth, wool and linen and serge, and the woman behind the counter looked up, surprised to see a convent girl in a navy gabardine coat and school cap. She guessed that I had stolen a march. I had come to buy bed socks. A white shoebox stacked with socks, summer and winter, was flung on the counter, and I picked out a pair in wool and angora that was striped in contrasting shades of pink. The woman complimented me on my taste and said I had picked the most expensive pair of socks in the batch. All I had was two shillings, but since she knew where to find me, and was in on my transgression, she was certain to receive the remaining sixpence. Nevertheless, she wrote my name and the IOU into a big ledger that seemed to be full of names and IOUs written with a scratchy pen in heavy brown ink. She wrapped the socks in silver paper. It was not a flashy silver, more a dun silver, the same as used to be around a cake, called Oxford Luncheon, which my grandmother presented to my mother when she came on her annual holiday, never staying the full week, missing home and the mountains; somehow there was an estrangement between them, mother and daughter. The silver paper around the Oxford Luncheon smelled of raisins, sultanas, and candied peel, whereas the silver paper around the pink socks smelled of nothing. I placed it in the pew where my nun knelt.

I knew that she had received them and possibly loved them, because not long after, and quite irrelevantly, she spoke of the difference between angora wool, which is the down of the rabbit, and cashmere from the down of the goat, both being very sought after.

That term was one of ecstasies and doubt, the seesaw of love, the shiverings, depriving myself of the pleasure of seeing her in order to think about her and then flinging myself in front of her, like a fawning dog waiting for its reward. Our friendliest times were in the cookery kitchen, when after the class she would sometimes ask me to stay behind and help clear up. It was informal: white flour on her fingers and on her habit, stacking saucepans and colanders, as occasionally we would say small things to one another that meant multitudes. She seemed to guess that I had decided to become a nun, and that in a few years we would both be under the same roof, subject to the same rules, in our hair shirts, sleeping on iron springs, stoically immune to passions and temptations.

Then it happened. The coolness. She began to look pinched and pale, and was bad-tempered in class. She allowed other girls to carry her books. She swept from classroom to classroom like a creature possessed. I dreamed it before it actually happened, I dreamed that she would have to go away. One evening she was seen in the back of a motorcar, along with another nun, both in their heavy knitted shawls, obviously setting out on a long journey. I believed that she was gone forever, that she had had to renounce her vows and was being brought home to her parents in disgrace; it was weeks after, agonizing weeks, when from a young postulant who came from a parish near home I learned the truth. My nun had had a crisis of sorts, a bit of a breakdown, and was sent to the Sister house in Ballinasloe to recover. There was an entire term without her.

Yet when I did see her again, many months later, my hopes were raised. We had all assembled for the Head Nun's evening homily, when she came in softly, so softly, whispered something to the Head Nun, and then, when our eyes met briefly, I felt that I had reason to be euphoric. But it was not so. I would never see her alone again. I had moved to a higher class, where a different, brisker nun took geometry and maths. Our paths rarely crossed, but one evening, in the chapel grounds, I saw her coming toward me, alone. There was no one but us. She was whispering her prayers, but as she sighted me, her hands came out from inside her copious sleeves and flew up in defense, as if I were an enemy. She passed swiftly, her praying much louder.

Because of my seeming devoutness and obedience, I was given the honor of playing Our Lady of Fatima in the school play. It was not a speaking part. All I had to do was stand with hands folded as in prayer and gaze at the three shepherd children of Fatima, who knelt below and to whom I was secretly to impart the third secret. My throne consisted of four wooden butter boxes, all covered in pale blue tulle. I, too, was draped in blue tulle. Another girl, who stood at the side of the stage, informed the audience of the first two secrets, which were to do penance and pray for the conversion of godless Russia. The third secret was preceded by lights, to represent a trembling sun, a sun that moved outside cosmic laws, a sun surrounded by scarlet and purple, which had stretched the abilities of stage management, who had only a flash lamp and some bicycle lamps to rely on. While I was pausing to impart the third secret, the three children recited the rosary as the audience waited, or were expected to wait, in thrall. The prophecy itself, which was most significant, was conveyed by the narrator, who somehow divined the secret words I had transmitted to the children. It predicted a dreadful calamity upon the Church and the martyrdom of the Pope, at which there was wailing from a chorus of girls in their navy gym frocks and the shepherd children lay on the stage, disconsolate. My sole duty was to stand utterly still, not to wobble, as befitted the profundity of my message. Many compliments were bestowed on me for the first two nights, but it was the third night that mattered most, because priests and the Bishop of Galway were attending. Nerves and excitement spiraled. Even as I climbed the butter boxes, I felt unsteady. They seemed not so solid as they had been before, and the distance between myself and the shepherd children seemed enormous. I began to shake, to shake uncontrollably, gripping the blue tulle, which was in itself sacrilege, since I was supposed to remain with my hands folded. I could see the children underneath were also becoming a bit distraught, but I was unable to stop it. All I begged was to get through those forty-five minutes and not disgrace myself, and I had almost regained composure when it started up again, only worse: the sun trembled and indeed made movements outside cosmic laws, as I too began to see things, lost consciousness, and like Humpty Dumpty came tumbling down, to the dismay of the children and flurry as the narrator and a nun hefted me off. The curtain had to be brought down. My understudy, who was not wearing tulle, mounted the butter boxes, and the performance had to start again.

In my cubicle, where I had gone to hide, I could hear the applause, and later a lay nun brought me a jam tart, and though I could not be sure, I imagined it was from *my* nun, to indicate that she had lived my shame with me.

He was known to be a hobo, and yet, when he arrived off the evening bus in the town, things perked up and word went round that Roland was here. Even his name, Roland, had the ring of legend. He was from somewhere in County Limerick and came to stay with a bachelor in the town who owned a hardware shop and kept several greyhounds which he half-starved, yet in his booming voice he would call out, "Roland, give the dogs some water." It was at the Sunday-night "hops" that Roland came into his own, in his navy blazer and open shirt, bell-bottomed trousers, and hair slicked back with Brylcreem. His technique, as it was known, was feigned casualness as he watched the form, then tugged at some girl's arm, this being an invitation to dance, along with the usual "Righty-ho?"

The "hops," for which admission was sixpence, was in aid of a new altar for the chapel, which was to be in Italianate marble with mosaics of gold and modeled on an altar in the Vatican. The parish priest stood near the entrance, where one got the ticket, and afterward he sat on a chair inside the hall to ensure that couples did not make free with one another when dancing. The floor was slippery from some new miracle powder that had been discovered, and it was no longer having to endure the awful smell of paraffin oil with which they used to douse it.

I was waiting for the results of my exam. After the shame of Fatima and my nun's coolness and other restlessnesses, I made up my mind to cut my education short and sit for my final exam one year early. It entailed endless studying, including with a torch under the covers in my cubicle at night. I kept reading, devouring all these facts. I had graduated to a private cubicle and, because of my endless studying, became something of a favorite with several nuns. When I got styes or nervous turns, the Head Nun would call me aside and give me valerian, which she dropped from a little pipette into a beaker, that and boric powder to bathe the eyes.

It was the first time I had attended one of the hops, and I was excited by it. A boy called Percy asked me up for a waltz, and as we moved along to the strains of a very sentimental tune, he inquired what color my eyes were and how far I lived out of the town.

This was an oblique way of deciding whether or not to ask to walk me home. The men were always angling to walk girls home, and if things went as they hoped, it meant they would desert the main road and go down the Dock Road or to a path under the bridge, across fields where there were unused cow houses and lime kilns. But no local girl could hope to compete with Dolly the crooner. She was a peroxide blonde with black fishnet stockings and black suede high-heeled shoes. She also wore black velvet gloves that reached to her elbows, and men, watching her hold the microphone as she delivered the slushy song, nudged each other, wondering if they would score. But she was always accompanied by a bruiser, a rough diamond who had metal rings on several fingers, enough to dissuade any upstarts. Toward the end of the evening her songs centered on heartbreak and infidelity. There was "After the Ball," in which many a heart was broken, "Jealousy," and "The Tennessee Waltz," in which, gallingly, a friend steals another man's sweetheart.

One night, before my last term at school, I somehow guessed that Roland was going to ask me up, which he did, with the expected "Righty-ho?" I cannot remember how we conducted it, except to know that, when the dance was over and lights extinguished, we left and hovered on the street until there were no longer any car lights or any flash lamps. Not a word was said. I went with him half-willingly, and we climbed the town under a sky that was a feast of stars, outglittering each other. There wasn't a soul in the street, the townspeople fast asleep in their beds.

Once installed in a siding, by a galvanized door that led into a yard, I began my procrastinations. The upshot was that I opened my coat and allowed my skirt to be bunched up around me. That part of himself that he exposed he half-camouflaged in a handkerchief, and his exertions were so robust that they might just as easily have been spent on the door itself, which shook and rattled. I feared it would alert some holy Mary who might be on the prowl, with a flash lamp, for such indecency. The headlights of the car at the bottom of the hill showed the sheen of wet on the street, and everything was then hurried as he unbolted the door and pushed me into a big yard. In the bit of light from the moon I saw that the yard was full of blue chip stones, as the shopkeeper was a supplier of them.

Roland did not convey me home.

Back in the convent I studied constantly, not wanting to fail my final examination, as it would mean incarceration for another year. The world with all its sins and guile and blandishments was beckoning.

PART TWO

Big Time

After stumbling along country roads and fields at night, the beam from the flashlight fitful and the battery forever in danger of conking out, I found Dublin enthralling: the street lighting was as marvelous as the illuminations said to have lit the sky with *Laudamus, Adoramus,* and *Glorificamus* during the Eucharistic Congress of 1932. Light flooded the pavements and glinted off the steel of the defunct tramlines, and sent a gold-threaded haze up into a line of young trees where birds roosted.

It was a Saturday night in the late 1940s and my first walk into the city with my sister Eileen; Anna, the girl we shared digs with; and Maeve, a friend of hers, arms linked in pairs. We passed a fairly shabby-looking hotel, where they said hurlers and their followers drank after a match, and then a select grocer's with cooked hams in the window, so tempting, the bread-crumb crusting of mustard and brown sugar studded with cloves. I was ravenous. For food. For life. For the stories that I would write, except that everything was effervescent and inchoate in my overexcitable brain.

"There goes Bang-Bang," Maeve said. Each night, holding a key as if it were a gun, Bang-Bang would jump onto buses, throw himself on the platform, shout warnings, then jump off again, but no one paid any heed to him, knowing he had been shell-shocked during the war.

We stood to gape into the Gresham Hotel, the apogee of grandeur, with its overhanging iron and glass awning. Anna said that it was where priests from down the country stayed when they came to Dublin, so that it exuded both a sacred and a salubrious aura. The giant column of Nelson's pillar was so tall that it was impossible to see Nelson's face with his blind eye. Aldermen of the city had erected it in 1809 to celebrate his victory over Napoleon in the Battle of Trafalgar. But poor Nelson had yet to undergo more hazards. His column would be toppled by an IRA explosive, and the head, which was left intact, stored in a shed, only to be stolen, the thief then sending a postal order to the authorities, via an evening paper, to cover the damages for broken glass, padlock, window frame, and screws. Many, including the boxer "Strongman Butty Sugrue," coveted that head, and very soon it was stolen again and displayed in an antique shop in London, then later returned and laid to rest on the original site. There it was booed while an official from the Corporation took it away, only to drop it as he loaded it into the lorry, and after more skittishness Nelson was taken to end his days in the calm environs of a library.

At the base of the pillar, the women known as the "Shawlies" were putting the squashed fruits, flowers, and vegetables into their barrows, and the ground was slippy from the skins and the pulp. All Dublin knew them, shouting out their wares—"Cox's apples... blood oranges... blood oranges"—and then repairing to the pub on Saturday night, fighting like tinkers, the expletives more and more "choice," vowing to have each other's "guts for garters." One, by the name of Rosie, Maeve said, was a right card, known for her "Upperocity," every phrase beginning with "As de Valera would have it." De Valera was our Taoiseach, an austere figure who sat in front of the Blessed Sacrament for an hour each day, and so devout was he that he brought gifts of blessed scapulars to distribute among the heathens in foreign delegations.

There too, prancing about, was the dotty woman in a tweed costume and a hat with a red cockade, conducting her moral crusade, holding up the crucifix of large rosary beads for passersby to kiss, half-singing, half-speaking:

> All is in the hand of Mary,
> In the mighty hand of Mary,
> All is in the hand of Mary,
> Her legion marches on.

Opposite the pillar was the General Post Office, where the men of the 1916 rebellion proclaimed the Irish Constitution, raised the Irish flag, but soon were overwhelmed and summarily executed in Kilmainham yard. Farther along, a statue of Daniel O'Connell, the Catholic emancipator, an iron man in a black iron coat with iron angels guarding him. But I was finished with all that, with history and martyrs and fields and the seven woods and religious maniacs, being, as I believed, on the brink of daring emancipation.

The four corners of O'Connell Bridge were flanked by tall lamps on stout cast-iron pedestals that gave it an air of majesty. We were entering the south side of the city, thought to be swisher, and on toward the purlieus of Grafton Street, which was the "acme of fashion." There were more imposing statues, and in College Green, where not a patch of grass was to be seen, there was a sign for Bovril, so dazzling, so bewitching, that to stand before it, to absorb the red-gold glitter of each of the six capital letters, was to witness an earthly aurora borealis.

Trinity College took up an entire corner of a street, the stone gray and somber, the windows unlit, as if it had gone to sleep on itself. Far more fetching was the Bovril sign across the way, that medley of color flickering on and off, flickers that corresponded to the hope and wildness going on inside me.

We gazed in shop windows in Grafton Street, the styles so gorgeous, so enviable, but with no price tags on the diaphanous dresses. Then we came back on the opposite side, passing a beggar woman on the bridge who was holding a bunch of scallions, either because she had been given them out of pity or she was hoping to sell them. Her skin had a peculiar greenish hue from the rays of the lamps, and she muttered as we passed along. We stopped outside an Italian ice-cream parlor to look longingly at scoops of ice cream in dainty glass dishes, with melted chocolate or red cordial poured over them, and in taller glasses there were sundaes with crests of whipped cream in flawless whirligig. Having no money was galling.

The first awakening was to come the next day, the Sunday, when my sister and I visited cousins in Phibsboro and watched from the velvet sofa as they ate their Sunday lunch, relishing it, offering us nothing, not even a slice of the apple pie that a maid passed around on a palette knife, having already cut it in the kitchen.

Still, that Monday morning, I set out for the chemist's shop in Cabra Road with unwonted pride. I was wearing my best, pleated skirt and a navy cardigan, and luckily, as it was September, the lumpen tweed coat of which I was ashamed hung in the wardrobe. In the chemist's shop I would spend the next four years, training for a profession that was not my chosen one, but convinced that I would meet poets and that one day I would be admitted into the world of letters.

The chemist who greeted me, and under whose tutelage I would be, had a pale, pinched face and gold-rimmed spectacles, and the boss's wife was all pie at first, then peevish, when it transpired that I had come without a shop coat. Reluctantly she took two pound notes from the till and told me to go to the drapery along the parade, to get a coat, adding that each week half a crown would be deducted from my wages. My salary was seven and six per week, and with this eventuality it would be only five shillings for several weeks to come, which did not allow for much diversion. There was little room for that anyhow, as three nights a week I attended pharmaceutical lectures on the south side of the city and, two other nights, lectures to qualify as an optician, something my brother decided would be to the family's advantage. The optical lessons were in Kevin Street, part of the slums, so gaily immortalized in Sean O'Casey's plays, the Joxers and Fluthers drinking their wages in the pubs, as they philosophized on the planets while their wives pushed prams, like the legendary and ghostly Molly Malone, "through streets broad and narrow," to forage for a lump of coal, a crust of bread, a head of cabbage, anything to feed their children. Cycling through those dark streets, I saw no poetry, only loads of washing on makeshift clotheslines and on the crumbling wrought-iron balconies of the tenements.

"Soft morning, city! Lsp! I am leafy speafing," Anna Livia said, except that my mornings were neither soft nor leafy as I set out for work on a crock of a bicycle, trying to negotiate my way between the other cyclists, the buses, and people late for work. Once a month there was a cattle mart in North Circular Road; the beasts were hectored out of the back of lorries, roaring and bawling, an almost human plaint to their cries, chafing against their new confines, some refusing to be herded, running loose, as the drovers, with their ash plants and their bludgeons, walloped them on their heads and on their shins. At Hanlon's Corner I would have to dismount because of all this commotion, the drovers shouting and belting the poor beasts, which slithered, their wet scutters everywhere, and bus drivers honking their horns impatiently. The drovers, like myself, all hailed from the country and were either "bullock men" or "heifer men," carefree and galumptious. Countrymen, they had come to the city as youths and taken a liking to it, working in the knackers' yards and the mart and later driving the animals miles to the docks, lords of the streets, in their dirty trench coats and pliant ash plants. All of it brought back the reek and constraints of home, and I would remember the three unanswered letters from my mother and tremble at my remiss. Things in our house would flash before my eyes involuntarily, the orange papier-mâché bowl, with bills and Mass cards, and the bottle of ink tilted on one side, ready for the next letter and the next as she drained the last drops to set down the numerous things on her mind.

> Some have died for love
> Some for the nation
> But I met my death
> Through the Dublin Corporation.

Such was the rhyme I recited to myself on my perilous journey to one or two of the chemist's shops owned by my employers. In Cabra Road the clientele was poor, chiselers rapping the glass counter for "tuppence or thruppence worth of gentian violet for me sister's worms," whereas in the Navan Road the clients were more effete, bluff men in tweed jackets and wives with husky voices, who came, or sent their chauffeurs, to collect Dexedrine tablets, which were reputed to be "uppers" and also good for slimming. My duties in both shops at first were fairly menial. I would stack the shelves, weigh packets of Epsom salts, Glauber salts, borax, and boric acid into small paper bags and label them, and gradually acquaint myself with the prescriptions of two rival doctors, which were written in Latin. My shop coat was a feature, since it had a stiff collar not unlike a priest's, with a panel of mother-of-pearl buttons across the left shoulder.

Dublin was full of stories, some funny and spry, and sometimes gruesome. A blond nurse, known for her flamboyance, who drove a red MG, provided illegal abortions in a dingy room, while ostensibly offering cures for dandruff and constipation. Her methods were primitive, injecting a solution of ergot and a flushing out with Jeyes Fluid, but unfortunately she fell foul of the law when a dead mother was found on a curb in Hume Street and a newborn baby abandoned on the side of a road in County Meath. She was sentenced to penal servitude in Mountjoy Prison, not far from the chemist's shop where I, longing for lovemaking novenas for love, was nevertheless haunted by the specter of Mamie Cadden, who to some was an angel of deliverance, to others a murderer, and who would die, declared insane, in a lunatic asylum in Dundrum.

There were as well the old codgers at street corners dying for talk, reeling off the names and nicknames of legendary characters, Zozimus, Johnny Forty-Coats, Paddy Bones Sweeney, along with the balladeers and poets and poetasters and pensioners with their "God be with the old days, the Glory days" and how Dublin would have been finished during the war, except for the horses and horsemen who ran their hearts out to be of service. Around the gates of Trinity College were the medical students, with their smart mufflers, among them a few foreigners from deepest Africa, who were all reputed "to be Princes in their own right."

First he tickled her
Then he patted her
Then he passed the female catheter.
For he was a medical
A jolly old medico.

I got to know the various customers in the chemist's shop, their ailments and their money worries, asking for "tick" until payday at the weekend. I acquired a straggle of admirers in the

Navan Road shop, boys and young men from the nearby deaf-and-dumb institution, who would come and just stand, striving for speech, like convicts with their shorn heads and rough gray uniforms, and if they chanced to catch sight of themselves in the mirror that fronted the weighing scales, they backed away. They didn't like what they saw. But their smiles were glorious, and they reddened when they saw me take down the big jar to nick a few sticks of barley sugar, which they sucked and sucked on, and outdid each other in craven gratitude. The boss's wife would not have approved, but this was harmless in comparison with what my mother was advocating: my devout mother, in one of her letters, said that in his *Summa Theologica* Saint Thomas Aquinas had recommended poorly paid workers to steal from their rich masters in necessity. How she came to know of *Summa Theologica,* or a twelfth-century saint, was beyond me.

A retired guard called Paschal, who had a duodenal ulcer, and who at first used to stand like a sentry while his prescription was being made up, got to learn of my interest in books and loaned me two of his. After some time he confided in me the fact that he was writing an article, intending to show up the country's bigotry and ignorance. There was, as he said, the utter disgrace of Rouault's *Christ in His Passion* moldering in some secret room. Friends of the National Collections stumped up four hundred pounds to present it as a gift to the Municipal Gallery, which refused to hang it on grounds of obscenity. They were not alone in their disgust, as the ex-Lord Mayor, a Mrs. Clark, described it as "a travesty that was offensive to Christian sentiment" and a Mr. Keating, a painter, called it "childish, naïve, and unintelligible." Paschal said that there were only a few enlightened people left in the country, one being the columnist Myles na gCopaleen, who had written mockingly of the farcical fate of Rouault, saying that, of course, no Irish man, with his "extensive knowledge of Sacred art and the bondieuiserie of the Boulevard St. Sulpice," could tolerate such abomination in his bedroom.

Yes, as Paschal said, regrettably the great gods were gone. Yeats dead and eventually buried in Drumcliffe; Joyce dead and buried in Zurich, next to a zoo; O'Casey living in England and writing acrimonious letters to the paper; and Beckett, "the bawd and the blasphemer," as good as dead, having moved to Paris. It was, as Paschal said, "all down to one man," the archdruid of Drumcondra, Archbishop John Charles McQuaid, who kept Ireland free from paganism and modern aberrations. Dublin was in thrall to him, with his distinctive aura, in red cloak and red biretta, wearing the "Borgia ring" of precious amethyst presented at his inauguration by the Knights of Saint Columbanus. If he attended a religious concert, the choir sang out "*Ecce Homo*" as a spotlight was trained on him. His powers were primordial, what with an acquiescent government, a vast network of spies and numerous religious sodalities. Such was his empathy with the Vatican that Ireland, poor though she was, paid the expense to keep the oil lamps of St. Peter's lit. His exigence was known to all, but the full and paranoid extent of it was only revealed in a marvelous and sometimes hilarious book by John Cooney, after his death. In it some of the more obscure vagaries of the archbishop are featured, such as the telescope he had fitted in his country seat, Notre Dame des Bois, to spy on couples and young men on Killiney Beach after dark, that and his penchant for sexually explicit medical manuals written in Latin.

The negative influences with which he was obsessed were British newspapers, evil literature, communism, and foreign soccer players. The cinema too was a hotbed of iniquity. Only instructional films, such as *The Fight against Tuberculosis,* or those showing the maneuvers of various local defense forces, were recommended, and at his bidding protests were organized outside cinemas; at different times Orson Welles, Danny Kaye, Larry Adler, and Arthur Miller were all denounced for their leftist tendencies. Even Cole Porter in time was censored. When, for *Hospitals' Request,* the words "Always true to you, darlin', in my fashion" were played on the radio, the archbishop insisted that the following week they be replaced by harmless instrumental orchestra music. For his "modesty campaign" he used to be driven in his deluxe Dodge through the streets of Dublin at night, looking for any sign of miscreance, and if there were nude mannequins in a shop window of a department store, he ordered that they be removed next day. When, mistakenly, tampons were introduced without consulting him, he immediately issued an episcopal censure to the government, so that an unfortunate parliamentary secretary for health had to explain that the sale of tampons was to be discontinued, as they were in danger of stimulating girls at an impressionable age and could eventually lead them into acquiring contraceptives (which were also illegal) to satisfy their dangerously aroused passions.

The craze for fashion was whetted when in the papers I saw advertisements for dinner gowns in banana cream, coatees embroidered with pearls and diamonds, black muskrat stoles, and whitener for "Milady's teeth." But I had saved only enough to get a pair of gold sleepers, believing the words of the song, "And if your love wears golden earrings, she belongs to you..." It was to Dr. Masterson I went, as I knew his name from the prescriptions, which were almost impossible to decipher. He was a gruff man. The method was rudimentary. A needle was bored through the earlobe, into a cork at the back, then wriggled and rewriggled to make a hole large enough for the little sleeper to be fitted. Before he began, he said that if I squealed at the first one, he wouldn't do the second. His dispensary was crowded and pierced ears were a frivolity. For a week or so, little crusts of dried blood could be seen on my earlobes, which the dummies examined and fretted over.

I was on my bicycle when I saw a group in Baggott Street that had surrounded a tall woman dressed completely in black, like a nun. It was outside the Unicorn restaurant, and being so tall, she had stooped to address them. Someone said that this was Maud Gonne, the fairy queen about whom Yeats, laboring in ecstasy, had written poem after poem. She was the Woman of the Sidhe, who long ago on horseback, with her dog Dagda behind her, rode all over Donegal to give heart and fire to the evicted peasants as their cabins collapsed under the assaults of the battering ram. It was the nearest I would ever come to a myth, because not only had she served as Yeats's muse, she had also married Major John McBride, a hero of the Boer War, and one of the men executed in the doomed 1916 rebellion. History and literature had meshed and were embodied in her loftiness—"Pallas Athene at Howth station, waiting a train."

As she walked away, an older man, shaking with emotion, recited the prophetic poem that Yeats had written to her:

> . . . A crowd
> Will gather, and not know it walks the very street
> Whereon a thing once walked that seemed a burning cloud.

Some years later I would meet her son, Sean McBride, who had all his mother's aristocratic air and mien, his temples like hers, white as alabaster, and his accent slightly French from having grown up in Normandy. He took me to lunch in Jammet's, Dublin's grandest restaurant, and afterward he smoked a cigar and had a cognac, while I had a peppermint frappé, my first ever. I was married by then and lived in County Wicklow, and McBride offered to drive me part of the way, toward the Wicklow Mountains, to Kilmacanogue. I was too frightened to let him hold my hand on the journey. That rectitude, combined with my longing, was what made him the protagonist in my first novel, *The Country Girls,* the aloof and mysterious barrister whom Kate would moon over and lose her heart to, in fiction.

As Christmas was approaching, the head of the transport company announced that railway stations no longer needed to resemble Victorian ones and, moreover, to banish the ghost of rationing stations, would be lit up to generate a "festive atmosphere." Ornate greeting boards, hanging flower baskets, fairy lights, and garlands went up. The tallest tree ever seen in the capital was in Westland Row. But I was going home from a different station, "Kingsbridge of the bitter winds," with the borrowed volume of Sean O'Casey's autobiography in my suitcase. I had the same old tweed coat with, however, an added touch of flamboyance, a gentleman's scarf of white silk with sumptuous fringing that I had bought in a secondhand shop for a song. As I arrived home, the welcome was effusive, and my mother felt the gold sleepers, as if somehow they reminded her of her own youth.

That next morning, not having to mount the bicycle, I slept till noon, and she wakened me with a pot of tea and fingers of toast cut very daintily. She was curious about Dublin, the style in the shop windows, the altars in the numerous churches, the friars in their brown robes hurrying through the streets to minister to the sick, and our cousins who, though they came each summer and ate like gluttons, were too stingy to give us a cup of tea.

Later I went out into the fields. It was frosty, the grass crisp and dry, and you could hear an animal's moan a mile off. I had forgotten how much I loved those fields, my breath almost blue in the clean air, our two dogs trotting along beside me and sometimes scampering off when a rabbit had darted from some hole and in a crazed stupidity came first their way and then ran for its life. Birds flew and dipped with a jauntiness, sometimes perching on the telegraph wires, from which there came a low, zinging throb. Then suddenly they would take a bold flight off to somewhere else and possibly resume their concert. I knew that I would always come back to Drewsboro and yet that I would never come back entirely. I felt carefree, stayed out a long while, went up the hills to see the river, the icy water crystal clear, with wild swans shivering in the rushes.

My mother's eyes were seething, even before she spoke. She was holding the volume of Sean O'Casey's autobiography, open at the incendiary page. Was this how I spent my time? Was this their reward for the sacrifices they had made to get me to Dublin? I was flustered, having read only the first forty pages, which were about family and the trade union movement and the backstage rivalries in the Abbey Theatre. I nearly fainted as she started to read aloud:

It was commonly reported by those who were close up to the inner circle, that, if a monk was to be kept from straddling a judy he had to be shut up in a stone coffin and let out only under the supervision of a hundred halberdiers while he was having a snack in the first, second and third watches of the day, but as this guardianship of the ladies was too costly and too troublesome, the monks had it all their own way, and there wasn't a lassie in the whole wide world who didn't know a codpiece from the real thing, even when her eyes were shut and her mind wandering.

She was about to burn it. I begged her not to, saying it was not my book and that I must return it. I begged her and I hated her.

Back in Dublin, debauchery was thriving. An unemployed laborer from Crumlin was fined two pounds for offensive behavior in the Olympia Ballroom after he had been caught jitterbugging. The end of the world was predicted. One thousand pilgrims who had traveled to Knock Shrine in County Mayo were warned by a Father Declan of Inchicore of the mounting avalanche of infidelity and apostasy that threatened to submerge the world in blood and tears. In a pastoral letter the Pope was forced to admit that it was "the darkest hour" in history since the Deluge. A third message from Our Lady was due to be conveyed to the children in Fatima, prophesying this Armageddon. Chapels were packed. On the appointed day and at the given hour of three o'clock, in a swish golf club outside the city, players and caddies lay on the damp turf pleading for mercy. Except that the hour passed uneventfully and people resumed their wicked ways.

Funds permitting, I would twice monthly, on my half-day from the pharmacy, go to a stage show in the Capitol Theatre, billed to be Ireland's answer to the Folies Bergère. It was a veritable Mecca, the stage with gauze backdrop and lurid Technicolor, peroxide blondes with flashy suspenders kicking their thighs and their legs to the heavens, their flesh so beautifully, so evenly bronzed; their faces, in contrast, a stark alabaster white. They were the mere backdrop to the main event, when a crooner, in a fawn suit and with a dazzling smile, strolled on, the goddesses already having formed a semicircle, their arms making a balustrade for him to lean on. Then he came downstage to ravish rows of us besotted women and girls, who had paid one shilling for this thrill. The collective swooning in that audience would be impossible to measure as his first song came as a signal to each yearning one of us:

> Brush those tears from your eyes
> And try and realize
> That from now on
> I'll always be true.
> I went away
> But I didn't mean to stay
> And I will regret it until my dying day.

By then the handkerchiefs were out, and sometimes he would sing the last verse again, as a sop, while the chorus girls, the goddesses, shrugged and pouted in a mimicry of huff.

At the stage door, where we, the adorers, hovered, he would emerge smiling, whistling, proud of his little audience. One or two might be lucky enough to get a hurried autograph. I was disappointed to note that his handwriting was slovenly. As I watched him go down the lane, it never occurred to me that he might single me out, except that he did. It was brief. It was a beckon of the head to detach myself from the others and his asking if he should call the following Sunday around two, then making a note of my address on the North Circular Road. Already I was negotiating the minefield of getting my sister and Anna out of the flat, and my hopes hinged on the fact that they did corporal works of mercy, visiting sick people in hospitals.

Sunday, and the coast was clear. I had made a sponge cake and laid a tea tray. "Nice place," he said, as he climbed the three flights of stairs covered in dark linoleum and entered the kitchen, which doubled as sitting room. He was in a shabby suit, unshaven, and without the pancake makeup, but still irresistible. He had never seen a tea cozy before. It was one of my mother's, made of mohair, with a mohair picture of a white cottage and a small red hall door. He thought it was nifty. "Nifty" was a favorite word of his.

As we sat on the sagging horsehair sofa, exchanging sweet nothings, an unfortunate thing occurred. The door of a washstand, in which we kept saucepans, colanders, frying pans, and a drum of Vim, crept open of its own accord, revealing our ramshackle domestic life. He didn't seem to notice, as he was already exploring the nape of my neck, my throat, saying ordinary, but in that context amazingly poetic, things, and I was thinking to myself how lucky to have been singled out after weeks of patient pursuit. The hooks of my brassiere yielded to his touch with a willingness. When he removed my silk stockings and flung them into a nether corner, two unnerving thoughts arose, one that my sister or Anna would return early and the other that the stockings, which had been twice to the invisible menders, would not survive this brawl and could not be repaired with nail varnish.

But circuitousness could go only so far. He was now begging for the comforts of the bedroom, and as his entreaties intensified, so did my balk. I was skirting matters, jumping up to make tea, except that he had no interest in tea. He drew me back down quite roughly, and I was now on his lap, trembling, him telling me not to tremble because it would not hurt. The dilemma, I tried to tell him, was that my sister or Anna, both highly religious, would be returning at any moment. Why hadn't I mentioned that earlier? We could have met somewhere else. There were quiet dells in Phoenix Park. He was getting testy. In a moment of sheer madness, I suggested he might sing "Brush Those Tears from Your Eyes." Sing to you! There was nothing for it but candor. I spoke of my fears, and sensing them, he cradled me in the crook of his arm, called me "Baby," and said there was nothing to be afraid of as "he could go through me like butter." It was shocking altogether.

Pointing to the wall clock, I said they were due back by three, which allowed for a mere eleven minutes of canoodling. Holding me fiercely, he said he was "game ball" and it could all be over and done in less. Love's dream, that mystic linking which binds souls as well as bodies, had snapped and I hauled myself out of his embrace. What did I want? "What do you want?" he asked, saying my name, which he must have remembered from the day he gave me his autograph, prior to this first rendezvous. The spell was broken. He saw that it was a waste of time, moved to the kitchen chair, took out his bicycle clips and snapped them around the ankles of his navy gabardine trousers. Then, standing before the mirror that was next to the holy water font, he took out a broken white comb and ran it through the spill of his beautiful, soft brown hair. "Tolloll," he said, as he had got his smile back, and hurried out and down the stairs.

The phrase was new to me, and I reckoned it was Dublin slang. I would come across it again before too long, when I began to read James Joyce and found a Mr. M'Coy spoke it to Leopold Bloom after some aimless conversation. Naturally, because of the fiasco that had happened, I was too ashamed to go back to the Capitol Theatre, so my free half-day was spent in bookshops and at bookstalls.

Dublin was a more trusting town in 1950, and secondhand books would be left on trestle tables outside the shop, with canvas awning above to keep off the downpours. Anyone who might want to could appropriate a book and walk off. It was at a stall in Bachelor's Walk, overlooking the Liffey, that I found a slim volume called *Introducing James Joyce,* by T. S. Eliot. I opened it at random. The paper was a pale lemony color, the print was small, the letters in a deep, indented black. A sentence shot up at me: "All blessed themselves and Mr Dedalus with a sigh of pleasure lifted from the dish the heavy cover pearled around the edge with glistening drops." The scene was

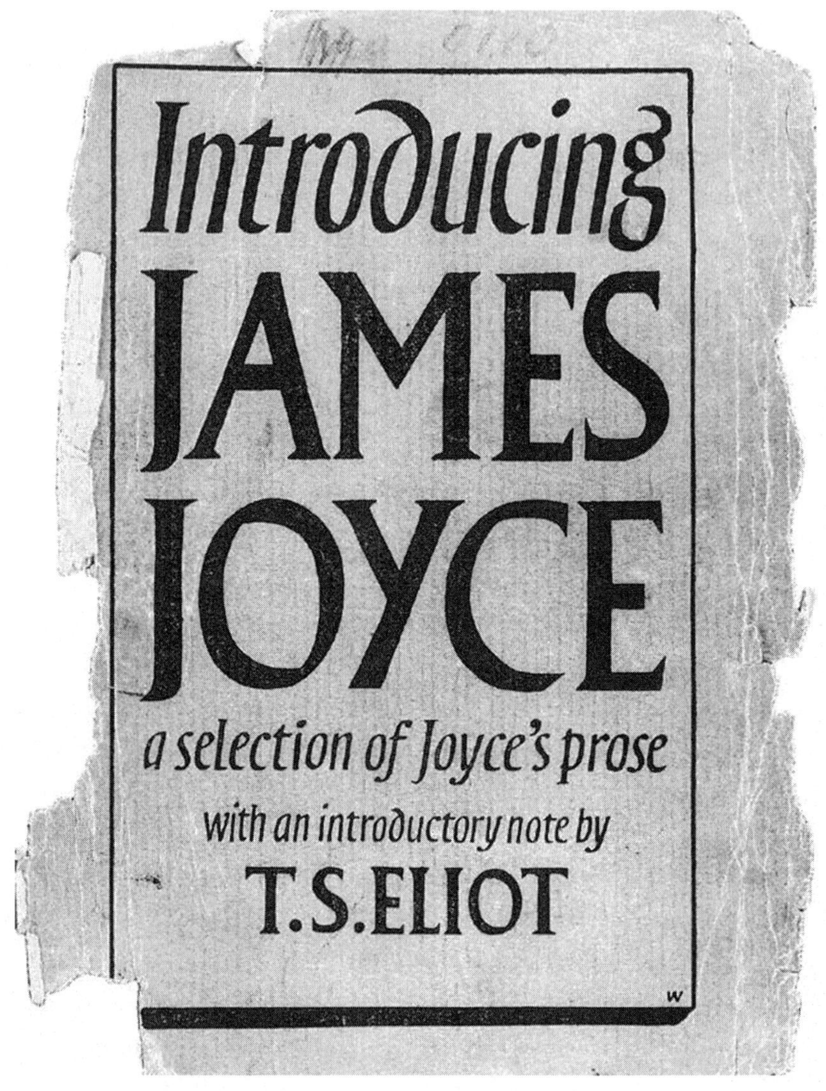

My introduction to literature. Published by Faber & Faber in 1942.

the Christmas dinner in the Dedalus house, seen through the child's eyes of young Stephen. There was the great fire banked high, heartiness and witticisms, the plum pudding studded with peeled almonds and sprigs of holly, merriment, glasses replenished until the sudden dispute arose about priests meddling in politics and the church's hounding of Charles Stewart Parnell once it became known that he was an adulterer. Reading it, I realized that it could have been a Christmas dinner in our house or many a house in Ireland, maybe not with the same erudition but with the same bitterness that split people and made them spiteful and unforgiving. I bought it for fourpence and carried it with me everywhere, including to pharmacy lectures, so that I could read it at will and copy out the sentences, luminous and labyrinthine as they were. It was when I copied them that I began to realize how great they were, the short, flawless snatches of dialogue, lush descriptions of corpses and steers and pigs and kine, of sea and sea stones, and then the extraordinary ascensions, in which worlds within worlds unfolded.

The pawnshop with its three golden balls was in Capel Street, and it being Monday morning, it was busy. My good Gor-Ray skirt was getting known in the Crystal Ballroom, and as I hardly ever got asked up, I decided to pawn the skirt. I took the morning off from the chemist on the excuse of being sick. Only twice in the four years of my apprenticeship did I take a morning off, one for the pawnshop and one for the morning I had my ears pierced. The counter was full of stuff, old clothes and suits, basins with sheets and pillow slips, good suits, blazers, false teeth, and a skeleton that a medical student had brought. It was a sickly yellow, like the keys of an old piano. People pawned on Monday morning and usually managed to retrieve their stuff by Saturday. A man kept aiming his snooker cue at each of us, calling it Gilda, which he had named after Rita Hayworth, "the good-bad woman Gilda." Then we were treated to a rigmarole of how he came to get it, having suffered an accident on a building site, his trousers getting caught in the wire mesh, ending up a cropper, unemployed, and having to wait two years for the compensation money. Quite suddenly he took issue with the pawnbroker, called him a usurer, a feckin' usurer, and said we were all being shafted. That was the thing about Dublin, stories abounding and so many of them hinged on poverty. I got a five-pound note for the skirt along with the blue docket to redeem it, except that I knew I would not go back, as it would never feel the same again.

What with my expiring virtue and limited wardrobe, I was storming heaven, this time not for love but for money. My prayer was answered. My sister was a secretary and worked for someone "high up" in the railway company, and I received a commission to write a weekly column for their magazine. It was to be six hundred words in length, lighthearted, and of interest to women. I would receive the exorbitant fee of a guinea. I chose the pen name "Sabiola," not knowing how I came by it, except, I dimly recalled, it was the name of a concubine in the court of King Farouk of Egypt. An image of a vamp with bobbed hair and a cigarette holder, supposed to be a likeness of me, was featured at the top of each of these nonsensical jottings. My pieces had to contrast with more serious features, such as The Plaint of a Pensioner, Strange Rail Crashes, Tributes to Dublin Busmen, Illegal Haulage, The Knock Shuttle Service, and the dawn of the Dandy Diesel since "the sun was setting on the steam locomotive." With no time to walk the city or interview people, my topics tended to be somewhat generalized and ranged from the joys of golden autumn evenings to the culinary skills for tossing a Shrove Tuesday pancake. I would go into the dress shops to inquire from buyers the latest trends in fashion and learned that as hair was expected to be longer, due to our incontinent skies, the Dublin ladies were soon to adopt the American craze and go "beret-mad." It was a long way from James Joyce.

From the outskirts, Dublin seemed like a fairy-tale city, with its necklace of lights lending a pink flush to the sky that paled the farther one moved from it. We had gone there by bus, Peter Abelard and I. I think it was clear that it was to be the night when something momentous would happen. I had first set eyes on him in a newspaper office, where I went again and again with articles, in the hope that one might be accepted. Through the long plate-glass window in the newsroom I could see the journalists at work, and he seemed the most thoughtful, his eyes always lowered and his eyelashes long and sandy. In secret I had called him Peter Abelard, who for the love of Héloise had been castrated by the medieval clerics of Cluny.

Then one night I had occasion to speak to him. An article of mine had been accepted by the women's page of the paper. It was about a seaside resort as yet undiscovered. I had gone there and simply wrote down what I saw, the big waves, green and vaulting, and the long spit of wet yellow sand and a lonely-looking tower in the distance. My pride in having it accepted was very great, knowing that people at home would read it and that my mother might forgive me my literary aspirations. On my way from pharmaceutical lectures, I had gone to collect the guinea that was due to me and which the editor said I would find on her desk. There to my delight was the warm sheet of newspaper, the ink still wet on it: "Portrane has not yet been discovered," but instead of my name, it was my sister's. Deprived of my moment of glory, I went into the corridor to search for an editor, a subeditor, anyone who could right this wrong. I could see them all through a window, editors and compositors, all at work, Peter Abelard among them. He saw me wave the page, somewhat agitated, and came out. He took it and withdrew into an inner room, and after some time returned, my own name now in bold, black print on the heading. He asked if I might like a drink sometime and we met in a pub in Drumcondra on three occasions, hands touching one another under the table, and the whiskey, to which I was not accustomed, like fire

VOICES OF SPRING.

What was that sound I heard? "Violets—6d. a bunch; cheap violets, Miss." Yes, the wind that blew up from the miserable side street carried with it the glad tidings of violets, and though the flower woman tightened her shawl in around her just as I pass, her harsh familiar shouts were a challenge to the passing winter. Shy, though her basket of violets were, they were still violets, and with them came the split-second hope of long evenings and soft weather and life creeping back into a million buds and a million flower beds.

That began spring for me, because no matter what snow or what gales come the way now I can weather them as sturdily as the Moore Street violets battled the January frost.

Funny, but that first moment when Spring taps you on the shoulder, is the most exciting moment that seasons can give. The mind is full of delicious disturbances and unguessed hope fills the heart. It is that first sweet sup with no sourness to destroy the taste. It is just a flash this advent of spring, or love, of success, or . . . In fact a modern song has quite unexpectedly caught that introductory delight. When one sees a stranger—you know the song "Some Enchanted Evening."

But as I was saying, the violets were a stage in the affairs of the season. I suppose now, too, the ploughman is bringing life to the earth, the lambs are wondering at the new green hills and the clocks are asking one another when they may skip over that hour?

You too? The winter coat is only a necessary evil now and unconsciously, even innocently, you're looking in the windows at this season's suits.

FOUNTAINS OF YOUTH.

My friends travel—at least most of them do, and in their much-travelled minds they think of me as the geographical Cinderella. So generous are their thoughts that, when they return, they long to tell me of the sights they have seen, the food they ate, the wine they drank, the nice things strangers on Continental trains said to them. And they are certain to tell me about the fountains.

I imagine the whole of England and France, not to talk of Spain and Italy, covered with fountains, propelling jets of water like wine, or blue sea, or green fire too, or diamonds or rainbows. Because everyone who comes back talks effusively and elaborately on fountains —especially the fountains after dark when lights play queer tricks with them almost as queer as the tricks (or miracles?) cosmetics can play.

But their leaping fountains never really fascinated me. Instead of that they remind me of our own village fountains that were as much a landmark as the square of the chapel gate or the cross-roads. When I was younger, fountains played a part in the life of every house. The richest memory I have is of hurrying from school to plunge our mouths under the fountain or to cunningly spurt huge water jets on to passing cyclists.

The fountain was our plaything just as it was a gossip halt for the women when they went to fetch water at dusk. Old men tapped their pipes against the fountain, young boys taught each other water tricks there, and drovers always turned on the fountain after a fair day to clear the dung from their boots.

The time has come now when every house has its own fountain, now an aristocratic water supply! The gifts of advancement or civilisation and good County Councils. The village fountain has gone dry, and now I have none to admire unless I start travelling, but even then the fountains will not be the same.

Extract from a weekly column for a railway magazine, early '50s.

in my gut. One evening the friendly girl behind the counter who got to know us asked if we were getting engaged and he smiled the most beautiful, inscrutable smile.

Having got off the bus, we went through a gateway and into a field, then along the side of the field and down into a hollow, where, under a clump of low-hanging trees, he spread his raincoat on the dampish grass. As he took my hand, to help me down, I thought how chivalrous it was, and saw that he too was shy. This giving of myself had assumed a primordial importance, but soon my musings were cut short. Peter Abelard, with his trousers down, was about to make love to me, and it was too late to say "I want to know you better" or "I want to talk" or "Can we put our clothes on and go back to the road?" Most of all, I wanted the magic syllables of "I love you" to be said there in a field that I would never know the name of.

My gaze inclined upward. Branches and tiny twigs, so placid against the night sky. The first thrust broke the phantasm of love, but my reasoning, which was somewhat askew, was that this brutish initiation had to be gone through in order to set us on the true path of love. I clutched at the thin grass and looked up at the few stars, wan and isolated, and thought that there would be happier lodgings and starry nights, and did all I could to stifle the sobbing. Soon that sobbing was stifled even more by his cries, which cut through the surrounding hush of the night. I asked him to hold me, and he did. Then in a while we stood up, each looking for a tree to lean on, silent as we put our clothes back on.

Later, in an upstairs room of a pub which was a distance away, we sat at a folding table, hinged to the wall. We were alone. Either I was too constrained to eat or else too concerned that Peter Abelard might not be able to afford two dinners. As I drank tea, I watched him cut away a rim of fat from a large chop and then commence to eat it, along with boiled potatoes and peas, which were served in an egg saucepan. The peas kept slipping off his fork, and this seemed to annoy him slightly. I was convinced, though I would never know, that the love he had intimated in Drumcondra, and the literary link between us, was no more. Since he worked in the newspaper, he saw all the novels that came in from overseas before they were banned, and I inquired about Alberto Moravia's *The Conformist,* which was deemed an offense to the Irish nation. But Peter Abelard was disinclined to talk. Two words kept repeating themselves to me—maidenhead and maidenfern, words that sounded the same and were so very different. Maidenhead, "a membrane that was the entrance to the gate of woman," and maidenfern, "a plant with capillary leaves." I remembered that in the bookshop I'd read half a play, *La Celestina—The Spanish Bawd,* where a defiant woman employed her time mending maidenheads, so that future swains would be foolish enough "to get mixed up in their skirts again." But that was Salamanca in 1502 and this was Dublin in the 1950s.

We took the bus back into the city and parted casually at the terminus. It was only walking home that I began to relive it, moment by moment, but other, lesser things kept intruding, such as the damp of the grass, a diamanté hair slide I had lost, the peas that kept slipping off his fork, his blond eyelashes, his beautiful priestly voice, which, were he not such a sinner, could enthrall congregations in Cluny or Paris or Salamanca. Getting closer to our digs, I got the wind up, fearing my sister and Anna would sense this vast change in me. They were already suspicious, believing that I was falling into wanton ways, wondering, Why a gentleman's dress scarf, unless it was for gallivanting? Moreover, the late hour would need some explaining, but that was nothing to the explaining that I would have to do to myself. When I got in, I would soak my knickers in a basin of cold water with bleach, and bleach all the evidence away.

The following Saturday night, after work, I cycled to a church on the Quays, hoping that the priest there would be more lenient than the demon in the Church of the Most Precious Blood in Cabra. I thought of my own blood on the bit of field that cows would sniff at. In the privacy of the confessional I gave a sketchy account of my "fall," whereupon he raised himself up, his bulbous cheeks flush against the narrow grille, saying that there was no muffling of this sin, this loathsome sin, which must be confessed in full to God and to his ministers. As it came out in shaming snatches, it seemed even more loathsome, and he seethed with anger. I thought the partition between us would give way. He then asked how sorry was I for my sin and did I acknowledge that Christ, the Fisher of Souls, would have to fish me out from the pestiferous, vile, slime-ridden pool of transgression? He reminded me then that there could be no salvation, no fishing out, unless my atonement was utter and I resolved henceforth to avoid the sin that in the hierarchy of sins was the most damnable of all. He asked if marriage had been discussed, and fearing repercussions, I said that the man had gone to England leaving no address. The penance he gave me was astronomical, decade upon decade of the rosary, daily Mass and Holy Communion, which I knew to be out of the question, as I had to be in the chemist's shop by eight-thirty. I came out of that confessional box completely confounded, eyes glaring at me as to why I was so long in there. Knowing that I had told him a lie about Peter Abelard scooting to England, I would now have to go to another church on the Quays (there were five of them) in order to get a second Absolution for the Holy Communions that I was to receive.

Despite the fiasco in the field, I sent Peter Abelard the one book that I treasured, *The Charwoman's Daughter,* by James Stephens, which Paschal insisted that I keep. On the flyleaf and to create a mature effect, I had copied a line of scripture, which

Peter Abelard had spoken in the pub in Drumcondra: "Honey seems bitter to them that are sick with the jaundice."

It was not until November, the month of the suffering souls, that he rang the chemist's shop and invited me to Sunday lunch with his wife and children. There were toys and a tricycle thrown down on the gravel, and even though it was winter, the hall door was wide open. The inside was a bit ramshackle. What has stayed in my memory is his sharpening the carving knife on the stone ledge of the kitchen window and then with aplomb carving the roast. It was five months since I had seen him, and he barely looked at me; his eyes were the same guarded blue that I had fallen in love with. After the lunch he took his jacket from the hook on the back of the door, since he had to go to work, and his wife asked me to stay behind. It was then I quaked, thinking she was going to question me, but she didn't. All she said was that they had been childhood sweethearts and that no one would ever come between them. She was a thin woman with freckles, and on that Sunday she seemed in command of things, getting her children to eat up and asking at what hour might she expect him home.

Then one day she rang the chemist's shop and asked me to come and see her. I went there, believing she had found out, but it was not that at all. He had fallen in love. She learned of it because, when searching his pockets, she found various epiphanies extolling this new love, which had come as such a shock to him. Winnowing out the excessive words, he wrote draft after draft, until he had found the perfect one: "After that dark woman, you search for someone who will fit into the irregular corners of your heart." She produced a bottle of sherry that had been there since Christmas, and we drank tumblers of it; then in her grief she cracked the empty bottle to pieces on the porcelain of the kitchen sink, repeating the words that had eaten into her, "After that dark woman, you search for someone who will fit into the irregular corners of your heart."

I could not tell her of my deception, and instead, to prove my somewhat dubious loyalty, I went into embattled verse.

> Oh dark woman
> With a shawl and ribs
> I could have served him better
> With my shanties.
> But men do love the shimmer
> And so his ghost
> Is hacked in half between us
> The dark me and the dark you.

I had made a new friend, Rory, who worked in the Palace Bar next to the *Irish Times* where the literati came.

"Ah, Boccaccio isn't in it," he would say, recounting everything he overheard, improvised poems and odes and the fact that a man called Alan C. Breeze had returned from England with a set of false teeth, which he claimed to have belonged to T. S. Eliot. But that was nothing compared with the conversation that ranged each night from matutines and nocturnes, to syllogisms, spondees, dactyls, the intrusive apostrophe, the broken lines of Virgil, and Aristotle's tabula rasa. According to Rory there were two kinds of drinkers, the loquacious ones out of Joyce and the quiet ones out of Beckett, the Belacquas, solitary men, precursors of Krapp, beholding a pint, "drowned in dreams and burning to be gone."

The savants spoke in alexandrines (whatever they were) and threw quips of Greek and Latin at one another, drank "Niagarously," the toast being "I drink to the thirst to come." Mr.

Cartoon of the all-male Dublin literati in a hostelry, 1940.

Smiley, the editor, in a green sombrero hat and canary waistcoat, would arrive around ten at night, sometimes singing parts of the leader article, which he would later polish, brushing aside hangers-on with "Out of my way, pismires, warlocks, stand aside." Rory said the nail of Mr. Smiley's finger was pared to exactly resemble the nib of the pen that had belonged to Keats. Around him in the private snug were his cohorts, his few favorite journalists, including Roger Casement's brother, Tom, who was the somewhat dilatory chess correspondent for the paper. The two geniuses were the poet Patrick Kavanagh and the author Flann O'Brien, who also wrote a column for the *Irish Times* under the name of Myles na gCopaleen, where, according to himself, "the meek and tireless music of his quill set down on parchment the goings-on in the country." Meek he was not, but with a rapier wit he mocked the Dublin Corporation, the wife, the Civil Service (of which he was, surprisingly, a servant), bicyclists, the Abbey Theatre, insurance fellas, and the plain people of Ireland, otherwise known as "Godridden gobdaws and galopes."

Patrick Kavanagh, with the Monahan hills and the twisted

boughs still in his veins, claimed that unless the clay was in the mouth, the singer's singing was no good. It was hard, as Rory said, to connect the man with the poet. The poet had written evocative lines such as:

> Leafy-with-love banks and the green waters of the canal
> Pouring redemption for me, that I do
> The will of God

Yet the man could be boorish. He had made a date with a lady to have tea in the Gresham Hotel, a spinster who lived in the Midlands and a devotee of his poetry. A shy man in his gruff way, he decided to bring along a few bowsies to liven the conversation. From behind a screen and some tall castor oil plants, they spotted her, by herself, mousy, with a knitted cap and matching knitted mittens. With ne'er a word, they retreated, back out into the street, Kavanagh buck-leaping, saying, "That craythur would never crack a man's thighs."

Their lives, as their friend John Ryan wrote in his beautiful memoir, *Remembering How We Stood,* were shambolical. Kavanagh, "in wifeless existence," had a bedsit in Pembroke Street, the bath full to the brim with empty sardine tins, the salon with a typewriter and secondhand chesterfield suite, and attached to the window a rear mirror, stolen from a lorry, by which he could appraise welcome or unwelcome callers. One night shortly before Christmas, and to the amazement of all Dublin, Archbishop McQuaid, "honouring the holy condition of poverty," decided to call on the poet. It so happened that Kavanagh was entertaining a "lady of the night," so that the monsignor, who came up to say the archbishop was about to follow, had to be discouraged with sundry excuses, such as the condition of the room and the lavatory not fixed. The poet did, however, agree to go down and meet the archbishop, and came away with a hand-knitted sweater, a bottle of Power's Gold Label, and two hundred Sweet Afton cigarettes.

His daily routine was unvarying. Up at dawn, when he might compose a few lines, then off out to get the newspaper to study the racing form, a quick malt in some nearby lounge, a bus to Grafton Street, to McDaids, his favorite haunt, down to the bookies, and back to the bar at fifteen-minute intervals, all of it made possible by his surprising good luck at backing winners, mainly outsiders. In the evening he would make the journey to the pub, where Mr. Smiley presided and where Rory was witness to Kavanagh's bouts of silence or fury. When Louis MacNeice, who lived in London, dared to breach their circle, Kavanagh mocked him, singing, "Let yez go back and labor for Faber and Faber," to the tune of "The Bard of Armagh," the evening descending into blows between rival poets and their foot soldiers.

Joyce was constantly spoken of in these circles, and not always favorably. Granted he had his epiphanies, but his work was full of smut and he had looked through a "gloss" darkly. Moreover, a lot of his stuff was shamelessly cogged from *Thom's Street Directory.* Myles, when asked if he resembled Joyce, would say "that nothing could be further from Detroit," and that *Finnegans Wake* was a "wallet of literary underwear." That book, along with *Gone with the Wind,* were the two that he started five times and couldn't finish. His harshest gibes, however, were for the Prairie professors, Americans, talking through their "caubs" and descending on Dublin to write their theses on Herr Joyce, comparing the key motif in the Ithaca section with the door lock at No. 7 Eccles Street, in homage to Mr. and Mrs. Bloom.

I went for the first time to the Abbey Theatre with Paschal, the retired guard, and stood in the lobby, giddy at the thought that Yeats, Lady Gregory, and Synge had once stood in that same place. The play was *Cathleen Ni Houlihan* by Yeats, and Siobhán

McKenna played Cathleen, the lamenting woman, the embodiment of Ireland, who was recruiting young men to fight for her cause. It was mesmerizing. I decided, there and then, to forsake the path of writing for that of the stage and remembered my wan attempt to join the Travelling Company, which had played *Dracula*. But now I was more determined.

Hilton Edwards and Michael MacLiammoir ran the Gate Theatre and were two of the most scandalous figures in Dublin. I had not seen them onstage, but I had the good luck to be at a bus stop once, where, to everyone's amazement, Michael joined the queue. He was like a demigod, in a voluminous cloak, fully made up, and wearing an auburn wig, exuding an air of theatricality and replying in a velvety voice to a woman who was showering him with compliments. By what devious means I got his home address, I cannot recall, but I still have the postcard telling me that I may come to No. 4 Harcourt Terrace at 11:30 a.m. on a particular Sunday.

Theirs would be the first theatrical house I ever set foot in. It was exotic. A red chaise longue, the dark violet wallpaper with a tracery of plumage, framed posters and photographs of the two actors in their various costumes, their eyes evil and dark as molasses, their eyebrows roguish. No matter where I walked in that room, Michael MacLiammoir's eyes followed me from every conceivable corner. I was jittery. In he swept, again fully made up and wearing a flowered silk kimono, which went just below his knees, the serge of the trousers prosaic by contrast.

The lines I had chosen were that of the old woman in *Cathleen Ni Houlihan* who went from house to house, recruiting young men to die for Ireland, lines that Siobhán McKenna had spoken with such conviction and such feeling:

Many that are red-cheeked now will be pale-cheeked; many that have been free to walk the hills and the bogs and the rushes will be sent to walk hard streets in far countries; many a good plan will be broken; many a child will be born and there will be no father at its christening to give it a name.

I murdered those lines. It would not have been surprising, what with my untoward and reckless gesturing, to see pictures slide off the walls or decanters wobble on the silver trays on which they stood. He endured most of it and then, with a staying hand and a surprising gentleness, said that he believed I was descended from one of the great, ancient Galway tribes and, excusing himself, hoped that I would be able to find my way out.

Coming out into the daylight, I felt crushed, believing that life was a gray road, an unending literary limbo, where I would never reach the Parnassian heights that, in daftness, I had aspired to.

The Literary Bessie Bunter

Because of spouting bits of poetry, I came to be named "The Literary Bessie Bunter." It was a journalist at the radio station, whose pet name was Bunny, who christened me so. I had met him the day I did my first-ever broadcast. It was on Saint Bridget, patron of country women and of butter, whose feast day fell on February 2. "The Literary Bessie Bunter." It is how I would have been described to the man I would marry, although marriage did not feature in my ruminations.

After Peter Abelard I had taken a vow of chastity, but nevertheless I had a few lackluster dates, one with a man who delivered bread and cakes down the country and who would walk me the three miles from the Crystal Ballroom in South Anne Street to the digs in North Circular Road, just by Phoenix Park. There was I, devouring books and yet allowing a man who had never read a book to walk me home for a bit of harmless fumbling on the front steps. Another time, in a hotel in Kilkenny, a gamey, curly-haired rogue who had plied me with champagne took me upstairs and into the one bedroom that was unlocked, where providentially a housekeeper stormed in, arms akimbo, and shouted, "A bishop slept in this room last night and ye want to defile it," at which he scooted.

It was December when our landlady called me to the pay phone in the hall. It was Bunny ringing to invite me to have a drink with an author who had had a film made of his book *The Plymouth Adventure,* starring Spencer Tracy. Would I join them? To smarten my appearance, I took a red muff, which my sister had borrowed from a wealthy woman, knowing it would liven

In Lake Park, County Wicklow, 1952.

the drabness of my black coat (the tweed one long since discarded). This black coat was going green and had moth holes.

When I came into the crowded pub in Henry Street, Bunny greeted me effusively, as if I were an old flame. There was Ernest Gébler, handsome beyond words, sallow-faced, with dark brown eyes and granite features. I had seen a picture of a German actor, Conrad Veidt, and saw a resemblance in this man, whose voice was so hypnotic that others deferred to him, as did I. He spoke of his trips to Hollywood, of which he was scathing, and a play that he was meant to have had produced in New York, starring Sam Wanamaker, except that producers and producers' wives had argued interminably over it and the project was scrapped. He was so cosmopolitan and so cultured. He spoke of James Joyce with familiarity and referred to Leopold Bloom as Poldy. I was elated. By chance we discovered we had something in common. I mixed two stomach medicines each week for a German man, in long black overcoat and black Homburg hat, who spoke with a European accent. It happened that it was Adolf, his father.

Next day was my birthday, which he must have overheard me mentioning to one of the group. To my astonishment, after I had shut the shop for the lunch hour, I found him tapping on the window for me to come outside. In his sports car we drove to a shop in Grafton Street, and there I acquired a coat that surpassed anything my mother or her friends, the beautiful Gavin girls, or the doctor's wife, had ever worn. It was gray astrakhan, with a red velvet collar, and it fitted like a glove. Already I was saying adieu to The Literary Bessie Bunter.

On that spring day when I first visited his house in County Wicklow, the gorse was just coming into bloom with the daffodil flowers, buds in tapers of folded green under the trees, up along a winding avenue. He drove slowly, for me to be able to see everything, and he was proud at showing me these things, and even in those early days, though half in jest, he referred to me as his "child bride." The house, a shooting lodge, was not so very imposing, painted white and set down in a hollow with youngish woodland behind it; he told me there was a lady's garden and a rose garden. It was called Lake Park, though it did not overlook the lake, which was about a mile down a twisted track. In the fields all around I could hear the bleating of sheep, and standing on the front steps, I saw a second valley where he said a bohemian poet, who had poisoned one of his many wives, also lived. They had not yet met, and I got the feeling that he kept mostly to himself.

His housekeeper, Nancy, opened the hall door, sleeves rolled up, her arms strong and pink. She scolded him for not having come the two days previous as he said he would and, taking one look at me, believed that I was the reason for it. As a peace offering, he handed her a brown glazed coffeepot that he had bought in Bewley's in Grafton Street and the choice things from a delicatessen, for our supper, which she looked at and then snorted.

As I waited alone in the sitting room, I looked at the portrait of him hanging on the wall. It was in green, his skin a sickly greenish hue and his eyes with a livid light in them, as if the painter had not liked him. It was a darkish room, the walls painted oxblood red, and the half-drawn brown shutters obscured most of the daylight.

How could I have known that in six weeks, I, the future "child bride," would be living there, wandering through those unfamiliar rooms, yet not mistress of the house, because he was still married to a wife who had returned to America with their son? I would be living there, going from room to room, a little lost and out of my depth, and curious about the life and the love that happened in it before I came.

It had all been so precipitate, too precipitate, and I thought that it would take months, if not years, for us to come to know one another. I missed the life in Dublin, the customers, the Saturday evenings, tearing to get to a shop to buy something, to buy anything, because ironically, two months before I met him, I had qualified as a pharmacist and was promoted to a salary of three pounds ten shillings per week. I missed hearing the latest from Rory about the literati and the woman, a dazzling American, who had breached their poetic circle and who, because of the color of her hair, was called Marmalade. Although he was a writer, Ernest was an outsider in these circles, his one friend being J. P. Donleavy, who had written a novel of bohemian Dublin, not yet published, but rumored to be a sizzler.

It so happened that I had run from the chemist's shop, still in my white coat, run from the family who were coming to bring me back home and, as I had overheard in the conversation between my boss and his wife, if necessary, to put me away. The "putting away" meant nothing other than the lunatic asylum, and I had a momentary image of Mad Mabel. They had learned of my transgressions, my sinful life with this evil stranger, and the two weekends alone with him in his country seat. It was an anonymous letter, left on the saddle of my mother's bicycle as she came out of morning Mass. Someone who knew me well had betrayed me, and that someone had carved the future path of my life.

There was consternation in the chemist's shop the morning the news came, what with the boss ringing around to find a locum to replace me, and his wife in high dudgeon because my mother had telephoned him and not her. I resolved to do the only thing I could do, which was to bolt. The chance came when they repaired upstairs to have their lunch and I, as usual, passed in and out through the kitchen and down the back garden to the shed, where the stocks of medicine were kept in Winchesters, to fill the smaller eight-ounce medicine bottles. Making my escape into a back alley, I ran the length of the parade and then came out onto the main road much farther up, and so as not to be too noticeable, I took off the white coat and carried it on my arm. A bus for County Wicklow left St. Stephen's Green each evening at seven, and I waited under cover of trees, not knowing what the welcome might be when I arrived at the shooting lodge.

My future husband embraced me, almost childishly glad to see me, as yet ignorant of the looming furor. He had missed me, and on his mantelpiece were a few loose hairpins that had fallen out of my hair in bed, which he kept as reminders. In a welter, I told him that I would be followed, dragged home, and put away, but he was disbelieving and said poetry had gone to my head, and that such things happened in the dark ages of long ago.

As the plane landed on the Isle of Man, I saw gorse in bloom, and it seemed to me to be a continuation of the gorse that bloomed in County Wicklow, as if the distance was not too great for my family to find me. Ernest had yielded to my entreaties and decided that we should go away, for a week or so, until tempers died down. He contacted Donleavy, who, with his wife, Valerie, was staying on the Isle of Man in his mother-in-law's house, which, as he said, was so secluded that we would never be found.

Except that we were. The next morning I am marched out of a garden by a strange policeman, and on the other side of the wooden gate a group of people was waiting for me: my father, an abbot from a Cistercian monastery who is a friend of his, my sister's boss, who hired me to write the Sabiola column (now scotched), a neighbor of ours, and my brother. My brother steps forward and grips my arm, saying, "You're coming with us." But I was not coming with them, and I spoke rash words of never wanting to see them again. Yet it was also true that the night before I had been having misgivings, hearing Donleavy and Ernest talking, so blasé, about books, exchanging literary gossip, stories concerning publishers that they seemed to know about. Donleavy talked of Gainor Crist, the man from Ohio, a demobbed GI who had come to Trinity College to study but instead was an habitué of various pubs where he made friends of motley boozing companions. He was the inspiration for Donleavy's book *The Ginger Man,* which at that time was being considered by a publisher in Paris. For my part, I would begin to say something and then find myself inadequate to finish the sentence. Donleavy's wife, Valerie, sensing my awkwardness, would cover up for me, as she saw that I was out of my depth.

The abbot, in an endeavor to calm things, held up the gold crucifix that was around his neck and made the sign of the cross over me with it. He was the one I feared least. I told him to reason with them, to tell them I was not going home. The two policemen stood farther up the road, somewhat aimlessly, and my brother took my arm to steer me to a second car. It was boiling hot, so hot inside that car that I could feel the perspiration from my armpits oozing out onto the pink seersucker dress. It was a new dress that Ernest had bought for me on our way to the airport, when we stopped at a small town where the owner of a drapery store was called down to admit us. My brother asked me if I was pregnant. Could I be pregnant? I didn't know. Had I had intercourse? I had. He said there was no other solution but to take me to England. The word "abortion" was not spoken, but it was implied, and before my eyes ran images of Mamie Cadden, the dingy room, the bucket of Jeyes Fluid and fatality. By now I was hysterical, and he was about to slap me, when suddenly we heard shouting, and in the rear window he saw that, farther up, the party had come to blows. On impulse he rushed to defend his own, leaving the car door open, and I got out and ran to a nearby bungalow, where a man in a straw hat was watering plants, a golden retriever beside him. I asked if he would hide me, and surprisingly he led me into a hall where a woman gave me a glass of water. Once I heard the two cars go down that quiet road, I knew that they had gone, and I asked the woman to ring Valerie to come for me.

Back in the kitchen, the minutiae of the fight are being played out, half in excitement and half in repugnance. The visitors had called Ernest out and immediately set upon him. They had kicked him with force, while the abbot and two policemen looked on, whereupon Donleavy, who had trained under outstanding boxing coaches in New York, arrived, sleeves rolled up, and tore into them. The upshot was that they left, to repair to the hotel in the town, on the understanding that Ernest and I would go there at four o'clock and I would be returned. When I told them what my brother was intending, the idea of that visit was squashed and the police were informed that we would not be coming at four o'clock.

We heard the private plane go over soon after, and I wondered what it had cost and how my father could have scraped together that huge amount of money in so short a time.

It was in the guest bungalow that adjoined the main house that my husband-to-be made his feelings known. His ankles had been kicked, they were blue and black, and there were open wounds on both of his shins. Strips of skin, like strips of parchment, were hanging off, and at his instruction I was holding a steaming kettle to the various wounds. I still recall the arc of that steam and his seething expression.

He had already, on Donleavy's typewriter, written a letter to my parents which I was to sign. It was an ugly letter, unsparing of them in every way, and it was hard to reconcile it with the man who had bought me the astrakhan coat and kept hairpins as a souvenir on the marble mantelpiece. He seemed surprised by my small attempt at rebelling, and when I said I could not sign it, he asked indignantly if, perhaps, I was eager to be restored to their ignorant and barbaric ways.

I signed it, and in the doing I knew that, by going from them to him, I had burnt my boats.

We came home to the shooting lodge and, in the language of benign fiction, settled down. He gave me money to buy new clothes. I bought a pleated skirt and a salmon-pink cardigan, its tiny sleeve buttons covered in the same fetching pink, and flat ballet shoes, since he said high heels, which I loved, were bad for me. He opened a subscription for me in a library in Dublin where I could get all the most recently published books, and so, in truth, began my real apprenticeship as a writer. He took a photograph of me with my long hair, standing by the hall door, somewhat self-consciously, and with pride sent it to his first wife. I learned to cook. I copied out a line from Elizabeth Bishop, "Christmas trees, waiting for Christmas," although it was only April.

I was lonelier than I should be, for a woman in love, or half in love. There was this gulf between us, so much about him seemed strange and distant. Sometimes I would notice such a sad expression on his face and wonder if it was for the other wife, or his child, or his early life, which I was learning about gradually. Theirs was a fractured family; his father, who played the clarinet, was a traveling musician, and they had moved with

With Ernest Gébler, London, 1959.

orchestras from Ireland to Wolverhampton and back to Dublin again, by which time he had parted from the wife who had borne him six children. She was a diminutive woman with a sharp tongue, and having paid us a cursory visit once with one of her daughters, she looked me up and down and said, "You will never be Mrs. Gébler in this house." His ancestors, according to what he had been told, were carpetbaggers from Armenia, who had migrated to Bohemia, where they merged and married with Czechs and Germans, so that he was of mixed blood on his father's side and Irish on his mother's, which is perhaps why he was nettled when by chance one day I read aloud a poem by Bertolt Brecht:

> I, Bertolt Brecht, came out of the black forests.
> My mother moved me into the cities as I lay
> Inside her body. And the coldness of the forests
> Will be inside me till my dying day.

It was not the first time I saw that cold resentment, as if something that was his had been taken from him, or, more grievously, he had thrown it away, and it was the source of his writing.

There was a room on the opposite side of the landing from where we slept, and one day I ventured in there. In one corner there was a pink cot with an abacus of colored beads and a folded pink angora blanket. In the wardrobe, as if she had only recently left, there were some of his wife's clothes, slacks, scarves, shirt blouses, and various pairs of walking shoes, with shoe trees in them. In a side drawer there was underwear neatly folded and a variety of belts. From a hanger I took a tartan jacket and put it on, and as there was no mirror in that room, I went to have a look in the bathroom, where Nancy was lurking, always lurking, having increasingly taken on the scrutiny of Mrs. Danvers in *Rebecca*. The jacket, she said, did not suit me.

It suited the other wife better. Then she whispered something terrible in my ear. The other wife was coming back, and only she, Nancy, had been entrusted with the secret. It was to be a surprise. She had set sail for Cove in Cork, bringing everything, her son, her trunks, everything. I knew it was a lie and said to unnerve me, and yet I feared it like an omen. Ernest had been writing to his wife to get the divorce papers from their hurried marriage, and she had been writing back, talking of her new life, but things were more amiable between them. The pictures on the stamps were all of American heroes, and I would hold the flimsy, airmail envelope up to the light, hoping that I could glean something from it.

There were things I feared about him, small things with larger implications. A sheep had got in among our flock. Tom, who was Nancy's husband, reported it, and there indeed was a sheep with a pink stripe among all the other petrol blues. He guessed it was some farmer who drove it in, in spite, because he was not popular with the locals. Late that night, with a Tilley lamp, we went up to the field that was beyond the wood. At the very sight of us the sheep started to run, and dogs from farms at the far side of the lake began to bark furiously, something that undermined the secrecy of the mission. They ran in crazed circles, with the culprit in among the others, so that twice, because of the angle at which I held the lamp, he caught the wrong sheep and shouted at me to hold the lamp upright. It was a blustery night. Still running, he whipped them apart, or tried to, with a bit of rope he had brought up, and was shouting at me to follow close, a hysteria in his voice. They ran as fast as greyhounds, without any cunning, kept running into one another and scattering, and twice he had the pink sheep by the haunches, only for it to escape, and finally, when he almost tripped on a hole, it too tripped, so he caught it and knelt down, holding it with both hands. He told me to put the lamp down and tie the feet with the rope, which I did, though it resisted in frantic and impotent little thrusts. Then he carried it down in his arms, as it continued to bleat haltingly and pitifully, while the remainder of the fold had scurried off away from us, lying prone under the low stone wall, where they huddled, in fear for their lives. It was still occasionally bleating and struggling when he bundled it into the empty turf sack and put it on the back seat of his car.

We drove down from there into the second valley and along a road that forked into a littler road toward a vast stretch of bog. Once loose, the sheep rushed through a tangle of bushes that were at the entrance, and though haltered, it ran and ran, and the last we saw was its strange mad jigging, no doubt in an effort to free itself of the rope, just jigging on the first knoll that it came to, gray like a boulder, against the dark of the bog and the deep night.

Not a word was spoken as we drove home, along deserted roads.

Things began to go missing. The pink cardigan that I saved to wear in the evenings was gone, and so was the gold chain and cross that had belonged to my mother. Then it was his things, shirts, jackets, and finally the coffeepot. He guessed it was Nancy's doing, and one Sunday when she and Tom had gone by bus sixty miles away on a pilgrimage, we went across to their quarters, which were in the yard. There, on an old blanket, as for a bazaar, were the several items, along with things we had not even yet missed.

Nancy was summoned and told she was sacked. She marched around his study, screaming that it was an injustice; her hands spoke, her fat arms spoke, every bit of her body spoke, as she vowed that she would not be turned out onto the road or dumped in a bog like a stray sheep. She alternated between fury and anguish; then, seizing her trump card, she reminded him of his dismay, his heartbreak, the morning he got up to find his wife with their child had fled.

She painted a picture of him going from room to room, opening wardrobes, only to find that some were empty, then the stripped cot, searching for signs that would tell him it could not be true, and then driving like a madman to the post office in the village to make a phone call that was all in vain. She recalled his sitting in his study for months and months, leading the life of a monk, while she was the only one to give him his meals, to cheer him up and to sing, "How much is that doggie in the window?/The one with the waggly tail." Then, rounding on him, she said, "You had no one, only me, until you met *her*." Her husband had appeared in the doorway, totally abashed, bowing, holding the blanket with the stolen booty, which somehow, when he opened it out, looked pathetic. They were given a reprieve.

The day we brought them to Dublin was their first time ever to the city. Nancy wore a straw hat bedecked with artificial cherries and a linen jacket that she was bursting out of. As we entered the outskirts of the city, they were disappointed to find the houses so small, higgledy-piggledy and too close to one another. When Tom sighted a tall black man, he slapped his thighs with excitement and wanted to get out and have a conversation about *Uncle Tom's Cabin,* which he had seen with a traveling picture show, believing that the man in the street and the man in the film must be cousins.

We had lunch in a tearoom in Grafton Street, and as there was a pianist, Nancy requested "How Much Is That Doggie in the Window?" and hummed it to her own satisfaction. She had a gift for me. It was a white flannelette dribbler piped with a blue border, and spreading it out on the table, she winked. Cunningly, she had concluded that I was pregnant, as she saw me in the early mornings going up into the woods to be sick and knew the reason for it; but nothing was said.

It was in the study that night that I told my husband, and the transformation in him was miraculous. His happiness was boundless. There was something so gentle and astonished in his whole being, all his hostile traits put to one side, a new life, the life he had been meant to have; the old, sad world put down to sleep.

My sister Patsy and Ruth, the woman's editor whom I had worked for, came on me unawares. I was in the garden putting down a row of young lettuces. They both had beaver-fur coats, absurd in the heat, and it may have been to impress Ernest, who was down at the lake, tarring and painting the boat for a trip we were to take. They shook hands, apologized for coming unannounced, and then, embracing me, my sister called me "Poor Coppers," saying she would wait in the car, as Ruth had something important to tell me. It was an envelope with my mother's handwriting, and she read it to me there and then:

My dear Ruth,
I do not remember if I have written to you since this unhappy incident of Edna's. I meant to but everything I did for the last weeks seems to be all out of mind. Well, Ruth, wasn't this an awful tragedy. Poor dear Edna, whom I loved with all my heart and soul. She has broken my heart and I cannot just tell you how I feel. It was the greatest shock I ever got and still I can hardly believe Edna could be so cruel to us. What has come over her or is she accountable. Her father asks me to write to you and go and see her with Pat, so Ruth please do go and see how Edna is and what you think could be done to get her away from that

awful man. If she could be got to get out of there, then she may see reason. Ask her would she like to see me and when and where and tell her from me I love her as I always did, only I can't understand why she was so cruel to break my heart and her father's. He too loved her and is as deeply grieved over all that she has done to us and worse to herself. God help and pity her and I feel sure He will. I know you too got a shock but Ruth, there is no one feels this as a mother does and Edna whom I thought could not do a wrong, as she was so full of fun and so good-hearted but I suppose she is not to blame. She has been foolishly led astray and was too innocent for the man she met. I will look forward to hearing from you and I know you will do this for me and let us know exactly what you think of Edna. Poor Eileen has taken this thing very badly too and it seems she had been worried over it for a long time but to us it came as a complete shock as we never knew of any of it until the last minute, otherwise we would have stopped it in time. I even went to meet the bus two evenings to meet her as she wrote to say she was coming home but at the same time I now believe she had run to Lake Park and had no notion of coming home, it was only to prolong time to get to that terrible man. From my heart I say may God help her in this awful trial and tell her,
Ruth, that my love remains the same for her and beg her to see me.

Yours very sincerely,
Lena O'Brien

As she was reading it, I stared down at the row of lettuces, so pathetic in the dark bed of clay, darker still where I had watered them.

"I'll see," I said, taking the letter from her.

"But I can't go back to them without an answer," she said.

"I don't have an answer," I said, thinking that she would understand, but she didn't. She was annoyed at being thwarted and ran off in the direction of the car, refusing the offer of tea which I so plaintively made.

It was a sunny morning and I was about six months pregnant, the feet regularly kicking on the wall of my stomach. I had brought out two kitchen chairs into the yard, their seats facing each other, a basin of hot water on one and a basin of cold water on the other, to wash my hair. Afterward I sat on one of the chairs, running a towel through my hair, totally unaware of my surroundings, as I was coming near the end of *Madame Bovary.* It was the deathbed scene of Emma Bovary, her sitting up in bed like a galvanized corpse, hair undone, eyes fixed and staring, when the blind man (the presager of death) passes under her window, singing a trite love song that causes her to rise up briefly, "her heart bursting through her ribs in a terrible upheaval."

I could not stop crying. Why could life not be lived at that same pitch? Why was it only in books that I could find the utter outlet for my emotions?

When Ernest discovered the draft of a story I was writing, which many years later would come to be called "Small Town Lovers," an argument flared up. The opening line was "It was a country road tarred very blue and in the summer, we used to walk there." He erupted, saying there was no such thing as a blue road, but I knew that there was. I had seen them, I had walked on one, the hot tar smearing the white canvas of my new shoes. Roads were every color, blue, gray, gold, sandstone, and carmine. He was categorical about it. It was as if by saying it, I had defied some inalienable truth. He had to be right about everything, and if he was crossed, a look of hatred came into his eyes, but to be crossed by me, a literary flibbertigibbet, was ridiculous, believing as he did that he owned me.

But in secret I clung to the blue road, while knowing that somewhere in the distance, like a glacier, it would come between us.

I wrote my mother the first letter that I dared to write since I had run away:

Dear Mother,

It was a green silk dress pleated, the little pleats gliding into one another, and there was a matching jacket with it, part of your trousseau. My life has changed and yet in many ways it hasn't. If only I could talk to you, if only I could confide in someone. The man I am with is something of a mystery, he has his seasons and his dark moods. His father's people hailed from Armenia, carpetbaggers, who made their way eventually to Bohemia in Czechoslovakia, where they settled. They were a musical family, music ran in their blood. A great-uncle or perhaps an uncle, who was a violinist in Prague, sawed off his right hand, rather than serve under the Gestapo. He never knew this uncle or grand-uncle except to know that he was called Herman, but he relates to him in some tortured way. He has inherited traits that he himself is a stranger to, being of Armenian, Jewish, Czech, and German and Irish stock. Sometimes I see such a dark, brooding look come over him, not aimed at me or not always aimed at me, and I cower. Love was something you put your foot down on, with regard to me, and you have won. He can be kind and thoughtful, some evenings we sit together in his study, with the lamp not on and everything fond and tender. But these are only interludes. For instance, he had this dream of my giving a party, a huge party, for which I hired a marquee and served caviar in glass bowls, along with gallons of champagne. When he wakened, he was as angry with me as if I had actually given that party and incurred such terrible extravagance. I am trying my hand at writing. I wrote about a blue road, he says, there is no such thing. My thoughts get somewhat scrambled. If I think ahead, to say ten or fifteen years, I cannot see this life going on in this way. I make jam when the medlars and the damsons are in fruit. He likes it when I make jam, it establishes me as the housewife. His friends tend to think of me as beneath him and a mope. When I recall Drewsboro, there is always frost, early mornings on our way to or from Mass, the high grass plumed and you calling out to me to pick my steps, so that my good Holy Communion, kid shoes would not get stained. When the child is born, you and I might become friends again, it might draw us together. I am so, so terrified. Your labour has got mixed up with mine. God grant that I do not disgrace myself when my time comes.

Eventually, the impediments to marriage were overcome, since Ernest had been baptized a Catholic and his first marriage, in a registry office, was not recognized by the Catholic Church. I got my own wedding ring in a pawnshop and wondered, would it be lucky? I was twenty-three. My marriage dress, which was fawn and drab, was also my maternity dress, with a panel along the front that could be narrowed or widened depending on the bulge of the belly. It was in a Catholic church in Blanchardstown, a rainy morning in July, and two workmen were called down from the scaffolding to serve as witnesses. Afterward there was a lunch in the Bailey restaurant, with my sister Eileen and the poet Val Iremonger and his wife. It was here that I had my first taste of champagne, and I took an undue liking to it.

Four weeks later I was in the nursing home in Hatch Street about to give birth. I felt safe there, the nurses were attentive, coming in and out, timing the length between the pains and telling me to breathe, to breathe. Though woozy from the drugs they had given me, I could feel the last stabbing bouts of pain, as the head started to butt out, and great tears of joy and emotion gushed out of me. Ernest was overjoyed to have a son, and it was as if he himself had given birth to it.

In the days that followed, I would get out of bed and look in at the cot. In repose, the baby, christened Karl Ernest, was pale as a snowdrop, then scarlet when he cried, the little fingers flicking, with the temper in them. The morning he was circumcized a bright berry of blood showed in the bag of his diaper. I could not keep myself from looking at him, at the little tuft of black hair and, underneath it, the gap in the crown of his skull, the two halves opening and shutting, like a hatch, all the while hesitating to pick him up, because I felt so unprepared as a mother.

The Doll's House

It was in London that I would find both the freedom and the incentive to write. We moved there in November 1958. I had two children now, Carlo and Sasha, who like the sheepdogs in their grandmother's house, whom they adored, would spar endlessly and yet remained allies against a baffling grown-up world.

After I brought them to school, I would race home in order to write, sitting at the wide windowsill in their bedroom, which was quite deep, and I wrote in jotters I had brought from Ireland which were called "Aisling," meaning dream or vision. Once, an insect, a little gnat, crawled out of the center-page binding, and I jumped in terror, so carried back was I to Drewsboro and its environs. The wash of memory, and something stronger than memory, was so pervasive that I forgot I was in a semi-detached house in London, with a small back garden that looked out onto another small back garden and an identical row of houses with red tiled roofs. Bleak suburbia.

The words tumbled out, like the oats on threshing day that tumble down the shaft, the hard pellets of oats funneled into bags and the chaff flying everywhere, getting into the men's eyes and their having to shout to be heard above the noise of the machine.

In my first month in London I had gone to a university to hear a lecture by Arthur Mizener on Hemingway. When he read the opening paragraph of *A Farewell to Arms,* of soldiers going down a road, the dust their boots raised and leaves that

Carlo and Sasha Gébler in the back garden of Cannon Hill Lane, 1959.

had already fallen, I saw in a marvelous instance how Hemingway had separated the oats from the chaff.

I cried a lot while writing *The Country Girls,* but scarcely noticed the tears. Anyhow, they were good tears. They touched on feelings that I did not know I had. Before my eyes, infinitely clear, came that former world in which I believed that our fields and hollows had some old music slumbering in them, centuries old. I would ask myself to dream of Drewsboro at night, to refresh my memory. Once, it was newborn calves butting one another to drink from the bucket of separated milk, another time it was of goslings, their feathers with the softness of flowers, and, fixed in my memory forever, is one in which I am holding my father's shins on a tongs, about to consign them to a fire in a little grate in an upstairs room where a fire had never been lit. Mother, father, field, and fort, makeshift fences, corn lodged in the rain, and bread rising in the oven. Indoors and outdoors. In the month of May the hedges a carnival of pink and white, hawthorn petals blowing about like confetti.

I saw again a dog lick the afterbirth of a calf in a hollow, lap it up, and the dark fort where Lady Drew was seen in her nightgown and where, one summer Sunday, a girl with ringlets lured me in for an "op," short for operation. It was quite dark, and we were hidden by the low-lying branches as we took off our knickers, then pulled up the stalks of the wild iris that grew in a swamp and stuffed the wet smeared roots into one another, begging for mercy. Our cries flowed together and were muffled by the drones of bees and wasps that swarmed in and out as we swore eternal secrecy. Then afterward, when we came into the daylight, her eyes were a queer, shiny black, the light making yellow slashes in her pupils, and she said that she would "tell" unless I gave her my most prized possession, which was a georgette handkerchief with a pink powder puff stitched into it. And so I did.

The novel's opening paragraph centered on the fear of my father—*I wakened quickly and sat up in bed abruptly. It is only when I am anxious that I waken easily and for a minute I could not remember what it was. Then I remembered, the old reason, my father, he had not come home.*

But it was my mother who filled the canvas and who infused that first book. Even as I was writing it, I guessed she would disapprove, as she was suspicious of the written word. "Paper never refused ink" was one of her more sarcastic sayings. I recalled seeing her as she was beating hot stirabout with a pounder, and I read her lines I had copied from a calendar:

When icicles hang by the wall,
And Dick the Shepherd blows his nail,
And Tom bears logs into the hall

She had looked up at me, her face wreathed in steam, and said if that was writing, "they got their money easy."

In London twenty years later, the words poured out of me, and the pen above the paper was not moving fast enough, so that I sometimes feared they would be lost forever.

I had received fifty pounds to write a novel. The advance was paid jointly by Knopf in New York and Hutchinson in London. Flushed with wealth, I splashed out, for my husband a pullover, for the household a sewing machine (sewing was not my strong point), for my children some plastic weaponry and tin drums, which their father objected to. For myself, a tiny bottle of perfume with an orange rubber stopper in the nozzle. It smelled almost religious. Sometimes of an evening I would dab a little behind my ears to cheer myself up, and seeing this, Carlo and Sasha would fret, believing that I was going out. But there was nowhere to go and we had made no friends. Sometimes, after they had gone to bed, I would walk as far as Morden and read the handwritten cards in newsagents' windows—*Black Cat Found... Piano Tuner Wanted... Cane Chairs Refurbished.* It was there that I got the idea for my first television play, called *The Wedding Dress.* The message read, "Widower wishes to dispose of recently deceased wife's clothing, as good as new, call evenings." That play, fifty years later, would mutate into the stage play *Haunted,* in which a Mr. and Mrs. Berry, in isolated Blackheath, lived in the marital crucible.

I had betrayed my husband, though not in deed. He had heard my future publisher, Iain Hamilton, and I exchange some words on the telephone that were decidedly tender. Iain, the one who had commissioned the novel, was fond of me and believed in me as a writer. But I was not in love with him. The truth is, I wanted to be rescued—a tall order for a man with a wife and children and a publishing house to oversee. We arranged to meet for lunch "up London," as I called it. First I went to a hairdresser's in Wimbledon, which was unfortunate, as the stylist insisted on putting small rollers in, so that the result was a frizzy old-fashioned hairdo.

Still, it was a day out, the very first since we had arrived, three months ago, at Waterloo station, which I found to be grimy and sooted, the waddle of the pigeons so ungainly, not supple like birds at home. It was November, and seeing the wreaths of paper poppies around the several monuments as we went in a taxi from Waterloo station to SW20, I thought England so dolorous.

Yet now I was seeing Piccadilly Circus: its teeming life, newspaper vendors at street corners shouting out the catchy headlines, and already early editions of an evening paper were being thrown from vans that stopped, regardless of other traffic. This was the hub of things. In Bond Street I inquired the price of a bronze horse, which I suppose was by Giacometti, and got, from a smartly dressed male assistant with beautiful lapis cufflinks, a supercilious reply. In a shop in Regent Street I tried on different pairs of high-heeled suede court shoes, such as the dancing teacher used to wear. Oh, the protocol, my stockinged feet placed on a sloping dais to be measured and a stout woman, no longer young, remarking on the fact that my feet were two different sizes, which made her job harder. I chose black suede ones which laced over the instep. It was not the narrow corded laces that I was used to but a ribbon of black taffeta, which she tied in a bow. Walking around on that carpet, I thought I would levitate. As I saw myself in the long mirror, the stout woman complimenting my calves, I was already wearing these shoes to literary soirees. Hearing the price, I almost fainted.

"Twenty pounds!" I repeated.

"Guineas, madam," she said tartly, and realizing that there was to be no sale, she unlaced them hurriedly and put them in the white box, with tissue paper that was the color of clean gray ash. I have never forgotten those shoes.

The lunch was in El Vino's in Fleet Street, which I took to be the last word in literary sophistication. It was very crowded, and we sat at a small table near the window. He ordered a bottle of red wine, along with steak-and-kidney pie. I was terrified that we would be caught out. He did not take to my new hairdo, and from time to time ran his hand over it to smooth it out and in that way to affirm his attraction. I had to tell him that my husband had heard our conversation, because of listening in on the extension in his bedroom, which I had not at first realized. I found out only because of one of the entries in his logbook, which he kept in a yellow strongbox that was always locked. I had found the key to it in the well at the top of his bookcase and read the many entries that had grown rancorous with the years: his lifting me from behind a shop counter, launching me into a world of literature and refinement, bringing me against his better wishes to live in London. Though void of intellect or cognitive powers, I was already passing myself off as a writer. I told my publisher only of the bit that concerned him, in which my husband asserted that he would publish any nonsense of mine solely because of his infatuation. He looked flustered, filled both our glasses, then held my hand gravely, realizing it was too dangerous for the friendship to go on. I would finish the novel, and that would be the link between us, and I thought of the picture of that pair of outstretched hands, destined to be divided, that was on willow-pattern plates.

At a quarter to two each day, when it was time to bring my husband his tray of Earl Grey tea and two slices of slightly burned toast sprinkled with olive oil, I put the jotter aside, hoping that the next day's chapter was safe inside me. Then after the children got back in, I made bread and sponge cakes, knowing that the smell cheered things up, but also knowing that I could not live forever in that mock-Tudor house that looked out on a common, mired in fog.

There were no rows and no scenes; the friction was mounting just beneath the surface. Sensing this at dinnertime, the children would do daft things, laugh uncontrollably, or tell tall tales from school; a fight that had developed into a bloodbath, big boys "milking" smaller boys, and the luring of a girl, called Janice Budding, into the shade. Their father read, usually from

Carlo and Sasha, mid-1960s.

the *New Scientist*, which he subscribed to. As he became more and more concerned about the poisons in the atmosphere and the poisons in food, our diets were strictly monitored. A favorite book of his was *The Culture of the Abdomen* by Mr. F. A. Hornibrook, from which he would read passages at random:

One cannot live over a cesspit in good health. How much more difficult to remain well if we carry our cesspit about inside us.... Food is taken several times daily, often too frequently and too freely and of unsuitable quality; but, as a rule, one occasion only is permitted for the ejection of its waste materials. And remember that all the time this lagging tenant of the bowel is retained the conditions favouring evil are at work; heat, moisture, nitrogenous refuse, darkness and micro-organisms. The slow poison factory is in full swing, and its output is turned into the highways and byways of the body.

Being the younger of the two, Sasha showed his discontent in mischievous ways. He scraped off the new turquoise paint with which his father had proudly painted the lavatory seat, and another time he interfered with the red plastic fob watch by which his father set his time for his breakfast. The two hands were usually set for a time between one and two o'clock, when I would bring him his breakfast. I was surprised to find the hour and the minute hands had been moved to ten o'clock and recognized that it was a ruse, because on a sheet of paper under it Sasha had written, "Hope you get the joke." He saw himself as something of an embryo writer and was proud that his was one of the essays on display for parents' day, with a little gold star at the bottom of the page. In it the dreariness of domesticity was blithely bypassed:

I live in a large cave with my mother and father and each morning my father goes hunting and if he is lucky, he catches a deer. While he is out, my mother dusts the cave.

My novel was completed in three weeks. It had written itself, and I was merely the messenger. I copied it in a neater hand and sent it to an invalid in Hastings-by-the-Sea to be typed. I had found her name in the back of the *New Statesman,* and when she returned it, she said it evoked moments of her own life in the north of England long before. If ever I found myself in Hastings, she would make me welcome.

My publisher was happy; his hunch had borne fruit, and their reader, the author Clifford Hanley, had written a glowing report, enclosing a personal letter for me with a quote from Robert Burns.

I had left the spare copy on the hall table for my husband to read, should he wish, and one morning he surprised me by appearing quite early in the doorway of the kitchen, the manuscript in his hand. He had read it. Yes, he had to concede that despite everything, I had done it, and then he said something that was the death knell of the already ailing marriage—"*You can write and I will never forgive you.*"

It was as if by writing it I had taken the ground from under his feet: I had sabotaged his inner belief in himself, and I could not completely blame him. In the six years since I had met him, when I so faithfully embodied the daftness of the literary Bessie Bunters, something had changed in me and he had played an important part in that change, and now I was poised for flight.

Yet we went on. When the check from the publisher came, I had to endorse it and hand it over to him. I would receive a small amount from it for each week's housekeeping. As a reward he bought me a hut, so that I could write in the garden. It was a wooden shed, fitted with a table, a chair, and an oil heater. On Saturdays, when the children were at home and playing in the garden, they would make faces in at me through the window or slip in notes saying, *We are missing you, We are ill,*

We are interested in the distillation of gin. They were both precocious and fearful, and knew all too well that we were living on tenterhooks.

Why I remained so passive may seem peculiar to outsiders, but not to me. I was petrified and wanted us, my children and myself, to survive.

A phone call from a stranger inviting me to a poetry reading in Dulwich. He had heard of my forthcoming novel from a friend in the publishing house and decided to look me up. Normally the poets met in a pub on alternate Thursdays, but this was to be in his house and, unusually, on a Sunday, since Ted Hughes was attending and it was his only free evening. At last! I had read of literary coteries: in San Francisco, the Beat poets assaulting the sensibilities of the bourgeois, Russian poets who met underground to recite their works when it was too dangerous to have them printed, and in a pub in Soho a few years before when bohemians, including Dylan Thomas, had convened. So now it was Dulwich and Ted Hughes, the living Orpheus, whom I would meet. It was clear that I had been invited alone, something I knew that my husband resented and that would incur a hefty entry in the logbook.

It was quite a pilgrimage from the hinterlands of Cannon Hill Lane to the poetic environs of Dulwich. I left our house abnormally early in order to negotiate the Underground, the two changes which I'd already studied on my miniature Tube map, and the connection to the overground train for Dulwich. From the station to the strange address there were some mishaps, but eventually I found it and looked through the window, as the curtains were not drawn. A tea trolley was laden with bottles, and an electric fire, with a large crenellated papier-mâché facing, glowed a candy pink. A woman was endeavoring, not very successfully, to herd children out of that room, running her hand through her hair in exasperation. A tall, larky man answered the door, a little surprised at my punctuality. Poets were not meant to be punctual. He followed his wife upstairs and said to help myself to a drink. I drank sparingly in those, my green and salad days, but I needed one after the fret of the journey; but I discovered that the bottles on the trolley were for ornament, several shapes and sizes, including two yellow liqueur bottles with long yellow spires, totally empty. The host returned swiftly, having changed into an orange velvet jacket, and from his pocket he took a naggin of whiskey, which was obviously his tipple. From a sideboard, he hauled out a bottle of Wincarnis and poured some for me into a tumbler. He was a flirtatious man, winked a lot as he chatted. What literary titans had I met? What literary "rag" did I read? Was I following the spat in *The Listener* between two northern heavyweights? Did I think Ted Hughes the reincarnation of Heathcliff? What was that thing on Haworth churchyard?

> On thee too did the Muse
> Bright in thy cradle smile:
> But some dark Shadow came
> (I know not what) and interpos'd.

Not once did he wait for an answer, so ebullient was he. He was hoping to get back to poetry himself and also get stuck into Dante for Lent. It was going to be quite an evening, what with getting the numero uno poet himself. Gigs in the pub often proved quite tricky, poets, who brought the heavies, the rough trade, demanding cash up front. The guests, apart from Orpheus, consisted of two Canadian poets, female, and a young man called Archie, an aspiring poet who worked for a mortgage broker. Archie was coming from Crystal Palace but was in a bit of a pickle about finding a babysitter.

The hostess returned in a sky-blue jersey dress with a string of pearls, clearly annoyed with her husband, saying something would have to be done about the children on Sunday evenings, as they were invariably incontinent.

"Incontinent," he said with a quizzical laugh and took another swig, whereupon she held out an empty glass for him to pour some drink. She said her name was Janice and she had a twin sister called Judith, they being so alike that there was a running joke among their friends, *Hello, Judith, How's Janice,* or vice versa. She asked if I had come a long way and if I had children, and as I said their names, I recalled the glares they gave me, the silent rebukes, as I left the house. She said she was determined that her children would not grow up to follow the Arts, as it was a mug's game, to which her husband said, "Touché," and took another long swig.

The first guests to arrive were the Canadian ladies, girlfriends, as was obvious by the way they stood so close and held hands. The older had a plait of her hair wound around her forehead, and since this was being greatly admired by Janice, I insanely mentioned the resemblance it had to a photograph of Ivy Compton-Burnett that I had seen in a bookshop. The host let out hoots of laughter: did we know that when Philip Toynbee was given the honor to have dinner with Ivy and her friend, he fell asleep over the soup? Over the soup! Ghastly, ghastly.

From time to time, he went to the hall door and opened it in the belief that Orpheus had materialized. He was clearly fidgety, and after a bit more small talk, and in order to assure himself that all was on course, he decided that he would ring Ted Hughes. The phone was on a side table, a heavy black receiver, and taking the number from a tiny slip of paper in his inside pocket, a number so precious and known only to the select few, he read it carefully and winked at the sheer joy of having it. We each watched him dial, and then, as he held the phone out for our benefit, we could hear it ringing at the other end, somewhere in Chalk Farm or Primrose Hill, and it was clear that Ted Hughes had already left his house and was on his way.

Since time was running on, he decided that perhaps we should start, an hors d'oeuvre, as it were. The elder of the two ladies agreed and with a bold stare took a sheaf of poetry from her brown leather music bag. She read several poems, all replete with images of waterfalls and rills and cascades, all metaphors for various heightened and erotic states of emotion. There was some polite clapping, and then her friend read two short poems that were clearly indebted to Ogden Nash. My host, who had been taking certain liberties, the odd nudge, a hand on my knee, said that he had tossed off a few lines, extempore, and was throwing his hat in:

And the green-eyed whore
In the red-eyed dress
At the shag end of the day
Counts her loves
In shillings and in sixpences.
Oh sweet sister
Oh green-eyed muse.

Janice let out a shriek before throwing the contents of her glass directly into his face, and things might have worsened were it not for the ringing of the doorbell at that very moment. We held our breath. It was Archie from Crystal Palace, who had been lucky enough to find a babysitter. He was awkward, kept his coat on and kept his head down. Asked if by any chance he had seen a tall man with a spill of dark hair at the turnstile of the station, he was too embarrassed to reply. He sat on the edge of his chair, and taking a folded sheet from his pocket, he studied it earnestly. Not a single vestige of beauty or feeling or fire informed the poem that he bashfully read, but our host nevertheless decided that this was the trend, the postmodern trend, that poetry was taking. There was a sinking realization in that room that Ted Hughes was not coming.

The younger Canadian poet read a few lines from "The Journey of the Magi" for us to deconstruct, which we struggled to do. Eureka! Our host had a brain wave: we would take a leaf from the surrealist's book, André Breton and all that gang, and we would each write a line, then fold the paper over and pass it on to the next person, and then we would have something avant-garde to deconstruct. At that moment Janice, who had fled the room since the debacle with the thrown glass, returned with refreshments. She had a pile of red paper napkins and a cheeseboard with a brand-new cheese knife, the label hanging off it. Meanwhile, her husband took six bottles of stout from the sideboard, which he opened, winking all the while, and stationed them there for us to help ourselves. But on Sunday nights, as I knew, the Tube stopped early and the last bus from Wimbledon station to the bottom end of Cannon Hill Lane would be at ten-thirty, so I had to excuse myself.

As I passed the river in Cannon Hill Lane, a few hundred yards from our house, the slurps of the mating frogs were deafening.

The furor upon publication of my novel took me by surprise, although there were advance rumblings. The head nun from the Convent of Mercy sent a letter saying, "We have heard that you have written a novel. We give credence an open mind." The sheet of paper shook in my hand, and I saw again her inquisitioner's eyes, with that little cyst on the lower lid of the left one. A friend of my mother's, a doctor's wife who was visiting London, invited me to supper at the Cumberland Hotel in Marble Arch, and quizzing me about the book, she smelled a rat, so that before long my mother wrote saying she hoped and prayed that I was not about to bring ignominy and disgrace on my own people.

Publication day was like any other, and reviews were to come in fits and starts, instances of praise marred by soundings from home. In her letters my mother spoke of the shock, the hurt, and the disgust that neighbors felt. I had sent her a copy, which she did not mention as having received, and one day, after her death, I would find it in a bolster case, with offending words daubed out with black ink. There would, she said, be many who would turn away from me when I came home on the annual holiday. The postmistress, who happened to be Protestant, told my father that a fitting punishment would be for me to be kicked naked through the town. Stoning would be next.

Luckily, in that tenuous state, I was unaware of the righteous correspondence that went on between Archbishop McQuaid and the then Minister for Justice, Charlie Haughey, both agreeing that the book was filth and should not be allowed inside any decent home. They shared their indignation with the Catholic Archbishop of Westminster, all three men in evident bafflement that the "Literary Lounger of the *London Illustrated*," who was normally sane, had let me off so lightly.

There were occasional excitements. I was interviewed on television by the actor Robert Shaw, who had been somewhat complimentary, and afterward when he and my husband met in the green room, they looked daggers at one another. Meanwhile, the author L. P. Hartley was being interviewed about the book by Jack Lambert, pronouncing it the skittish story of two Irish nymphomaniacs.

Home life was punitive. There were no rows, just silence and routine. In the logbook, which I now read when he took the children some afternoons in his vintage Railton for a drive on Wimbledon Common, I would discover his ongoing fury with me and with the world. He used to stay up till three or four in the morning, listening to music and, as he insisted, writing, except that I saw no evidence of it. There were only these caustic entries. Arthur Koestler, according to him, had sold out on his Marxist principles, and those who executed the Rosenbergs should themselves face the electric chair. I read how I was puffed up with newfound fame, my ravenousness for literary circles ever-deepening, the world blind to the fact that my book owed its being to the husband who had sacrificed his own talents to serve mine and indeed had martyred himself. I would be allowed to get on with the *scribbling*, while, in return, he was given complete control over the children, their welfare, and every aspect of their lives. A Faustian pact, of which I was hitherto unaware.

There was no way out.

It was after my second novel, *The Lonely Girl*, had been published that Father Peter Connolly, a professor of English in Maynooth College, wrote a long piece about both novels, praising the nature sections, the composite picture of rural life and convent education. In an anonymous letter, one of many which I received, I simply found a newspaper clipping with the heading "Priest praises her."

A cultural organization in Limerick called An Tuarim decided to have a public meeting so that my own people could voice their reservations to me in person. The hall was packed to overflowing, people still pouring in half an hour after we were due to begin, kneeling, squatting, while I sat on the platform next to the chairman and Father Connolly, feeling none too confident. The physical oppression in that hall, as was later reported, was such that for a while it seemed as if Ireland, just as James Joyce had described her, was indeed the sow that would eat her farrow—by which he meant piglets—or, in my case, would eat the "enigmatic thirty-year-old literary bonham."

Mr. Dillon, the chairman, opened the meeting by saying that at least *I* had probably read the books in question, something that was perhaps not true for all those present. He then went on to say that it was a rare thing for Ireland to talk to an Irish writer in public before he, or she, was dead or embittered. Father Connolly then stood up, holding *The Country Girls,* and began by suggesting that it be read in full before judgment could be passed. He was aware, he said, of the accusations of immorality, but in his estimation, it was amoral rather than immoral. He stressed the nature section, the sense of place, the ribaldry of rural life, adding that if there were passages less palatable to some, was it not the duty of literature to portray life, warts and all? He then spoke of the conversation he had had with me before the meeting and the reasons for my reluctance to live in Ireland because of its narrow-mindedness and robust censorship. The audience was not amused by his saying that Ibsen had been castigated by his own people in Norway.

At his request questions were invited, questions that inevitably turned into speeches. A woman began the proceedings by saying that the sexual imagery was unnecessary, shocking and indecent, and was there for no other reason except to coin money. Father Connolly felt it incumbent on him to get to his feet again and warned of the besetting temptation of judging a book by one or two paragraphs when a reader might well profit from what was "solid, substantial, and serious." He repeated his phrase of its not being immoral but amoral, and the audience seemed skeptical. The next questioner was also a woman, and she was shaking, saying what a sad day for Ireland this was. How much of my own life had I put into this stuff? How true or untrue were the descriptions of the convent? Had I no thought for my family and the shame I had heaped on them? Did I not think the decent and wholesome thing to do would be to donate my earnings to a charity? Then a dauntless young woman, wearing a green dirndl skirt and waving a green placard, jumped up and gave a spirited rendering of "They'll Be Hanging Men and Women, for the Wearing of the Green."

Mr. Dillon believed there was not enough male input, and so a man in the front row in a coat and hat put it to me in strong terms: Why did I live in England? Why did I write in England? Was there not enough experience for me in my own village and community? Was there not a rich furrow to uncover? I said that unfortunately, having drawn on this rich furrow, I was being punished. A woman, almost apoplectic, said that it was quite clear I had turned my back on a Christian society in order to live a life of sin and promiscuity. Father Connolly objected, saying he would like to remind people that this was a public meeting and not the confessional.

The debate widened then as to whether hard-core pornography should be kept out of Ireland. I said I had not read any hard-core pornography, either in Ireland or England, as it was difficult enough to try and write. This was met with some scattered applause. Another man, striving to be reasonable, asked if I would make it clear once and for all what my engagement was with my own country. Was I doing a Pontius Pilate and washing my hands of it? The audience deserved to know. I said my engagement with it was total, because for every writer the love of language begins in the place called "home." I quoted W. B. Yeats, who had said that the sea cliffs of Sligo gave tongue to his early poems, but this was met with scorn, my sheer audacity at comparing myself with William Butler Yeats, which actually I hadn't intended to do.

Mr. Dillon, sensing that things were getting heated, ruled that the evening should end on a positive note, and asked that all agree on the fact that, wherever I lived, Ireland had been the source of my inspiration and would continue to be so.

A leading article in the *Irish Times* paid tribute to Father Connolly's courage and voiced the hope that the meeting signified a turning of the tide. The banning and mangling of Irish writers, so it said, had for too long "marked the more shameful aspects of the forty years of Independence."

My mother was drawing a chicken on the kitchen table for us to take back to London after the annual summer holiday. The entrails were in a newspaper, and blood dripped onto the tiled kitchen floor. We were due to leave in an hour or so. My husband was polishing his Railton, having not exchanged a word with either her or me all morning. My sons, in a high state of bathos, were strewing farewells to their favorite haunts, to the tree house, the fort of oak trees, the hay shed where they had romped and the hay tram from which Sasha had fallen when the horse had bolted and the farm help, Eamonn, had sworn him to secrecy. Coming upon the bruises that night, my mother asked him when it had happened, to which he had replied gallantly, "I know but I am not allowed to tell."

I was in the back kitchen washing up while my mother went on drawing the chicken, and I was relieved to be leaving but fearful of what lay ahead. The marriage was at breaking point. I knew that, except that I did not know how it would end, in fact believing it was for eternity. I kept rinsing and rerinsing the cups and saucers, anything to be alone, when my mother said my name tersely, said it twice. I went in and stood near her. The pope's nose of the bird was pink and futile, and the long soft toenails were of a sickly yellow. Snipping out the heart and the liver for broth, she managed to cut the sac that contained the gallstones, and presently a green liquid with a foul smell spewed out. It meant that the insides of the bird were now poisoned. She was furious at her mistake and, throwing the scissors down, asked me curtly, "Are these children ever going to go to a Catholic school, or are they not?"

"I don't know," I said.

"Answer me," she said fiercely.

"I can't, I can't answer you," I said, because I couldn't. My husband made all decisions regarding their upbringing and had only agreed to their being baptized by indulging, as he said, a superstition of mine.

She became more and more insistent, and I too became more defensive as she wanted an answer, a resolution. It ended by her gathering up the newspaper that contained chicken, guts and all, and hurrying out the back door, up to a cellar where she dumped things and where dogs and foxes scavenged at night.

Our departure was brought forward by an hour. The tension was unbearable. Nobody speaking, everybody weeping, my sons crying uncontrollably, their goodbyes, their embracing and hugging of the two sheepdogs, their rituals, so brutally cut short, because my mother and I had fallen out completely. My husband sat in his car quietly seething. As I put our luggage in the boot of the car and looked back at the house, I did something stupid. I went into the unkempt garden and broke off a bit of honeysuckle to have as a keepsake in my book. As if I needed keepsakes!

My father hurried out of the house fuming and told me to go in there and put my arms around my mother and comfort her.

With my parents in front of Drewsboro House, 1966.

"I can't," I said, forcing back the tears that combined rage and desperation.

"You little shite...always were from the first moment you were born...and always will be," he said.

That was the last time we went there as a family.

It was in that frame of mind that I wrote the epitaph to my parents that would ever after dismay me, except that I wrote it when I did:

Shall I write and tell them that I hate them, these parents on the very verge of their extreme unctions, I hate him because he murdered me, in each and all of my tiniest inclinations, so that I walked with a stoop, thought with a shudder, and spoke the utmost untruthful, placating drivel, and she, she stitched me back on, she got a big packing needle that was her heart and a big bale of coarse twine that was her will, and whenever I walked abroad, she called me back, quick, quick, to the world of stirabout and bowel movements, to the cold dark rooms reeking of vomited drink, to the cold dark rooms waiting for their next hideous commission of sin.

It was about halfway on the journey when my husband stopped in order to have tea, which he had brought in a flask. We went into a cornfield where the harvest had already been taken and the ground was spiked in stubble. There were geese at the far end, and a gander with its neck craned, hissing and determined to drive us away. The story I was reading was Chekhov's "The Steppe." The parched plain, the sunburnt hills, the peasant women binding the sheaves of corn, and the terrible stagnancy in the story resembled the place I was in. To my astonishment, I fell asleep in that cornfield and dreamed that a group of people, including some of the characters in the story, my husband and my parents, were all crammed into some shelter, waiting. A girl, well known to be a thief, picked up a sack of potatoes and walked off with them. It might have been a religious service that we waited for, certainly it was deliverance of some kind, and then we heard that the actors who were due to come and entertain us had stopped along the way for a boozy lunch. My mother sat, utterly silent, with a hen in her lap. It was a Rhode Island Red hen, and she ran her fingers repeatedly through the folds of its feathers, searching for something she had lost. I went to her, to apologize, but found that I had lost my speech, and yet when I wakened, I let out some cry of dismay. My sons were shaking me, saying their father had started the car and it was time for us to go.

An envelope, addressed to me, containing a huge check. It was almost four thousand pounds and was for the film rights to *The Lonely Girl.* Enough to allow me to flee, with the children, to rent a flat, to engage a solicitor, and so on, but I was paralyzed by my own fears. My husband was asleep. I looked at the check again and again, held it up to the light, incredulous at the large sum, then reading the name of the bank and the two signatures, which were almost illegible. This time, I would not endorse it over to him, as I had done with all the previous checks from both novels. I simply put it back on the hall table, which was of black cherrywood with a latticed panel across the front. Every detail of those culminating hours has stayed with me.

In the early afternoon I took the children for a walk on the Common, knowing that sometimes their father would watch through binoculars, so that he could follow our movements. But he was still asleep. The children were playing a war game with two sticks—they liked war games—when, as ill luck would have it, Carlo hit another boy who was intrigued by the game and almost grazed his eye. A furious parent rushed to grab the two sticks, saying his son's eye was destroyed for life and demanding compensation, there and then. I had only my latchkey in my pocket. He insisted on taking down my name, our address, and our phone number, which, quakingly, I gave him.

Ernest had materialized as though out of thin air, and I was surprised that he had got up before being brought his tea and toast in the bedroom. He met us just as we joined hands to cross the road, and I saw the dagger look and thought that he had witnessed, through his binoculars, the near-accident with the other boy, but it was not that. The children were told to look at television, several hours earlier than normal, and Carlo went "whoops,

whoops," which was his favorite word at that time. He used to pick up certain words that appealed to him and savor them.

"You haven't signed it," he said, pointing to the check on the hall table. There was pen and ink bottle beside it.

"I haven't," I said.

He stopped, and for a moment he didn't say anything at all. Endeavoring to be calm, though in a rushing burst, I said, "No... and I'm not going to."

He stood motionless for a few seconds, realizing in that instant that I had never before openly defied him.

"Come upstairs," he said. I went upstairs, knowing that for years I had anticipated this defining moment and somehow I must go through with it. He stood with his back to the door, a simulacrum of power, his eyes blazing, saying that yes, the marriage was over, that I had killed it with my schizoid personality and vaunting ambition, but I was being given a last chance. I was being allowed to live in that house and see those children, provided I played by the rules.

"I won't sign it," I said, and he rushed toward me, almost soundless, and sat me on the bed. His hand came around my throat, a clasp so sudden that I thought I was already dead, yet cravenly fighting for words, the words still stuck in my craw, but waiting to be said. The words "yes, yes."

I came downstairs, endorsed the check on the back, and laid it facedown on the big sheet of blotting paper he had put there. Like a sleepwalker, I put on my coat and went out, surprised to notice that dark had fallen. It was late September 1962. It smelled of autumn, though I could not say exactly what the smell was, leaves and leaf mold and the remembered smell of bonfires from the back gardens. Smell attaches itself to a particular moment, and that autumn I knew that I was walking from the past, from the twin governance of parents and husband, but that my steps were as yet unsure.

I went first to a police station and then a hospital. The policeman who saw me was surly; hearing my wifely story, he simply kept asking, Did he or did he not molest you, and did I want the matter taken further? Limply, I said no.

From there, I went to the outpatients department of the Nelson Hospital at the end of the lane, where it seemed the dregs of the world had descended. People calling, people bleeding, people shouting, a drunk couple wrangling and then all of a sudden cuddling, a dog that seemed to belong to no one, bawling children, a taxi driver stumbling in, holding up his badge, searching for the bastard who had picked a row with him, and in a corner, all by himself, a dwarf with a look of utmost desolation. I was not sure why I was there. It was something to do with getting through a given number of minutes, and they would be followed by another given number of minutes, in which time passed, like walking along stepping-stones. The nurse who eventually saw me was motherly, but she said she could not prescribe sleeping tablets, and her advice was for me to go home, make up, have a gin-and-tonic, and mend the marital fences.

I went to Waterloo station, the place I had first seen when I arrived in London. I sat on a bench and curiously felt no fear. The men around me were mostly Irish. One, a talker, kept walking around, saying the same thing, "Oh, I'm tellin' ya, wah . . . oh, I'm tellin' ya," but whatever it was had slipped his fogged memory. They had a bottle of drink which they passed around. Another man got out a coin for the weighing machine and had the others in stitches as the machine spoke his weight back to him, and his friend jumped on to avail himself of the penny's worth. I was not afraid there that night, or rather, I was less afraid than in the house I had vacated. Many years later, in a taxi to Portobello Road, the driver swore that he had been one of the people on one of those benches that night and he remembered me, cowering into the collar of my coat, remembered my accent.

Woodfall Films was based in Curzon Street, and it was they who had bought the rights to *The Lonely Girl,* later called *The Girl with Green Eyes.* A man in their office loaned me some money and then rang Penelope Gilliatt to ask if I could go with my sons for a couple of days to her house in Sussex, where she and John Osborne lived. I picked them up from school, having brought a supply of chocolate, a Dinky car each, and some plastic swords, all of which they thought exciting. The excitement mounted when, soon after we arrived, John enlisted them to smash the greenhouse, which was already falling down. It was an old greenhouse on a cast-iron frame, and the panes of glass were covered in thick, black-green splotches of moss. The sound of the breaking glass came through the open window as we sat having tea, and I poured my woes out to two people who were evidently besotted with one another. Not long after, they left for their flat in London, linked and jocular, and I had such a stab of envy, because I feared I would never be so at ease with a man, like that. Penelope gave me two sleeping capsules that were a bright turquoise, like the beads of a necklace, except that I was afraid to take them, in case I would never wake up again.

My husband and I had one mutual friend, the Canadian writer Ted Allan, who for me was the last word in sophistication, because he had a play that ran in Paris for over a year and starred Jacques Brel. To my astonishment, when I rang him, he began to shout and rant, asking how could I do it to their father, how could I allow a man to go to the school gate, only to learn that his children had been abducted, a man who had had the same nightmare experience from a previous wife. He said then that Ernest was asking to meet me, and he assured me that everything would be all right, that there would be no recriminations, none. The meeting was in Ted's flat in Deodar Road; it looked out on the river Thames. Ernest seemed a changed man. He had obviously not slept, his eyes hollow, and he wore the old green jersey that zipped up to his throat. He inquired about the children's well-being, and then Ted offered to repair to his bedroom, hoping we would appreciate the trouble he had gone to with the tea, two pottery mugs and a brown teapot with a broken spout. Ernest spoke very gently, said he accepted the fact that the marriage was over, he realized that I was young and, as he put it, needed to sow my wild oats. He said we were both reasonable people and that we would share the children, but for the time being, I should bring them back to his house, until I got a place of my own. The matter of money was not mentioned.

I went back to the country to fetch them, and that night we stayed with Trix Craig in north London, a woman I had met at the parties given by Dr. Jerry Slattery, a Cork man who saw to it that all Irish people, but especially actors and writers, met one another under his roof. Trix made apple fritters for the tea, and we played ludo afterward, and the children and I slept on a blown-up rubber bed that she put in the sitting room. They had no idea as to what was going to happen. She gave me a fiver to replenish my funds, which were running low. In the taxi from Wimbledon station, they fretted about catching at least the second half of *The Man from U.N.C.L.E.* They argued fiercely over the plot, so I could not reasonably work out who was the good agent or who was the bad agent, the Russian or the American, except I did glean that they had ganged together, were in some HQ in New York above a tailor's shop, where they waited to confront the enemy who coveted their weapons. I told them that I would not be coming in, that their father and I had amicably agreed to separate, but this news was secondary to the cliff-hanging moment of the two agents above the tailor's shop in New York.

As the taxi pulled up, they ran in through the open door, throwing their coats down and making for the dining room, where the television stood in one corner. Their father remained in the doorway, smiling a cold, mad smile. He was thanking me. He said, "Thank you, Edna, you have just legally deserted them," and with that, he closed the door. Forever after, I have associated the closing of that door with the closing of a lid of a coffin.

It was September and the first few leaves had fallen; a few clogged the grille of his vintage Railton car. A thin fog filled the gulleys at the side of the common and drove itself onto the road in random shadowy pockets as I stopped on the bridge to think. There was really nothing to think about, only the irrefutable fact that I had deserted them. Legally. I leaned over the bridge and looked down at the dark sheet of water, where, in summer, men on camp stools patiently plied their fishing rods. Looking as I might into a ravine, I cried my numb and balked fury. I still believed that something dramatic might happen, that the children might have escaped and be running down the road toward me. I would see that bridge only one more time in my life.

It was a question of where to go. The money I had borrowed had almost run out. I had a few shillings, but not enough to take a room, should I see signs farther on that said BED AND BREAKFAST. Although we had lived in London for almost four years, I knew so little of it, the wine bar in Fleet Street, the huge conference room in my publisher's office, the local doctor's waiting room, and the school gates. I did not have enough money to get back to north London and the blown-up rubber bed.

I found that I was walking toward Putney, as Ted Allan lived there. In the streets I could skulk behind other people, but it was on the long stretch of Wimbledon Common that the fears multiplied. Little sounds. Little scurries in the grass. A clump of high fern was alive with creatures, and as I ran from it, I almost lost a shoe in the tangle. All the fears and foreboding of night were contained in that night, that walk, the streetlamps at the edge of the common too far apart, and peril in every fat shadow. I think I would have liked to die, yet something drove me on.

Putney High Street had more bustle, people in cafés, others queuing outside the cinema, and from somewhere the warm vinegary smell of chips.

I walked as far as the bridge, where the beams from the lamps shot down through the fog into the water. Somewhere on that bridge, in 1787, Mary Wollstonecraft, the feminist philosopher, feeling rejected by her lover Gilbert Imlay, soaked her skirts and threw herself from the bridge, but ended up being ignominiously dredged from the mud. From where I stood I could see the blocks of flats where Ted Allan lived, but I was not sure whether his was one of the lit or one of the dark windows. This was my one sanctuary for that night.

At the corner of the street, before the turning for Deodar Road, there was an auction room, and for at least a quarter of an hour I stared in at secondhand furniture, not knowing why.

Ted Allan was not home, so I knocked on the door across the landing. A woman called Beth opened it, and I remembered having met her briefly on the day I came to mediate with Ernest, believing things might be resolved. Without my having to explain anything, she understood and drew me in. While perhaps not being as palatial as I recall it, that room seemed to me to be the warmest, safest, and most inviting room in the world. The rays from the table lamps and a tall brass floor lamp picked up the mother-of-pearl grains in a black table and the rich, soft pile of the several rugs.

To be admitted as I was and told I could spend the night weakened all the strength in me, far more than the frightened walk had done, and so I blurted it all out, the overnight stay in north London, the loan of the fiver, the taxi ride, *The Man from U.N.C.L.E.*, and the children's running into the hallway, oblivious of the fact that I had just deserted them. She sat me down, gave me wine, and talked. Life was a bitch. Love also was a bitch. Later on, she made up the divan bed that was under the window and then covered it with a handmade quilt that had all the beautiful patterns and motifs of her native Canada. She said, yes, she knew, she understood, knew it all down to its savage guts, and then, embracing me, said, "With this kind of stuff, pet, there is no one in the whole wide world that can help you."

The picture window looked out on the Thames, and the lights from the flats on the far side gleamed and sent pillars down into the water that broke and meshed in a haphazard dance. The theme of my next novel came to me then. That is the mystery about writing: it comes out of afflictions, out of the gouged times, when the heart is cut open. I heard Baba's declamatory voice and her intemperate words as she dilated on their lives and their ruined marriages: *"It's not the vote women need, we should be armed."*

I rented a room for twenty-nine shillings a week in a house along the road and wrote my novel, often in transit on the bus, when I went to meet the children at school or at Wimbledon station, where they came on Saturdays: I sometimes had to wait for an hour or more, as their father relished the fact that I would get agitated and think that they might not be coming at all. They would fly out of the Railton and run to where I stood. He and I did not speak, and all communications were now by letter, which Carlo, being the elder, had the task of handing to me.

The novel, which I called *Girls in Their Married Bliss,* was deemed not as lyrical as my earlier works, but with the money and the help of an accountant called Walter, at Woodfall Films, I was able to buy a tiny cottage up the street which I furnished with bits and pieces from the auction room that I had stared into on the night of the fog.

They were allowed to stay three nights a week with me, and sometimes four, depending on their father's whim. By their woebegone expressions when I met them, it was clear that there were lamentable tales to tell, but they didn't tell them, and in recompense for that grim time, there was extra pocket money and comics and sweets and all the things that were forbidden in the other house. We called it the "Other House."

Then, briefly, my near-empty life had a sparkle. I knew it would only be for a night. It had all the ingredients of a ballad, a wild man riding by, a damsel, if not exactly in obvious distress, was certainly in waiting, and the setting a grand room in Mayfair with high ceilings and long windows that opened onto a wrought-iron balcony. Though I have lived in London for over fifty years, the name Mayfair still conjures up a region plush with promise and privilege. The party was being given by the American producer Charlie Feldman, and I was brought along by the photographer Sam Shaw, who was working on his latest film. I was wearing a short-sleeved sheer dress in ice blue, my going-out dress for that summer. It was its second outing, its first having been something of a disappointment. That was when I had met the singer Richie Havens through Sam Shaw, and was captivated by his rendering of the lines "She takes just like a woman... but she breaks just like a little girl." Afterward we met him, and he invited me to his hotel in Park Lane for the following evening. When I arrived, the concierge handed me a letter, the wording still so very clear, still etched on my memory: "I am not here, I have made two promises both to transpire on the same mountain." What mountain, what promises? I asked myself as I walked back across the marble floor through the revolving door and out into the busy street.

Feldman had approached me to do a rewrite on a script of Mary McCarthy's novel *The Group*, but I felt I was not experienced enough and turned it down. Nevertheless, he invited me to a summer party, where it was thought Robert Mitchum might or might not turn up.

Except that he did, arriving with his cohorts amid gales of laughter. He then passed through into the throng, and seizing his audience, he continued with the joke he had been telling all the way up the street from the Dorchester. He was wearing a soft brown hat on the back of his head, in deliberate guise of a hoodlum, and he looked even more handsome than when I had seen him in films. Robert Mitchum, in person. He crossed the room to where I was standing, took my bare arm, and said, "I bet you wish I was Robert Taylor, and I bet you never tasted white peaches." It was clear that he was going to take me home, regardless of my situation. He gave himself for a little while to his various acolytes, male and female, debunking his own legend of being known as the actor either with the gun or without the gun, then, suddenly, nodded and called out to me, "Let's go... baby," and we left.

Out in the street we paused to take a look at each other; my hair under the streetlamp looked redder than it was, and reminded him of an actress he knew, who had had her hair dyed for a movie and willed it to grow naturally red ever after. One of the bewitchers, he said, and laughed. There were visits to a few hostelries along the way to the Dorchester, then a pub in Mayfair, its lights beguiling as a brothel, then to a less fancy one where, unrecognized, he took turns with the men at a game of darts. When I turned on the light in my modest house in Putney and he saw the small, varnished table and kitchen chairs, guessing that I was impecunious, he said we should go back to the antique shops in King's Road the next day and get the place fitted out.

Taciturn in film, he was a fluent talker in life, proud of hailing from Norwegian seafarers on his mother's side and laboring men on his father's side, the father who had been crushed to death in a railroad accident in North Carolina. He wasn't like a movie star at all, more like a street poet, with that hectoring charm. He ran through his crowded life: digging ditches, being part of a chain gang, spending a week in a county jail in California for possession of marijuana, and being lucky to have known a few lovely ladies along the way. I played my favorite records, Tommy Makem, Ewan MacColl, and he sang the words back and we danced all the way up the stairs into the tiny bedroom, a white gauze curtain billowing in through the open window, we with all the shyness of besotted strangers in syrupy songs.

In the morning the hammering on doors and windows might have been that of the *Macbeth* porters. The film company had tracked him down to my house, and a tentative young man had arrived, saying that Mr. Mitchum was supposed to have been at Shepperton Studios some hours earlier. He dressed at his ease, kissed me several times, and, recalling his brief stint as a ghostwriter to an astrologer, he read my hand and with joking sincerity said, "We'll meet again... my lovely," and then he was gone.

It was almost a year later when, from the top of a number 14 bus, I was seized with an irrational and remaindered fit of jealousy. Passing Wimbledon Common, with which I had so many associations—the dreary walks when married, the fearful walk that night I left home, and once, an impromptu game of snowball—suddenly through the window I caught sight of my husband's car. The hood was down, and sitting next to him there was a young woman, her hair flying in the breeze, the very picture for a perfume or cigarette advertisement. I ran down the stairs of the bus and jumped off, only to find that his car had sped out of sight. After I had collected the children, I left them on the swings on the common, saying I would be back in a few minutes. Turning the key, which I still had, I let myself in. I felt like a criminal. What was I looking for? The woman's name. My husband's feelings for her. Her feelings for him. The evidence was there on the desk. They had found each other through a newspaper advertisement, and I also learned her name and the hamlet in Suffolk where she lived. In the log-book that was also on the desk, no longer needing to be locked, he had written a glowing description of her character; she was, as he put it, a kind, intelligent, thoughtful human being, free of insanity and literary ambition.

That night, after I got a babysitter, my friend Beth drove me to the address where we believed the girl lived. It was a long drive: pubs were closed in high streets, gates and shutters were down, then out into the country where lorries were parked in lay-bys, their drivers fast asleep, and there was one eating house with a crazy, gaudy light and a sign that said, OPEN EVERY DAY OF THE YEAR. Parts of the journey were countryside with trees or saplings, and other parts bare ground full of litter, with here and there a lonely telephone kiosk. Long, long after that we arrived in that landscape where the low land stretched out to meet the sea, land and sea as one, empty and whitish and with a forlornness that was telling me my journey was in vain. We arrived in the small town that was fast asleep. The houses were all of a piece, dotted in between with a coffee shop, a bookshop, a cake shop with a huge wedding cake in the window, and a shop that sold secondhand clothes. At the end of that street I saw Ernest's gray vintage Railton car. It stood out, so stately, so incongruous, parked there, with a small rime of mist on it too. This was the evidence I required to get custody, it was within a whisker of me, except suddenly I did not know what to do. I became very agitated. Beth had brought a small amount of gin in a tonic-water bottle and we each had a slug while we debated the next course of action. She said that she could pose as a detective and storm in there, but then decided it was too dangerous and too dumb. How impulsive and unthinking the whole episode had been. I went to the phone booth at the end of the street and looked up the woman's number. Surprised to find it, I dialed, and after a few minutes a voice answered and she simply said, "Fuck off."

Custody

"I crave leave to refer to my petition therein..." Pomp and circumstance. I am entering one of the great legal institutions of England, which I know of only through reading Charles Dickens. A large notice reads PROBATE: DIVORCE: ADMIRALTY, and I go through a courtyard to Court No. 23, Case No. 10706. I had come to get custody of my children. It sometimes recurs in a dream, that solemn room, a handful of people, the judge in a suit and white shirt, sitting on the bench, his clerk sitting directly beneath him, and in the dream the judge is looking at me, trying to decide whether I am or am not a suitable parent.

After three years of a precarious arrangement, with the children spending some nights in my house and some in their father's, things worsened, his thesaurus of rules and stipulations ever increasing and impossible to abide by. *They must not be driven in any private motorcar, they must not be bathed by either adult or minor, they must not be allowed into the room where I wrote, since my writing now reeked of the perverts and lunacy of Krafft-Ebing.* I was repeatedly warned that if I rocked the boat by even one fathom, he would emigrate with them to New Zealand, where his sister lived.

Then, in the post, a dossier of over six thousand words arrived. An obituary, charting our relationship from the day he had lifted me from behind the shop counter, thinking he had procured a decent, honorable companion but instead had found a "vainglorious monster, divested of all human traits," who had destroyed everyone and everything she touched, including her own bartered children. It ended by saying, "If you run to lawyers and courts, I will fight you. I am absolutely determined about that and I will fight you in my own way. Foul deeds beget foul deeds. A hundred thousand Arab children need a cup of milk a day to save their lives. The address of Oxfam is in the telephone book, you might still have time to save yourself."

My solicitor, Bernard Main, was of the old school, courteous, slightly absentminded, his desk a jungle of papers and folders, scummed in dust, reminiscent of *Bleak House* and its forlorn petitioners. He wore a worn, oatmeal-colored tweed jacket with leather patches on the elbows, and for street wear he donned one exactly the same, but he seemed not to notice the similarity. We had been on a bit of a mission, hoping to find a few friendly people who would swear to the fact that I was not a monster, a nutcase, a nymphomaniac, or insane. My husband had compiled a dossier from evidence he accrued from the local doctor, the headmaster at Hill Cross School, and the Irish girl who had worked for us.

Bernard and I were in a cold tiled hallway in a house in south London. A woman I knew from home had agreed to be a character witness. We were escorted into a small sitting room full of toys, where half a train set snaked around the curb of a fireplace and there was a hatch door to the kitchen, where the wails of one child were being drowned out by the yells of other children.

"Are they boiling a horse?" Bernard kept saying, as the smell of the stew from the kitchen became more pronounced; he doubted the wisdom of our quest. Maura, who knew my family and who was normally garrulous, came in flustered, then sat on a pouf, wringing her apron as if it were a dishcloth. She had never talked to a solicitor before. She looked from one of us to the other, wondered aloud what her husband would say if he knew, and then in nostalgic vein recalled Drewsboro, the lovely kitchen garden with different kinds of apples and pears and boys stealing them. One kind of apple in particular she remembered, with reddish flesh, as if there were dye in it, and she dilated uselessly on this. Finally he took a short statement, which she signed, hoping it wouldn't land her in jail.

It was a bitter cold night as we walked down a hill toward the luring lights of a pub. We were sitting in a corner and drinking mulled red wine when Bernard, dropping his guard as a solicitor and referring to the sheaf of threatening correspondence, asked why I had married such a madman. It was something I could not answer, not even remotely, and all I thought was that if anatomy is fate, as Freud has said, answering the pay telephone in the hall of 58 North Circular Road on the night that I was first invited to meet him was also fate. Indeed, as I would later learn, Bunny had a list of desirable girls whom they could ring, so finding me was merely part of a lottery. Sitting there with Bernard, who could not give me any guarantee of the outcome of the case, I was beginning to crack. I asked him who decided on the custody, and he said it was down to one person, one judge only.

The night before the case was to be heard, the children were in their father's house and were subjected to an inquisition that I would learn about only in time. I was in my house in Putney with the phone off the hook, a black phone coiled along the kitchen table, like a python ready to spring. Going up to bed, I was astonished to find a letter on the mat inside the door, an envelope with my husband's handwriting. It said, "I am not fighting it any longer, your methods are too dirty and too devious. I will not be in court tomorrow morning, so the children are yours to destroy."

Very early in the morning, I rang the barrister John Mortimer to impart the good news, and very relieved, he said that he would send his junior. I wore nothing stylish, though stupidly I put on long, giddy earrings with feather pendants that had the dip of catkins.

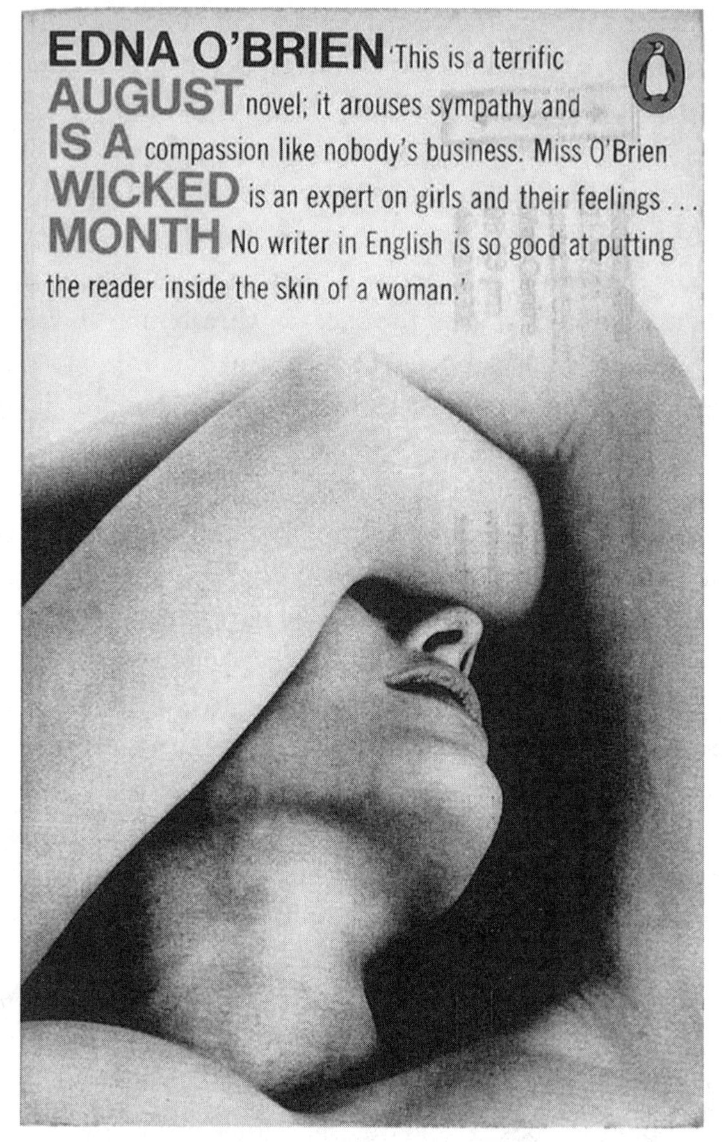

August Is a Wicked Month, *published 1965.*

The first person I saw as I crossed over the path, along the grass toward the courtyard that led to the court proper, was my husband in a dark suit, curiously animated, talking with a great excess of energy to two men, presumably his barristers.

An usher in a black gown showed me to my seat, and across from me I saw my husband arrange a series of plain white postcards on which he had written the incriminating evidence that was to come.

My junior was kind, but somewhat at sea, staring down at his notes. My husband's barrister then called him as witness, and with alacrity he climbed to the witness box and swore on the Bible. He was fired up, like an actor given the great part that he had always dreamed of. He told the judge that he had assembled his evidence in three categories: my character, my attitude to men, and my writing. The thought came to me that Moll Flanders, were she sitting in that court, stood a better chance of getting custody.

My most recent book, *August Is a Wicked Month,* he said made Krafft-Ebing's portrayals of perverts and lunatics pale by comparison. It had been banned in South Africa on the grounds of its being "obnoxious, indecent, and obscene." When I saw him hand a copy to the clerk, with two fetching photographs on front and back which had been taken by Lord Snowdon, I quaked. My attitude to marriage could indeed be gleaned from it, as indeed it could from a magazine (which he now waved) with the incendiary heading "O'Brien Tosses a Molotov Cocktail Through the Stained-Glass Window of Marriage." In the article I had said that the marriage vows should be rewritten in favor of the wife; this in a room full of males did not bode well. The pith of his argument, however, was that I did not really want the children at all, they were merely "decor" for my life. Faced with the responsibility of having them seven days a week, I would back away and disappear for months, as I had done before, having fled to America soon after I abandoned them. My junior's face reddened at each disclosure. Fighting this custody case was another example of my revenge toward men, part of the schizophrenic side of me that felt it must fight the entire male element in the world. From being a nymphomaniac, I was suddenly a man-hater. The children, if they were to be left to me, would, he assured the judge, become mother-smothered, emotionally sick homosexuals, my favorite group of people. The judge was then invited to read a particular passage from *August Is a Wicked Month,* which, somewhat irked, he did; he then turned a few pages onward, closed the book, and, looking around, said, "It seems to me that boys of nine and eleven would not be interested in this kind of literature."

My barrister was then asked if he wished to call me as a witness, and hearing him decline, I found that I was already standing, the words tumbling out. Without going to the witness box, I said that if I did not love them and if I did not want them, I would not have fought as desperately as I had done for three years. He asked if there was anything else I wished to say, at which I merely shook my head, powerless to refute the various charges that had been hurled at me. When I sat down, not only my ears but even the gold sleepers on which the catkins dangled were also burning like mad. There was a pause as the judge consulted the numerous notes from both sets of barristers, peering into them, then brooding at times, allowing his glasses, which were on a black cord, to slip off. I believed that I was doomed. The short wait seemed interminable.

"Pray, silence for the judge."

I was hearing the words, but they were like something coming from a great distance, and only by the junior squeezing my arm could I fully believe their impact. He had decided to give me custody, with due consideration for the petitioner's rights regarding visits and holiday arrangements. The years of agony had come to an end. I looked in my husband's direction and saw that he had stiffened with outrage and disbelief, and then he looked toward me, and I felt a terrible judgment descend on me, as with Lot's wife when she was turned into a pillar of salt.

I collected the children from their separate schools and told them the good news, which they barely responded to, and that evening in Putney at the supper table they were quiet and bewildered. Then suddenly Carlo, being the elder and feeling guilty for the father they had left, turned on me, saying, "Dad says you're a snob and you'll send us to a snob school and not a decent socialist school, where we would have grown up to be responsible citizens." According to their father, choosing to send them to school in Wimbledon, where the traffic was greater and where they risked being run over, was part of my death wish for them. Carlo was crying as he said it, crying and befuddled. Sasha placed our three hands together in reconciliation, and all that evening we were grasping for nice things to say to one another.

It was much later that I learned of their last ordeal in Cannon Hill Lane. They had been put in separate rooms with an affidavit sheet before them. They were given pen and ink, and their father, holding a long stick of red sealing wax, asked them to write a letter which he would bring to the judge the following day. They were to say that they wished to remain with their father and not under the unstable influence of a sick mother. They were left alone for this.

Carlo wrote:

Dear Dad,
No doubt when I am older, I will want to be with you for shooting and fishing and hunting et cetera, but just now I want to be with my Mum.
Love, Carlo

Sasha wrote a perfunctory *"Putney"* and his signature.

Their father would never forgive what he saw as their betrayal of him.

They had gone to visit him at Christmas, which was two weeks later, and had brought gifts, but they were met with an icy reception. As for gifts, he said he knew other children, better and more loyal, and so handed back the pullover and the mugs with the wrapping unopened.

In the embattled times which followed, it angered him that I was writing ceaselessly and that I was given what he called undue flattery in newspapers, primarily because of being perceived as glamorous. A friend in Ireland, an author called John Broderick, was enlisted to do the dirty work there, and in a journal called *Hibernia,* quoting my husband's exact words, he said that my "talent resided in my knickers." As Ernest saw increasing signs of my affluence, his bulletins became more incensed and he was furious at the fact that I moved from the little house in Deodar Road to a larger house in that street, to act, as he put it, "the part of the chatelaine." The new house had a front garden, with lilac and laburnum trees, like a house in the country, and the back garden ran right down to the river.

The Thames, its name derived from the Celtic word Tamessa, meaning dark, rose in Gloucestershire and obligingly passed the end of our garden on its way to the estuary of the East End and out to the North Sea. Most days it was brown and sluggish, porter brown, with black barges and coal boats chugging quietly by, an aimlessness to it, like a still life.

But to Carlo and Sasha it held dreams of treasure, of fleets, of merchant ships and invasions. The fact that it smelled made no difference. Once, a convoy of pigs' heads floated by, fresh from the abattoir, white and bloated, their ears limp as empty pods. Another time it was a dead, speckled puppy, a perfect simulation of a Christmas toy. Rats that came up from the water and into the garden were a source of terror and adventure. The boys had been given a gift of air rifles from John Huston, whom we met in Claridge's Hotel, where we had been brought by Sam

Shaw for a buffet party and where Sasha, seeing all the spread laid out, said, "What's worrying me is who's going to pay for this big deal." Not too long after, the air guns had been shipped from Rome, where Huston was working on a film. Pat Lobey, the builder, who was working on various things, taught them how to load and how to fire them, so they shot at cans along the back wall until their heroics were abruptly terminated as our nearest neighbor came through the side door, outraged, asking, did I not realize that bullets could ricochet and kill somebody? The guns were put away for an envisaged safari.

With his friend Adam from his new school, Carlo came up with the bizarre idea that, even if they could not shoot at the big rats, they could drive them away by smoking cigars. Metal hooks on the back wall served as a stepladder, and with their friends, who included Roc Sandford and the ever-spirited Hodge family, they would clamber each evening to delve into the river for loot. One evening, without their noticing, the tide had

With Carlo and Sasha at a swish lunch in Mayfair, London, 1966.

swept in, so that suddenly they were marooned on a bank of higher mud and shingle, calling out, "Rescue, ship ahoy!" and another neighbor had to lower his boat into the water and ferry them in. This adventure led to an extensive essay from Carlo about tidal activity, the unwonted gales from the North Sea, and Mistress Fate.

It is impossible to convey the exuberance of ten rowdy children in Trader Vic's restaurant in London. It was for Carlo's twelfth birthday, a belated salve for all the unhappiness they had been through. Never had they been in such a charmed place: ship's lanterns and wooden canoes hung from the ceiling, waitresses such as might be in Polynesia floated around in sarongs. Chafing dishes with all sorts of Oriental delicacies were set down, and the drinks were in wide glasses with gardenias floating on top. They ate ravenously, the savory dishes followed by coconut ice cream, and they then swooped on the fortune cookies, tossing aside any messages that did not live up to their, by now, exalted expectations.

Then came the moment for the pyromania, as they set fire to the tissue paper around the macaroons and watched the ash rising in random swirls and becoming one with the air itself.

A second birthday party had to be organized at home, since friends had not brought presents to the hotel, and this too had its rumbustiousness. The tea, the sandwiches, and the cake were but a mere prelude to a sort of barbaric hunt, both inside and outside in the garden, the ambushing of girls who in their gauze skirts with wide sashes ran and shrieked as they were pelted with water pistols and flying meringues. These assaults were afterward ameliorated by brief and blushing snogs.

For Sasha's birthday party I arranged a screening of *Cat Ballou,* their covert practice with the two air guns proving invaluable, in imitation of the fast draw, and the hilarious sequence when Kid Shelleen, played by Lee Marvin, not only missed his opponent but drunkenly staggered as his pants fell down. Lee Marvin was to be the surprise guest at the end of the screening, as Sam Shaw had been briefed to bring him, except that Lee Marvin had gone the way of Kid Shelleen and was in the bar of his hotel, reluctant to travel.

Either through Ted Allan or Sam Shaw, my two most influential friends, I met the director Jack Clayton, who played poker in Ted's house on Saturday nights with a batch of men. Jack was casting the children for the film *My Mother's House,* and Carlo was granted an audition, then brought back for a second one and given the lead part. The headmaster in their new school gave permission for him to be away for certain dates during the six-week shoot, on the understanding that he would have private tutoring on the set. Feeling a bit above himself and acknowledging that he was weak in Latin, he asked for tutoring in Latin and, if possible, in Greek.

A week of filming had started, and his happiness was infectious, along with a feeling of superiority over his brother. Then came a phone call from his father to say that I had broken the law concerning the stipulations over custody, and that he was taking me back to court, having already, through his solicitor, informed the film company that Carlo would not be returning to the set. He had learned of it through a newspaper article in which Carlo was photographed with some of the other children in the cast. After I put the phone down, I was in tears. How to break it to him? He guessed and shook with rage. This, his first, big, boyish dream, he had been robbed of. "I could kill Dad, I could kill Dad," he kept saying, and I knew by the way he shook that that murderousness was extended to me also.

"There will be another time," I said, but in his eyes there was a mistrust, as if somehow he had been expecting this all along.

But there were excitements and surprise visits, as one night in their bedroom, with all their clutter and paraphernalia, painted soldiers laid out on trays for battle yet to be, Paul McCartney entered. I had met him on my way out from a party that Kenneth Tynan and Quentin Crewe had given; the party was still in full swing, and both hosts, as I later learned, were understandably seething because Paul McCartney had decided not to go up to the drawing room to join the gathering but instead to see me home.

The children were asleep when we got in, and Elizabeth Lobey, the babysitter, while telling me they'd had their supper and their bath, was in evident danger of seizure at the appearance of Paul McCartney in our hallway in Deodar Road.

He asked where they slept, and then it was up the stairs into the bedroom, where he picked up Carlo's secondhand guitar and began to play and sing "Those Were the Days," a hit song by Mary Hopkin at that time.

> Those were the days, my friend,
> We thought they'd never end
> We'd sing and dance forever and a day
> We'd live the life we choose...

Sasha sat up dazed and, like Aladdin in the story, began to rub his eyes fiercely so that the genie in the bottle materialized. Carlo was angry at being wakened and said, "Go away, Mother, you must be drunk," and buried himself under his big floppy quilt. Presently I was hearing an improvised song, which Paul McCartney strummed on the guitar:

> Oh, Edna O'Brien,
> She ain't lying,

You gotta listen
To what she gotta say,
For Edna O'Brien,
She'll have you sighing,
She'll have you crying.
Hey,
She'll blow your mind away.

That next day at Ibstock School a bitter feud ensued, Sasha boasting about the visit from a Beatle and the song he had composed and Carlo calling him "Fibber, fibber," until Sasha, to everyone's disbelief, produced the plectrum that Paul McCartney had given him.

Nocturnes

It was sometime after that I decided, albeit reluctantly, to send them away to boarding school when they were eleven and twelve. I chose Bedales, which was coeducational and whose founder, John Badley, was a visionary who had cultivated the ideal of an education that encompassed "head, hand, and heart."

Letting go of them had been a big wrench, and the first parting as they walked with their luggage toward the redbrick building, the leaves on the trees turning russet, was well nigh unbearable.

The house in Putney felt like a mausoleum, their bedroom still with the painted lead soldiers laid out on trays for battles yet to be and two Oxo tins with their clobber, and everywhere masterful signs saying PLEASE DO NOT TOUCH.

I visited several times during the term, bringing hampers, which made them very popular for binges in the dormitories late at night.

That Christmas was the happiest ever: on Christmas night I cooked a dinner for over thirty people, and one of the guests was Len Deighton, who had brought the children a gift of the seven volumes of *Lloyd's Encyclopaedic Dictionary,* which had been printed in London in 1895. It was a marvel of language and information, strewn with quotations from great writers through the centuries, and when the time came for them to return to Bedales, I found that it was left for me on the dining room table.

We were at Waterloo station, with the several Bedales pupils hollering to one another, flinging questions that went unanswered, and stocking up with Crunchies and bags of sweets. Among them was a girl called Wanda. She wore a bright Gypsy skirt, a man's hat, and a patterned shoulder bag made from carpet material. Young men waited upon her. "Wanda. Wanda. Wanda." Sasha whispered to me that his brother had a crush on her, but judging by the multiple acolytes, Wanda's dance card was full.

She moved among them like an empress, and as soon as the barrier gate was open and we were allowed in, they followed, her satellites, and I followed too, somewhat tentatively, knowing that I must not show the merest jot of emotion. My main function was to carry one of the requisite hampers with cooked ham, pickles, and Stilton cheese, along with a clandestine bottle of port. In the carriage, which Wanda imperiously chose, there was a space next to her on the seat, which I knew that Carlo would have liked to take. He was being encouraged by his friend Norrie, who was on her other side. But with a proud, sad gesture, he declined and went on down the carriage to sit alone, where he took out his book, *Piers Plowman,* immersing himself in the humble Plowman's allegorical search for a heaven.

It was through their letters that I began to get to know my children, the different them, already forging their independence. Carlo wrote:

I am composing this elegy in the Bedales School Memorial Library, which normally exudes silence and the overpowering smell of wax. But as you will know from our garden, flowers can mitigate that smell and moreover the librarian having planted daffodils and crocuses in the garden beneath, the fragrance has improved the library's somnolent air. I think that partly due to you and your examples and education and partly through my own experience I have learned that there is in this world so much that one can fill one's life with and that we must become our own enrichers. Now that I have discussed the philosophical implications of my maturity, I propose to discuss the financial. I forgot to ask for money for the Common Room's new regime which comprises of myself and Jeremy Phillips. We would like to buy some posters with our own money also spiral folders for the extensive notes I have taken on my six academic subjects. That being so, is it not wiser to have your written permission to get money from the Bursar and have the entire sum paid at the end of term. Also my pyjamas is in flitters, I am practically a pauper. Love.

A letter from Sasha was contrite. After I took them to the film *Performance*, he was so enamored of the psychotic hero Chas, played by James Fox, that he began to imitate Chas in voice, mood, and inflection, and tended to monopolize conversations with gangster talk. When I mentioned this in a letter, he wrote back:

I have taken to heart what you have said. It is not a question of my not seeing the wood for the trees, it is a question of my seeing neither because of foolishly looking in the wrong direction. I am turning over a new leaf. Are you coming this Sunday?

He decided he wanted to go to France to improve his French, along with a boy called Anthony. Anthony had a heart condition. He was to stay in Tonneau, in western France, and accommodation had been found by the school. In the one letter that I exchanged with their future landlady, everything seemed ideal. They would attend classes in the morning and then return home in time for lunch, becoming part of the family, so that they could polish their French pronunciation. The family consisted of mother, father, who was a postman, and two children, who resented their being there at all. The family had roast for lunch, while Sasha and Anthony were given some sort of rabbit ragout. Anthony had taken an instant dislike to the mother, refusing to speak to her, simply hitting his plate with a spoon and saying, "I hate this woman, I hate this cow, *cette vache*."

In Central Park, New York, 1968.

All this I would hear later when Sasha returned home, buoyant and full of aplomb. Life at Tonneau was lackluster. In the evenings they walked to the town, which bordered a lake, and then out of the town toward the dunes and beyond, to where there were clumps of pine trees. They had hoped to bump into girls and instead met families with their dogs. While he was there, I had received one imperious postcard, saying that if there was a letter for him, it was to be placed in the Oxo tin. This I took to mean that I must not open it. I guessed that he had fallen in love with a girl at Bedales, proof of the infatuation in a song he kept singing,

> There she stood in the street,
> Smiling from her head to her feet.
> I said, hey what is this?
> Maybe, maybe she's in need of a kiss...

Little by little I could feel that he was, inevitably, growing away from me.

Sean Kenny, the theater designer, brought color and diversion into my world. His father was a stonemason in a parish on the opposite side of the lake from us, in County Tipperary, but Sean had left that world and was sought after in London circles. I would read his name in the newspapers, and sometimes of scrapes he had been in at a club in Soho, of which he was an habitué. He was renowned for his theater design, and critics called his sets radical, revolutionary, but to me they were more than that, they were little temples, worlds of imagination brought to life. It was in Alvaro's restaurant in London, where Sean and I had been invited by a television producer, John Irwin, that we met. Sean arrived late, his sleeves rolled up, his jacket over his shoulder. He was not a city person: you could tell by his hands, which were broad and strong, and his eyes, the hard blue of cobalt but with a flinch in them. He was abrupt with us, and scornful of the glamorous clientele all around. Every other word was "bullshit." Writing, he declared, was bullshit. Francis Bacon was the presiding London genius, A for Apple and B for Bacon, he said loudly. He loved Francis Bacon, as he loved Hieronymus Bosch. Mellowing a little after a few drinks, he said he could tell that I was a cave person, whereas he was a tent person, ergo a wanderer. Nevertheless, he gave me his phone number, and for all of two weeks I rang, but got no answer. Finally, when I did get him, my fluster was such that I had to invent a reason for ringing and so heard myself inviting him and his friends to a party the following Saturday.

"I'll only come for the bread and the wine," he said, half joking, and so the precedent was set.

That day was all bustle, the kitchen like a hotel kitchen, pots and pans on the long table, cookery books open, meats marinating, the doorbell ringing with deliveries, Joe Langdon from the greengrocer's arriving with fruits and vegetables, and afterward he split the pale wooden crates and made kindling for the fires. With shyness he accepted an Irish coffee, sitting on a milking stool by the fire, recalling that first day when he saw me on the High Street and I stood out.

Around nine o'clock that evening an entourage filed behind Sean Kenny on the outer porch. There were several young blond women, all of whom entered in such a nuanced file that it was impossible to know who was with whom, and for me, most crucial of all, which of these might be his girlfriend. Among them was the composer Lionel Bart and his chauffeur, "Jim the Limb," who went around prodding people on the arm, advising on the benefits of alcohol over heroin. Andrew Loog Oldham, tall, supercilious, who had been a manager of the Rolling Stones, had also come and took a particular liking to the potcheen, the homemade brew which my mother brought on her annual visit. It was all the more disquieting for me to learn, years after, that he wondered what Sean Kenny saw in me, as I was patently a social climber. But then again, he claimed that Princess Margaret joined him in drinking the potcheen, whereas she always drank Famous Grouse whiskey. She came with her husband, Lord Snowdon, who had taken photographs of me which Francis Wyndham had commissioned for the *Sunday Times* and which he said had the serenity of a Corot painting. When he invited me to Kensington Palace, the taxi driver, who happened to be Irish, was dumbfounded at the fact that I was being allowed "indoors"!

From the cast of characters of those days, Tony and Francis are the two people I have kept in touch with over the years, mostly by telephone. We reminisce a bit, make plans to meet, but rarely do, and the last time I saw Tony it was in the Cromwell

Portrait for Sunday Times, *1970.*

Hospital, where we were both being wheeled down for x-rays and he blew a stream of kisses.

Marianne Faithfull was also one of the regulars at my parties, the archetypal flower girl with her long hair and her ropes of necklace, walking around barefoot, putting music to Yeats's "Had I the heavens' embroidered cloth." Diane Cilento would bring the *I Ching*, the book of ancient Chinese wisdom, and the special bronze coins for us to throw so that we could learn from the hexagrams and trigrams what the future held for us. Sean Kenny, clearly besotted with her, could be heard saying that Sean Connery, who was within hearing, was "a slow-burning turf fire." It still baffles me how I came to know all these people; some serendipity threw us together and united us in the chimera of the "Swinging Sixties." It was a more innocent time. The famous were not so famous, and were not surrounded by gloating cohorts. Coming from County Clare, I was excited by this galaxy of visitors, and yet I was never carried away. I knew it was transitory, we were all en route, heading for other places, orbiting up, up.

Roger Vadim and Jane Fonda had come to stay with me, as there was a producer interested in my writing a screenplay for Jane and her brother, Peter, from a novel called *The Blue Guitar*. Vadim presided like a Russian prince, and women were smitten with him. Yet he was also an extremely practical man who before the guests arrived would advise on my wardrobe and on my hair. He was also the one to come to my rescue in the kitchen when a minor catastrophe occurred, as I dropped the goose taking it out of the oven; we pieced it together to make it look presentable. Later I saw Judy Garland, the famed Dorothy, in the living room, wistful and perplexed as she looked around, then nudged her escort, who was also a stranger to me, to indicate that they should leave, which they did, disappearing without a word to anyone.

The children were allowed home one weekend a month, and to them those jamborees were a seventh heaven. They wore red embroidered tunics that I'd got them in the antique market (which two years later they would discard as being sissyish) and threw themselves into the celebrations, little monarchs in that heady acoustic of song and talk and stunts. They answered the door, carried crates of champagne up from the basement, acted as barmen, and obviously Carlo took an exceeding interest as a joint was rolled and passed around to those who wanted it. Oh, the hilarities they witnessed! Shirley MacLaine, taking my hand to read my past lives, pronouncing in all seriousness that I had been "mother and prostitute, many times." Then it was George Melly's *Man, Woman and Bulldog*, a silent tableau for which, naked and with a deft maneuvering of the genitals, he accurately portrayed man, woman, and bulldog, an unlit cigar dangling from his lips.

The news from Bedales was unsettling. Carlo, obviously led astray by the revels, had been found with another boy smoking cannabis at the end of the paddock. This was conveyed to me in a health farm in Hampshire, not far from their school, where I was spending four days on a punitive diet of grapefruit and herbal tea. Though not feeling hungry, I was thinking longingly of Dundee cake, which I don't even like. I was sitting on my bed looking out at the rain and the lake, to which I had walked the evening before and listened to the ducks going quack-quack and stood on grass that was sodden and strewn with their gray-white droppings. Hearing the voice of Tim Slack, the assistant headmaster, I took fright and asked if there had been an accident. No, it was not that, he assured me, though I realized something must be amiss. I heard myself rave on about the effects of fasting and how everything was altered and clouds resembled camels, as they had to Hamlet. Then he blurted it out. Carlo had been found smoking "cannabis regis." I was furious, I was flabbergasted, I was apologetic and promised to give him a stern scolding.

"The thing is..." Tim said, mastering his intermittent stammer, "he says that he turned on with you, Miss O'Brien." Things began to fracture. I saw, as in a lurid flashback, Diane Cilento throwing the *I Ching*, Jim the Limb miming the heroin needle, and remembered the brown sticks of hashish being warmed, then crumbled and lit as the clean smell pervaded the room.

I assured him that home life from that moment on would be more rigorous, and put the blame on some tearaways who would not be invited to my house again.

As it happened, the children were coming to the health farm for lunch the next day. I had arranged that they would have a cold chicken salad, while I persisted with the grapefruit. As they came up the steps, Carlo lagged behind, and then in the dining room our voices had to be muted, since law-abiding people sat at nearby tables. I asked him in a hoarse whisper what in Christ's name he was doing, smoking a joint at the end of the paddock. He was contrite, admitted to it, but said it was the evening of the dance and his friend Norrie had asked him if he would like to "turn on" before the dance. It was mostly to get the courage to ask girls up. His eyes, which were large and blue-gray, were now overflowing, and I could see that we had drawn attention to ourselves. Intending to be stern, I said that I would cancel their weekend home, which was soon due, but they well knew that I was sure to relent. It was a cheerless lunch, and they trotted off, very unfulfilled and without daring to ask for extra pocket money.

My mother visited once a year and did not like the tempo of the parties. Why, she inquired, had Joe Bushkin, whom I had met only once, hired a swankier piano for a particular Saturday jamboree? Why had I, on impulse, bought a second sideboard, when bottles and spare glasses could easily be kept under the table in the kitchen? Sensing wanton extravagance and sexual innuendo, she sat in the winged chair, her hair swept up in tortoiseshell combs, sizing up the guests. She would retire, waiting for my step, which would be some hours later, her lamp still on. I would go in, and once, sitting up in bed, reprovingly, she asked, "Are you or are you not a good girl?"

It was Sean Kenny who succeeded in persuading R. D. Laing to come one Saturday night. Laing, half Lucifer, half Christ, pale and aloof, sat apart, refusing food, seemingly bemused by his surroundings. But that, I told myself, was the outer him; there was the him who had written *Bird of Paradise,* with its jangled ecstasies, reminiscent of Baudelaire's *Flowers of Evil.* In it he described a pivotal moment when, as a medical student in

Glasgow, he was on his way to the laboratory with the remains of a grotesque infant, wrapped in newspaper, and he went into a pub and had this sudden desire to unwrap the paper, to make them see, "to turn the world to stone."

He came most Saturdays, maintaining the same half-mocking aloofness, and surprisingly, one evening a row erupted between him and Sean. I saw Sean bristle with rage, sleeves rolled up, goading him to a fight, calling him "Black Teeth Laing" and threatening to throw him down a long flight of steps. Laing met the barrage with the calm of a Buddha and afterward took a rug off the chair and went into the garden, where he lay down on the damp grass and slept. Later, when he came back in, he danced, alone and in a trance, like a reincarnated Nijinsky. That was the night he told his wife that he could not go home because I had taken his keys, the keys to his car and the keys to his house, and so it was that night I felt he had thawed somewhat.

The parties, which went on for almost two years, always ended abruptly. In the small hours Sean Kenny would curl up on a kidney-shaped sofa and, mid-sentence, fall asleep. This would lead to a sudden exodus: blondes, having lost patience with him, would holler out the addresses of other gigs in far-flung regions of London, even as far out as Petersham. I would be alone with him, which is what I wanted. Once, however, a predatory girl called Chrissie decided to sit it out; she and I knelt by him, the two pagan Marys at the foot of the Cross, a little spent, but indefatigable, not exchanging a word, looking at that face that, in sleep, was so boyish, the light from an oil lamp that sat on a ledge just behind him giving a soft brilliance to the dome of his head, his high forehead, and the blond hair that was tousled. He was fast asleep, far away from us, a deity newly varnished. From time to time he muttered something, but he did not waken. It may have been the chimes of the grandfather clock in the hall that caused her to remember the hour, as suddenly she jumped up and asked abruptly where the phone was. It was in the kitchen, and I went on tiptoe to eavesdrop. I heard her say, "How's Kafka?," listen, and then slam the phone down. As she gathered her belongings, miffed at having to concede her place beside him, I asked who Kafka was. It was her dog, which her mother was minding, and she was in a foul mood at having been wakened at that ungodly hour.

Always when he wakened, Sean looked around at the chaos, glasses and dishes all over the floor, white lilies wilting, as faithfully he would say, "Have the people caused the flowers to die?" He would have a dram of cognac in his coffee, then pour a few drops onto the palm of his hands, which he rubbed briskly, and then inhale. I think I knew that he would not live long, life in its ordinariness was not for him, he was like a meteor which needed to consume itself. We would sit and listen to Dion on the record player, over and over again, the words that I hearkened to, "Sit down, old friend, there's something in my heart I must tell you," believing that he too had something to tell me. Then he would get up to go, making the same joke about coming the following Saturday, but only for the bread and the wine.

"But you will come," I would say.

"Of course . . . darlin'."

I lived for those Saturdays.

There were nights when people came unexpectedly. Richard Burton rang the doorbell one Monday evening, late, and said he was in the neighborhood, which was unlikely, as no one was in that neighborhood by chance in those days. Never on any stage have I been so mesmerized, so entranced, as I was that night, hearing Richard Burton recite Shakespeare, torrents of it. As a boy he had memorized those speeches and spoken them down in the Welsh valleys, and vowed that all his life would be devoted to Shakespeare, a vow he reneged on and felt sorry about. He loved language and loved writers. He had written *A Christmas Story,* in imitation of Dylan Thomas's *A Child's Christmas in Wales,* to keep Dylan happy in Parnassus. A story of mine, *The Love Object,* was a favorite of his, one in which the spiritual and carnal ramifications of a love affair were laid bare. Maybe because of it, he took me to be more libertine than I was. He could not understand why I did not want to go to the "bed chamber," wanting instead to sit and talk and be mesmerized. Men for me were either lovers or brothers; the lovers were more intimidating and often unobtainable, and though I dearly wanted to, I could never combine the two qualities in the same man. Richard Burton was a brother, and a bard brother at that.

At the London Evening Standard Theatre Awards, 1970s.

Increasingly I met people in the film world. Leslie Caron was intending to buy the rights of my novel *August Is a Wicked Month* for herself and Laurence Harvey to star in. One night she asked me to dinner in Montpelier Square, and I found myself seated next to Marlon Brando. Marlon Brando, with an intelligence so quick and lethal, his whole being taut, like an animal, ready to spring. He decided that he would take me home and, to my dismay, dismissed the chauffeur, despite my reminding him that black taxis did not cruise in Putney late at night. We sat in the kitchen, where he drank milk and I drank wine. Another bard. Stories. Of the vengeances he had wreaked on those who had thwarted him, including a judge who had sent him down for reckless motorcycling, and then, in boyish contrast, he spoke with reverence of Stella Adler, the acting teacher who had been his mentor and muse. He was playful and teasing, saying he wanted to ask me a question that I must answer immediately and with the truth. I could not imagine what it might be. I got more and more embarrassed as he teased out the suspense, merely saying in different, emphatic intonations that I must tell the truth. The question when it came was somewhat harmless: Was I ticklish?

It was a chaste night, as he ruefully confirmed in the letter he would write early the next morning, in the Connaught Hotel, where we went for breakfast. He took a long time puzzling over the words, in which he cast himself as Othello and, for good measure, gave me a spotted handkerchief, though it did not have the emblem of the strawberries. That, and a book by Abbie Hoffman.

We took a stroll in Grosvenor Square before he left to go to the airport, and quite unexpectedly he asked, "Are you a great writer?" The question, so sudden and daunting, caught me off guard. I did not want to boast, and yet I did not want to belittle myself, so that I heard myself say, "I intend to be." Nearby there were bucket swings, and he sat me on one and gave me a beautiful, dizzying, headlong push to the longed-for altitudes of language.

Each Monday morning I would go up to the top of the house to write. There was no connection whatsoever between the two worlds, the dizzy world of the parties and the wrenching world of the work. Then, in a dream, I came to see my divided self. It was still my own kitchen, only much larger, with red emergency bells along the wall, as if it had been converted to a hospital. On the long black stove were the pots of boiling water and shallower pans with hot sizzling goose fat. Without thinking, I picked them up and threw the contents over the throngs of startled, disbelieving guests. The era of parties was drawing to a close.

On days when I couldn't write a word, I took to tidying, emptying the hot press, sorting out clothes that the children had grown out of to take to the charity shop, and always I would come upon it, the forbidden cigarette. It so happened that Maurice Girodias had come to Putney to try to encourage me to write a sequel to *The Story of O*, and on leaving had presented me with the cigarette, suggesting the magic properties it held. This long white cigarette, such as I imagined Aubrey Beardsley smoking, held a fearful fascination for me. What might it do? Set me adrift in rosy nebulous places, or send me down into the fearful seas that I dimly knew I had once been to? I probably exaggerated its potency, but nevertheless I would put it safely back in the scarf and into the drawer. I attended workshops and seminars in search of the transcendental self, and numerous parties where there were people floating, claiming to have lapis lazuli visions and to have touched the navel of wisdom, spouting tosh that passed for real poetry. Deep down, I was afraid of losing whatever stability I had.

Once, in Philip Dunn's beautiful farmhouse in Mallorca, to which his daughter Nell had got me an invitation, there was another visitor extolling the alternative life. He was a Dutchman who carried around a veritable cache of drugs, and when I declined, he decided on a more drastic solution. Trepanning. With a Black & Decker drill he wished to bore a hole in the center of my forehead to give me the third eye and the enlightenment that I craved. From that too I fled, though unconsciously I was courting disaster.

The Sleeve of Saskia

The morning I had elected to take LSD with Laing was sunny and bright. Yet I had misgivings. It was 6 May 1970; the room was tidied, masses of peony flowers, white and pink, with blood-red spattering, in a big jug, and the river outside a picture of calm and tranquillity. Laing arrived punctually at ten o'clock, wearing a good suit and a collar and tie, which I had rarely seen him wear. I'd been a patient of his for about six months. The sessions, it is fair to say, were unorthodox, and sometimes he talked, and sometimes he would laugh, just quietly to himself. He was an admirer of the psychoanalyst Georg Groddeck, whose methods were equally unorthodox and who extolled the benefits of madness. Getting back to the original source, the family romance, was what mattered, and sometimes he told me some of his own infant memories, fearful figures to the left and right of the cot, an angry mother and his crawling over a mock-parquet linoleum floor. One day I brought a punnet of fresh figs, and he looked at their dark, aubergine skins, then got a knife out and slit them apart. He had us sit on the floor and observe them for the fifty-minute session, the opened figs, with the seeds in the pulp of reddish flesh.

On that morning in May when he arrived, I felt I should broach the dream I'd had, but at the same time I was hesitant. In it I was a very young girl on the way to school, when I tripped and fell on the road, a sharp stone splitting my forehead open. My brain tumbled out, and took the shape of a spinning top, when presently passersby, young and old, danced and trampled on it. As if that were not warning enough, I had learned from

Sean Connery, with whom I had had dinner the previous evening, that his trip with Laing, both being old friends from Scotland, had its freight of terrors. Yet I did not cancel the appointment. It was as if in some way I believed I could go through with it and yet escape the terrible ordeal. My reasons for wanting to take it were multiple. A secret part of me longed to be nearer to Laing, and another part of me believed, from various literature I had read, that my dreams and therefore my writing would be enriched.

I drank my potion from a glass. I do not recall it having any taste. As I sat there, I remembered that I must ask him to hold me, or at least hold my hand, but as the words came stuttering out, he had suddenly, in that winged armchair, metamorphosed into a rat, an executive rat, trussed inside a suit with a collar and tie. It was my last semi-rational thought on that day. The world was spinning, spinning, and the floor underneath began to sway like the waves of an ocean. I ran to the kitchen to escape it, only to find that it too was swaying and the walls to the touch had become flesh. I went back to the sitting room, where he was dancing, but I declined the invitation to dance with him, falling apart as I was. It went on for hour after hour. I was no longer sitting, I was on the floor, gasping, each onslaught more hideous than that which preceded it. Womb. Blood. Hell. Fire. The wounded pith of an opened fig.

At one point he picked the huge gilt mirror off the wall and showed me my purple-faced, mad-eyed, gyrating self. I broke water as when I had given birth, cascades of it gushing out of me, and yet I could not feel any damp on the floor that I knelt on. No sense of time or changing light. A garbled account of coming into this world with a memory and a set of despair, and then twice I said, *"The edges are splitting on and on, and that you have to die more than once, my mother, my mystery, my little children, I can only bear you."* I was dimly mindful of them in a boarding school in Petersfield, far away, too far away, ever to reach.

He left some time after that and I was alone, crawling around that room like a wounded animal. I would have liked him to stay. I would have liked him to hold me. I would have liked a biscuit, and I knew exactly the soft ginger biscuit I wanted, except that I could not reach the kitchen, where the tin was kept. I crawled to the telephone, which was on a little table, and attempted to ring Ted Allan. The face of the phone had a metal front, with the lettering and numbers in a recess, and as I tried to dial, it was like dialing into my own gums and it proved beyond me. That was when I cried, endless tears and an untoward and useless pity for a whole world that I could not get to.

Respite of sorts reached me. Just before dark, I saw the evening light fade, and as it did, I had intimations of resplendent colors, in the sky, on the river, colors shooting out of my mind, rich and streaming. I was seeing, as I once had in Vienna, Pieter Brueghel's hunters in the snow, and in that whiteness, the black trunks of the trees and the few crows were blacker still, while two hounds of velvety russet were asking to be stroked. The huntsmen with their spears dwindled in size as they went across a plain, toward the snowy peaks and the unseen gorge between mountain and whey-green sky. Then it was the sleeve of Saskia, the second wife of Rembrandt, as for ceremony, gold and dipping, and I suddenly wished that I had danced with the Rat Man. How long would it take me to get back to where I had been? As long, perhaps, as it had taken me to get there.

Eventually the doorbell rang and I found myself able to stand, then to walk, in order to answer it. Ted Allan and Sean Connery had come to see how I was faring, and as they later said, they were shocked to find a woman so drastically altered, talking daft, disconnected things and walking as if on stilts. My conversation ranged from bygone memories to snatches of learning, to prescriptions I had made up in the chemist's shop, to a line of a poem, *"O thou lord of life, send my roots rain,"* inevitably to the golden sleeves of Saskia. I asked for a biscuit and some red wine. The color of the wine was glorious. From the very meniscus down, I could see bands of different deeper reds, and I drank slowly as if it were nectar. They stayed for a long while, and by the time I went to bed, I was tired in body and in mind, having lived many lives in less than twenty-four hours.

The aftermath was frightening, as I became somewhat unhinged. Beth came with me to visit the children on the Sunday, and to bring the hampers, she doing most of the talking so that they would not notice the peculiarity in me. Some weeks later, in a shop in Bond Street, buying Hessian boots that were embroidered with daisies, I suddenly saw the yellow stamens stir and the flowers come to life. I, who love theater, could no longer go. In a theater in St. Martin's Lane I had to vacate my seat almost as soon as I sat down, as the crown of my head was being lifted by swords in order to reach the elaborately carved ceiling.

The trip to Paris was to countenance these various seizures, but instead it precipitated one. I was with Roger Vadim in his apartment in the rue de Rivoli as we discussed the possibility of doing a remake of Diderot's *The Nun*. Jane arrived from a day's filming with Jean-Luc Godard, but was not her customary wooing self, as she threw down a cardboard box full of oysters and said something dismissive to Vadim.

It was the next day in my room in the hotel that the hallucinations returned. On my mantelpiece at home in London, I remembered, I had a postcard of the painter Jacob Cornelisz depicting *The Adoration of the Christ Child* in a brown interior, the browns enriched with motes of gold and angels suspended from the eaves playing trumpets in tribute to the naked infant lying on a wooden trestle; but my visitors were different. It was in L'Hôtel in Paris, once known as Hôtel Alsace, which I had chosen for the fact that Oscar Wilde had died there and had left an unpaid bill. Tiny creatures, spitfires in little bibs, were swinging from every corner of the ceiling and hissing. Mere amoebae at first, they began to swell and multiply. I was doing what I could to evade them. I tried various strategies, reminding myself that in a guidebook I had read that the Eiffel Tower was held together by 2.5 million rivets and 18,000 pieces of metal, and bizarrely I thought of John Berryman in a hotel in Dublin drinking a quart of whiskey a day and trying to finish a poem. Then it was the turn of Salvador Dalí, whom I remembered as being in that same city but in a different hotel, jumping up to the ceiling to squash invading creatures with a towel. From the anteroom, which adjoined the bedroom, in order to give it the category of a suite, a grotesque figure appeared, a man with side whiskers, who lay above me, his whiskers frothed and wet with porter as the trolls in their corners laughed their little lungs out. I thought I was finished and rang a bell, which I found behind the silk pleating of the wall. A doctor was summoned, and it was he who diagnosed the cause of the hallucinations—I'd had a bad oyster. Medicines were got, and having taken them, I crept down into the center of the bed and pulled the quilt up over my eyes to ward off the invaders, whom I imagined to be skulking and muttering.

I had asked for no visitors to be allowed up, and yet, three times, they were. Marguerite Duras was the first; feeling my forehead and my pulse, she hurried out and went to the pharmacy for suppositories and lime-blossom tea. Peter Brook was next, as we were supposed to be writing a screenplay together. It had a title and a theme, but not much else. It was called *Vacant.* He had conceived the whole structure of it in images, and on large white sheets of paper there were drawings, a shifting kaleidoscope of ideas that I was too fuddled to grasp, so the meeting ended inconclusively. Then it was Samuel Beckett, no stranger to sickrooms and asylum rooms in his fiction, who opened the mini fridge, took out a miniature of whiskey and a glass, and sat down. It was some time before he asked me what was wrong, and I told him of the weird visitations, followed by the arrival of the two visitors, Marguerite Duras and Peter Brook.

"Ah, that could do it to you," he said, and continued in his meditative mode.

It had grown dark and the objects in the room were indistinct. It was a well-known fact that Beckett did not like too much talk. All his works are littered with the aggravation of the nonstop talkers, the quaquaquas. Finally I ventured to ask what he was writing, to which he replied, "Nothing much, and what use is it anyhow?" Somehow the talk came round to burial places. I told him of my grave on an island in the Shannon, so isolated, with its several churches, roofs opened to the skies, wild birds swooping in and out, tombstones chalked with lichen. He was surprised and wondered if I was going back for a perpetual "dose of disgust." He may have been remembering the monstrous treatment meted out to James Joyce, whom the authorities and Irish undertakers were so repelled by that his remains were never brought back. I remembered then that shortly after I had met Beckett in 1964, he had sent me a postcard—perhaps it was a manifesto he sent to many—saying he was in Dublin for the last time and had bought a black mourning hat in Elverys. Yet there remained so much of Ireland in him, in his voice, his walk, his stick, and in his writings, "the ruinstrewn land between road and ditch, the dear back roads, the daisies, the sheep, the lambs, the afterbirths," as he observed them on the mountain walks which he had taken with his father, all that and the silver-voiced hammer of the stonecutters heard in the distance. Not even Synge had captured

Ireland with such feeling. I always thought of Jack Yeats, Synge, and Beckett in the same breath, men of kindred spirit, tramps of a noble scion, who literally walked the ground they would enshrine in painting or in language. The very first thing I had ever read of his was in the London Library, on the fourth floor, in that darkish cranny, where by chance I came on a book with reproductions of Yeats's paintings, a book that I was very tempted to steal. In a brief radiant introduction Beckett had written that the artist who stakes his being is from nowhere and has no kin. I mentioned it and he looked up, pleased, forgetting that he had written it at all, instead remembering the long walks that he and Jack Yeats had in north Dublin, always taking their rest in some quiet pub to ponder. It may seem inappropriate to broach drink concerning such an exigent man, but most of the Irish geniuses, Joyce, Beckett, Flann O'Brien, and many others, were well-known habitués of the tavern, putting their sojourns to sedulous good use.

It was soundless in that room, except for the squeak of the casters of his chair on a bit of skirting board and chambermaids out on the landing calling peremptorily, yet gaily, to one another. He sat gazing ahead and sometimes up into the corners, where the freaks had earlier shown themselves.

"No need at all to go back," he said, with a kind of resignation, and I knew that he could not have written of the ditches and the daisies and the ruinstrewn land unless he had loved it with such a beautiful, sad, and imperishable loneliness.

Some months after I returned from Paris, the author Patrick Seale approached me about writing an article for a magazine about the annual pilgrimage to Mecca. Blithely I said yes. He pointed out that I would have to renounce my Catholic faith and become a Muslim in order to be allowed to take part, and again I said yes. Yet a dream told a different story. The heavens opened and I saw the bearded face of God, in all His wrath and all His omniscience. He had come to call mankind to account. A battle for the end of the world was being waged. The opposing armies comprised Jewish and Muslim opponents, battalion after battalion wiped out before my very eyes. Eventually they had run out of weaponry, and the improvised weapons became flaps of human flesh, cut up as pastry might be and filled with human blood that mysteriously acquired lethal powers. I was in the Jewish camp, but truth to tell, both sides were equally crazed and equally bloodthirsty. In death they were thrown upon one another in heaps, the very fraternity that appalled them in life thrust upon them in extinction. Just as I entered the front line of battle, I heard a voice, my own or another's, cry out, "It is not for earthly considerations we fight, we suffer so, it is to catch sight of God."

I telephoned Laing for an appointment.

"What could it be?" I asked him, as I recounted the various terrors and scourges, birth and death and the desert sands of Arabia, where I had never been. He said the trip itself and the subsequent "flashes" were a replay of experiences I had lived long ago and would have to live again. That was how it had to be.

I came away from that appointment more shaken than ever.

When his bill came, I suddenly saw things in more livid light. It was a large bill, covering the hours he had spent with me, and though somewhat nettled, I wrote the check and posted it at once. Then a strange thing happened. A call came after some weeks from his assistant to say that the bill was overdue. I said I had sent it, and fearing that she disbelieved me, I made an appointment for when he would return from his holiday. It must have been August.

It was a warm day when I sat in his flat, his wife and child out in the garden. With windows open all around I could hear sounds, and distinctly heard someone shouting his name and challenging him. He made no reference to it. I mentioned the check that he thought was not paid, whereupon, and with that strange half-smile, he produced an envelope from a drawer in his desk. The odd thing was that though I had the correct address and it was written legibly, the envelope went to all the other places he had lived in, in London, and was neatly readdressed. It was as though he was being followed by occult forces.

On the way out I asked him why it was that Freud had given Virginia Woolf a narcissus the day she visited him, also in rooms in Hampstead. He laughed his inscrutable, frozen laugh, and I never saw him again.

A long time afterward I was being driven from Edinburgh over to Glasgow when Laing's death was announced on the taxi radio. He had died of a heart attack, on a tennis court in the South of France. I owed him a debt; he had sent me packing with an opened scream, and that scream would become the pith of the novel I would write. It was called *Night,* the story of Mary Hooligan, in nocturnal lather, her mind raveled and excoriating, with all semblance of niceness gone. It was the dividing line in my life, between one kind of writing and another.

Chelsea

It was time to leave the house in Putney. In my fraught state, I began to imagine coffins in various rooms, the small white coffins of children, and soon it came to be that each room was filled with them and therefore uninhabitable.

Somehow, in all the turmoil, I managed to do some work and had written a screenplay called *Zee & Co.*, a sort of sexual flamenco featuring a spitfire wife, her husband, and the other woman. It was bought for a film in which Elizabeth Taylor, Michael Caine, and Susannah York would eventually star, but the result was a tame offering, with all the meatiness squeezed out of it. I received thirty-nine thousand pounds and so, with my housekeeper Elizabeth Lobey, I went house hunting. She could drive, whereas I could not. In the evenings we would drive away from Putney and on into Chelsea, to look for FOR SALE signs on hoardings nailed to gateways and piers. We would get out and walk around to see if this was the right street or the right house, and I would stand with the intensity of a water diviner to try to guess if there were any white coffins in there.

On Lower King's Road we passed the chandelier shop owned by two Russians, Dawna and Petrov. On my walks I used to be drawn to their window, which was bathed in light, as the chandeliers were left on all day. Scores of them, crammed together on low gilt chains, the pendants cheek to cheek, giving a shimmer to a bit of street that ran under a railway bridge, with a few small factories, a smelting works, and a garage that did repairs. Looking in, I could not help thinking of Anna Karenina at a ball in St. Petersburg, with fresh pansies in her hair, dancing the mazurka, turning round and round, about to leave the low earth of duty and routine for the higher and more terrifying peaks of love.

Then we came on my future mansion, No. 10 Carlyle Square. In the double drawing room, a young boy was playing the piano, and already I pictured my sons there. The fact that the asking price exactly tallied with the amount that I would get for the film was further proof that this house was meant for me. After some slight haggling with the estate agent, the price was reduced by fifteen hundred pounds, and in due course Petrov came and hung matching chandeliers in the downstairs drawing room.

My first night in that house was one of my happiest ever. I stood on the doorstep and saw a chain of fairy lights on a restaurant across the way, and next to it an art gallery and then a wine shop, where a young enthusiastic man called Ali would become my chevalier.

Before long, I met different people in the nearby cafés: a man in a black beret who claimed to be Marc Chagall's nephew, and another man, always tipsy, who came from Brittany and sold onions in the neighborhood. He would stagger into the café for a coffee and then bicycle off with garlands of pink-skinned onions around his neck and on the handlebars of his bicycle. There were two markets nearby that specialized in clothes and jewelry from the twenties, and in one of them, on a throne of cushions, was the Highlander seer Isabella Campbell, who became my friend and indeed foresaw love affairs that were looming. People were friendly. I would linger there and tell myself that I need never be lonely again. Adjoining one of the markets was a café where a very young shy girl made crepes, which she filled with either stewed apple or cream cheese and sugar. It was the bohemian life that I had longed for.

At the window of Carlyle Square, 1974.

Ali wore a kilt and was something of a jester, teasing his customers, calling everybody John. "Yes, John. No, John. Your wish is my command, John." There was a basement in Carlyle Square, and I asked him if perhaps he would like to live in it.

He was jubilant. "Yes, John." He moved in within twenty-four hours, and soon after his mother sent two rosebushes as a gift to me and for good luck. He stayed with me all those years with, it has to be said, some rowdy visitors at weekends. Frequently, on a Monday morning, a naval van, its blue light flashing, would be parked outside my house as an irate registrar came in search of laggard sailors who had not shown up for duty. Ali's paramours. I cautioned him about this, at which he would hang his head in remorse and say it wouldn't happen again, John. Then he would say he loved me, the way he loved his mother and Ella Fitzgerald, and that's the truth, John.

The actor Patrick Magee came to lunch and brought a bunch of red roses. A powerful man, his voice was a heavenly blend of ecclesiastical Armagh and the heightened rhapsodies of Anew McMaster in his great Shakespearean roles. Magee had toured Ireland with McMaster, and one of the troupe was a young Harold Pinter, who used to joke that Magee and he had shared minor parts, digs, and jockstraps. The evening I first met Pinter in the bar of the Aldwych Theatre, at a preview of *The Birthday Party* in the early sixties, contrasted so lamentably with the last day, a week before he died, in December 2008, when we had lunch. There were seven years of illness, which he heroically fought, almost disdained, except that it was there, and never so tellingly as in the lines of the poem "But I remember how to die, though all my witnesses were dead." He was a frail shadow of that other man, that earlier man, with the jutting jawline, eyes licorice-black that literally smote one, as he was having, as it happened, an altercation with the barman about the ice in his whiskey. At that very first introduction he spoke of his years of touring in Ireland, as he would on the very last day, Ireland, poor and bedraggled, and yet to him it was a golden time, which he enshrined in a little book called *Mac* that is a tribute to McMaster. In it he captured Mac the Thespian, Mac the Canny Manager, and Mac the Irate, who would brook no interruptions either from ignoramuses in the front row or actresses swooning during his soaring soliloquies.

But it was not he who introduced me to Magee, it was Samuel Beckett, in the bar next to the Royal Court Theatre. Magee was warm and expansive, yet one felt that he was in the grip of such turbulence that if any whelp were to try to muscle in, Magee would explode. He loved Beckett, it was plain to see, but so did all those who met him. It was not the fame, it was the sheer bareness, not a grain of untruth either in the person or in the work; it had all been whittled away.

Magee invited himself to lunch in Carlyle Square, and on the appointed day he arrived punctually, dressed like a toff. The roses he brought had sprays of white gypsophila, and when I said that hospitals at home never liked mixing the red and the white flowers, he bowed to tradition and the gypsophila was put in a separate vase. He was polite, almost genteel, and moved as big strong men sometimes do, with a daintiness. He drank vodka, and at first he drank slowly, but that was not to last. He talked of Ireland, mud and muck, trees dripping, fierce fathers and women's soft hearts, he bound from the youngest age for the boat, an émigré, with his svelte elocutions. Hating England at first, the provinces, dingy digs, playing to small houses with, however, some lonely and amenable landladies. He drank more and brightened, and grew melancholy again and raged, and was more theatrical by the hour.

It was now five o'clock, then six o'clock, and Magee was in no mood to leave. He was reciting Hamm's speeches from *Endgame,* putting a cold but furious madness into them. Nervously I said I had to be somewhere.

"Capital, capital." He would come with me. To augment the

lie, I invented the name of a family in a large house on Wimbledon Hill, one that I had noticed in the fallow times when I took the number 14 bus to Wimbledon to collect the children. I went to the bedroom, changed, and put makeup on, realizing the absurdity of all this. We left the house together, my trying to appease him, telling him they were quite uninteresting people and the dinner party would be formal. He tut-tutted that. He would lend some color. At the corner of King's Road I could see a taxi coming from the far end, and I ran, hailing it wildly, leaving Magee like a dethroned king uttering his harangues as to how disgracefully he had been treated, he who had dined with the nobles in the great houses of Ireland, England, and beyond.

It was three in the morning when the phone next to my bed rang: it was Magee, both lucid and furious, declaring love and hate in equal measure, upbraiding me, saying, "Woman, I bring you roses and the only gratitude I get is that you throw me out."

My nearest neighbors in Carlyle Square were somewhat fastidious, and I realized that I would not be borrowing the proverbial "bowl of sugar" from over the clapboard fence. They objected to Ali's rambunctious guests, and once, when Carlo, who was by now at Beaconsfield Film School, was loaned the school bus for the night, they complained by letter at having to sit in their drawing room and look out at something so vulgar. Others would take exception to the honeysuckle that I had brought from Drewsboro and that grew prodigiously on the front railings. Over the years many famous faces graced the place, including Robert and Beryl Graves, Robert bringing Jerome Robbins, who was led to believe that he was about to meet Edna Ferber, though he knew that she was long dead.

My play *A Pagan Place* opened at the Royal Court for six

weeks. I exulted in seeing my name in lights above the door. That was how I met Joan and Laurence Olivier, Laurence describing it as "graspingly human." They were frequent visitors, and for one Christmas party Laurence could be seen through the window conducting the hymn singing.

One evening when Sasha got back unexpectedly from Cambridge, he saw that the front door was open and there was a policeman standing there who asked him his name. Inside, he found his mother dancing with Prime Minister Harold Wilson, while his wife, Mary, and Marcia Falkender looked on. I was not a natural dancer, but Harold Wilson was gallant, unlike Lawrence Durrell, whom I had met in Paris and to whom I had accidentally said that I was unable to dance. A postcard that followed that infelicitous meeting said that if he had read anything of mine before our meeting, he would have looked for my single breast—in other words, he saw me as an Amazon. Feminists and academics, on the other hand, were tearing into me for my supine, woebegone inclinations.

On the opening night of my play *Virginia,* in which Maggie Smith was both radiant and prismatic, Carlyle Square housed a great galaxy of people, including Ingrid Bergman, who came in looking like an Ibsen heroine in a coat with a high fur collar.

"Dark cold mantles the land." Those were the unforgettable lines in a letter that Jay, the first of the two loves whom the Highland seer had sighted in the globe of her amber crystal ball, wrote to me. There had been a few breezy postcards that somehow conveyed the danger of the looming attraction. I met him by chance in Odin's restaurant in Devonshire Street, run by Peter Langan, another incorrigible Irishman who, because he was also from County Clare, felt he had the license to berate me, saying, "You aul whore you, you can't write," reminding me of how Anthony Burgess had slated me, had said that after Joyce and Yeats and Co., after the giants, came "the little people," such as me. Then later he would come over to the table with a bottle of champagne, unwilling to budge, and Sean Kenny would challenge him for his boorishness, but Sean Kenny was now among the shades. An Icarus, golden-haired, who had flown too close to the light, he was dead at forty-four. In a way, he foresaw it. The previous New Year's Eve, in Kevin McClory's house in County Kildare, he wrote in the visitors' book: "I have a habit of walking and talking. I have a habit of walking towards death." So that night, when I met Jay, a shy man, an embryo poet with a soft spill of dark hair, it was as if the ghost of Sean Kenny had brought us together. He had seen me at Sean's funeral in County Tipperary, had wanted, as he said, to cross the road and go into the pub where the wake was taking place, but instead he stayed with the men by the stone wall, holding their caps, paying their silent respects. One of Sean's four beautiful sisters showed me the model of the magic theater that Sean had made at the age of nine or ten. It was of matchboxes painted green, with cutouts of sandpaper for the glitz. He named it Kincora, the seat of a famous king. I told her how much I had loved him, to which she replied, "He broke hearts, that's what he did."

Jay was an Englishman who had gone to live in Ireland, and in his letters he would describe the walks that he took by the big river, cold and blue, and how he would then go off the beaten track and find a hidden spot where the older trees had got entangled and made a sort of house, so as to be alone with his thoughts of me. He gave me back the landscape that I had left. Then one day I received a copy of *The Collected Poems of W. B. Yeats,* with, on the flyleaf: "Suddenly I meet your face." An invitation to a love affair.

He would come to England once or twice a month, but I had

this yen to meet with him somewhere in Ireland, to recapture the time in my life before I met him, thereby bridging the years between us.

Castle Martin. Castle Keep. Castle Martyr. Castle Mary. Castle Hen. These were just some of the names of castles in Ireland which would appear in the tourist brochures. I found an advertisement for one that was on the Shannon Estuary and could rightly be called Castle Bullock. As castles go, it was not expensive, but then again I had not viewed it.

It was in the middle of a field, the gable wall gaunt, crumbling, and tilting from the winds. I went with my sons to view it. True, it was on the Shannon Estuary and it did have lookout windows to ward off marauders, but cattle had made it their abode, wandering in and out of the open doorway, dung everywhere, dry dung and fresh dung, and the smell of the beasts off the straw that had been thrown down in various corners. The boys found timber posts to make a haphazard scaffold up to the top floor, and having climbed up, I indulged my brief dream of entertaining Jay in this salubrious gallery.

Not long after I met him in Tipperary, and as it was a warm day, unusually warm for March, we sat on the grass that was pickled with daisies and made unrealistic plans.

That night, as we lay in a four-poster bed entwined in sleep, a figure, half-clown, half-satyr, came in, dressed in a white nightshirt and knitted nightcap. He was both comic and malevolent as he walked around the bed. Jay sat up astonished, then shouted, "Get out, get out," and the figure disappeared, smiling. But he was no spirit, rather he was someone sent to spy on us, and thenceforth we were shadowed. Yet we swore that nothing could come between us.

A few of his friends in England suspected that we were intimate. One woman, as I noticed from the one time I met her, by a needling in her pupils, resented it, and later on, lifting a rib of reddish-brown hair from the collar of his coat, she said my name, guessing his infidelity. Another of his friends invited me to lunch, saying mischievously that Jay would be there, three men to myself. Jay avoided looking at me and somehow gave the impression that we were strangers. I left early and went to nearby Portobello Road, where perversely, since I do not like fur coats, I bought a cheap fur coat. It had seen better days. It was a pelt really, with grisly patches of fur. When I got back to my house, he was already in the sitting room, pensive and contrite, warming his hands at the fire. He had wanted to tell his friends, he had wanted to proclaim our being in love, but somehow he couldn't. Seeing the coat, he said something unfortunate, how his wife might use it as a lining for a better coat, and I ran out of the room, appalled. How we must have chased and missed each other in so many of the back streets of Chelsea, because when we ended up meeting at World's End, in front of a shop called Granny Takes a Trip, we were both shattered, but reconciled.

His letters from Ireland were what kept me buoyant, and I would read them over and over again. Letters replete with promise.

Then one morning, unannounced, he appeared carrying a small bag with a few possessions, and without any explanation, it was clear that he had moved in. We were living together. We cooked dinners together. He sang Billie Holiday's "Here It Is Tomorrow Again" as he peeled potatoes. We read aloud to each other from Thomas Mann's *Tristan,* and sometimes we played Scrabble. Most evenings he would go out to the public phone to ring his family, but when he got back in, it was not referred to. It would have been a few months later when one night he was struck speechless with pain. He could only mime it. His teeth chattered. The pain ran from his heart up into his mouth, and in the early hours I called a doctor. In the Heart Hospital, where he spent two weeks, I would visit out of hours, and I came to realize that I was not the cornerstone of his existence. I did not bring calf's-foot jelly or arrowroot biscuits, I was not the wife who would discuss with him his plans for going home and convalescing in the morning room and possibly reading Thomas Mann.

Yet he did not go home when he was discharged, but returned to my house, and so it was as before, except that it wasn't.

June: the month that Virginia Woolf said mothers of Pimlico gave suck to their young. I wished that we would have a child and mentioned some women I knew who had had children in their forties. I wished for that. We were walking home from a party in Chelsea Embankment, discussing the guests and the humbug and the high-flown conversation, when I decided to get the key to the gate that led into the square, so that we might sit on a bench and talk, to prolong the night. One small thing had rankled. As we were leaving, a friend of his from his university days, who was now famous, asked for his phone number when in London, and pointing to me, he said, "I am with Madam for the moment," which stung me.

A new moon, silverish, its shaven rim the color of sulphur, and the smell of the lilac heady from thundershowers that had gone on all evening. There, on that bench, I am hearing words that I never wanted to hear and had never expected to hear.

"I will telephone you every day of my life from now on," he is saying. But this is an exit line, I say to myself, excusing it on the fact that he had had a drink too many and seeing his old friend, now famous, had revived his youthful days, his exuberant hopes and boat rides on the river Cam. Surely he was not serious. Yes, he was. He had decided earlier in the evening that it could not be. He was, he said, going home only briefly, and then to Germany, to places where the great poets that he had so admired had lived and that, when he was younger, had given him the rash idea that he too could be a poet. We sat there and cried at the fact that we were so suited and yet were on the brink of parting.

I waken very early the next morning and decide on a walk. A walk would be a salutary thing. In the Fulham Road, idiotically, I look in the window of an antique shop, where I knew he had looked and seen the very same things, a silvered tapestry, a gun chest, a prayer chair, and a faded green velvet portière. I felt the longer I stayed out, the greater the likelihood that things would have righted themselves.

Coming back into my own sitting room, I saw it, the stone of the green ring that I had taken off the night before reflected in the metal of his latch key, which he had left on the mantelpiece. He was gone. Nevertheless, I ran upstairs, thinking he might still be there, but it was not so. His favorite tarnished cigarette lighter was on the bedside table, and since its flickers were a matter of chance, believing that, if the flame caught on, all was well, I struck it and took a cigarette from the packet that he had also left. I probably smoked that cigarette. I had to keep moving. Into the garden, where even the roses seemed aghast, back into the house, going to the hall door to open it, to look outside, then to shut it again. Then I sat down and maintained an almost catatonic calm for the first half of the day, until the savage truth asserted itself again.

I remembered that his was an evening flight to Ireland and that he would be still in London, probably gone to visit the woman friend who had found the rib of my hair on his lapel. I looked her number up in the telephone book, and when she answered and I spoke, I could hear her calling him affectionately. He did come to my house, as I had begged, but I realized what a violation it was. The engine of the taxi was throbbing, as he had obviously asked the driver to wait. He was another person altogether, cold and perfunctory. The married man on his way home.

I waited and hoped, remembering all of it, and would humiliate myself by contacting a male friend of his for news of any kind, and then one day I wrote the vengeful Medea letter that is the inverse side of love.

At home for the annual holiday, I was unable to conquer the bouts of tears. My mother noticed this, and as we were folding a candlewick bedspread together, the flaps hiding now her face, now mine, she remarked that I was giving a bad and unwholesome example to the children, who had hoped to enjoy themselves. Later she called Carlo into the breakfast room on the excuse of carrying out a tray and asked him what was the matter with his mother and was she *at fault* about something. She knew it concerned love and she resented it. Since I had left my husband in 1962, twelve years before, she feared for the life of dissipation which she imagined I was living. Every letter of hers referred to it. She wrote:

You will always have my love and affection and never bother again with men outside of meeting them in everyday life or for work. I pray for you and each day of my life, I go down on my knees and ask Christ that you remember the words of St Paul, "Flee fornication."

I had turned forty, and I believed that by my mother's willing of it I would not find love again. Sylvia Plath had named it "the bone and sinew of [her] curse," and an au pair called Aurora, who had lived with us in Putney, then returned to Spain to get married and in a letter said, "Love is a malady of the heart." According to Gilbert White, the natural historian, love and hunger are the "great motives of the brute creatures," and the brute creature in me mourned Jay for many years.

The second prophesied love affair was even more vertiginous. When I think of it, I think of the first and last day that I met this Lochinvar, and yet the dimensions of it far exceeded those two pivotal occasions. It was at a party in a room in Pall Mall that emanated power, as did he. We shared our mutual admiration for Dylan Thomas, and I did not notice whether the walls were in gold or sienna, or that the marble columns had the rose, shamrock, and thistle emblems of the territories, so smitten was I. On my way out I asked for a booklet, to have a souvenir of the surprise encounter, and it was there that I read of the marble columns and the emblems of the territories.

On his first visit to my house Lochinvar said what every woman yearns to hear: "I will know you for a long time." With those words I pictured my marvelous future opening up before me, and nothing would have daunted me. I was on the high trapeze at the commencement of love, while not being totally blind to how things would transpire—surprise meetings, canceled meetings, devouring jealousies, the rapture and the ruptures of an affair. I should here say that I lack the cunning and the dissimulation necessary for a normal affair. I incline more toward the extremities of the Russian poet Marina Tsvetaeva, for whom love was both a transport and a purgatory. With Pasternak she had exchanged quatrains of eternal kinship, forever believing that the pain and torment could be discharged into poetry. Then it was Rilke, her Orpheus, who for her was the entire Rhine, the language they exchanged being the language of angels. They never met. In a last letter sent from St. Giles, when he was already dying, she suggests that he look on a map and pick a large town in France where she, a pauper, would meet him. It was not answered. Marina, by her own admission, created situations of isolating love so that she could write about it. James Joyce put it more bluntly, when after his dalliance with Amalia Popper, he wrote, "It will never be, write it."

Meanwhile, there was the vertigo of the affair, the many twists and turns, the reconsidered wisdoms, trade winds blowing hot and cold and hot again. It is impossible to capture the essence of love in writing, only its symptoms remain, the erotic absorption, the huge disparity between the times together and the times apart, the sense of being excluded. I remember a woman friend telephoning me to describe a party at which Lochinvar was the principal guest, and his running a comb through his hair as he passed a mirror in the hallway, and how all the ladies fawned over him. I would have walked on water to be there. Perhaps I wanted love too much ever to reconcile it with everyday life.

The worst time was the summer, summer when analysts leave their poor patients stranded and lovers go abroad on family holidays. It so happened that we were both going to Italy, though separately. The same sun beating down on both of us, on roofs and cupolas, on the jagged rocks along the narrow paths down to the sea and on the leaves of the olives that hung motionless and limp.

I had been invited by Gore Vidal to his villa, La Rondinaia, near Ravello. To get to the actual villa one had to walk, from the gate, a long avenue reminiscent of the one in *Last Year at Marienbad,* with a series of tiny steps. In moonlight, yes, it was moonlight, the white house on the bluff of the high rocks, overlooking the bay of Amalfi, was the enchanted castle. My suitcase was heavy, since I had been invited to another house in Tuscany, and not knowing the protocol, I brought every stitch of clothing that I had and too many pairs of shoes and too many books. It would be heavier by the time I left Italy, a testimony to my pining condition, which I think Gore sensed, as on the last morning, when he and I were leaving to take a train to Rome and I was clambering down flights of stairs with the suitcase, he called up in his inimitable voice, "Do I hear Sisyphus again?"

My bedroom was huge and the last word in sumptuousness.

When Gore's companion Howard showed me up, he reamed off the names of the famous who had slept there, and I particularly remember the names Tennessee Williams, Johnny Carson, and Bianca Jagger, and wondered if at siesta time they too might have wept on the pale green silk of the embroidered bedspread or leaned over the balcony, dispatching curses and endearments to an absent one.

The gardens the following morning, terraced and stretching for miles, were like those out of the Song of Solomon, hedges of aloe and box, pomegranate trees, fallen blossom, and the air veiled and silvery, as the sprinklers were all on. Such light. Such rightness. Such ripeness. And yet I was in moping mood, remembering that all across Italy in blistering heat tourists, including Lochinvar, were setting out, equipped with guidebooks and sun hats, scaling the high steps to the great cathedrals, or to the piazza in Siena for the Palio, as bareback riders outcouraged each other, or in Florence queuing to see Michelangelo's *David.* Michelangelo, another mendicant in the love department, who wished that his skin be flayed to make a garment or a sandal for his beloved.

I decided to walk to the town and do a bit of modest sightseeing, so that Lochinvar and I could compare our Italian sojourn when next we met. It was about a two-mile walk, and undone by the heat, I went into the big church in the square to mouth a few prayers, relieved by its relative darkness and its hush, away from the searing brightness from which there was no escape. I prayed that I just might bump into him and, in the next breath, wished that he was dead. Loving moments intermingled with aggrieved ones. Dangling, dangling. "I won't see you again, unless I yield to temptation."

The church was almost full, women old and not old, staring straight ahead at the altar, and still others caressing the various statues, pleading with them in whispers. There were, as well, vases of fresh flowers and withered flowers in different nooks, pink roses going milky white. From the sacristan I learned, also in whispers, that, around the Feast of the Assumption, the miracle happened. *"Miracolo, miracolo,"* she called it. The coagulated blood of the Martyr was expected to liquefy, and if it did not, it augured ill for the crops. There it was, in a glass reliquary, dark red in color like a piece of resin or sealing wax, and there were the faithful, staring at it, waiting for those first drops of shed blood heralding the Annunciation. The south of Italy, according to Gustav Herling, is "addicted to miracles as lonely people are to dreams," and they were all there, all these women, and I was one of them.

Sometimes I went outside to have a glass of fizzy water in the café, and then I would repair to an antique shop that also dealt in bric-a-brac and wander from room to room, looking at the price tags. Having gone in so often, I felt that I must buy something, and insanely decided on a set of fire irons, already envisaging the autumn and the fires I would light to rewelcome my lover. The set consisted of heavy brass tongs, a matching poker, a shovel, and two brass stands to rest these implements on. They were wrapped in various pieces of old newspaper, and it was clear that they would not all fit in the suitcase: some ingloriously would be hanging from the strap, making my arrival in the next villa humbling. It was the thud of that suitcase as I clambered down the stairs on the last morning that caused Gore in his sonorous voice to call up, "Do I hear Sisyphus again?" guessing that it was the age-old love sonata.

The miracle had not happened by the time I left, but I was certain that it would, what with all that mashing on bone and beads, the heaving sighs and the heaving chests and the faces, so imploring. It was certain to hasten the *miracolo* that would in some way extend to me, as it did.

It was on a train in England, about two weeks later, when my lover and I met, bumped into one another, he returning from the refreshment car with a brown paper bag that was leaking and I on my way there. It was where two carriages joined that we collided, the tracks rattling, the cars pitching about unsteadily as the train hurtled like mad through the countryside, where harvests could be glimpsed through the grimed window. Thrown together and apart; it was clear that summer absence and half-hearted resolve to end it had been in vain and we were starting afresh, all over again.

One morning I wakened to find that I was broke. I should have foreseen it, what with not writing regularly and keeping myself in readiness. It was my accountant who informed me of my situation, a City man, who put his bowler hat carefully on a side table. Broke. "But I have this house" was my reply. The house, he informed me, was not as valuable as I had thought. Prices were falling, and what had been worth X number of pounds would soon be minus X. How had it happened? I knew how it had happened. Love, generosity, the pipe dream. I was one of the foolish virgins who had not seen to it that her oil lamp was kept full. As with the two-headed Janus, before my eyes I saw Lochinvar's thankful expression each time I opened the door to him, and now his grieving expression as that door would be forever shut. We had known only a fraction of each other, but that fraction was sacred. I had fooled myself, living on emotional crumbs and now the inhabiter of Yeats's bitter words—I had "fed the heart on fantasies/The heart's grown brutal from the fare."

The estate agent was of the petit-snobbish brigade, suggesting I get a shears to the honeysuckle; then he tapped walls and window frames and through a skylight crawled halfway out to have a look at the roof. He re-emerged dusting his hands, saying that things were in reasonably good nick, but by the way he drawled over the word "reasonably" I knew it meant a reduction in the asking price.

The house sold quickly and for a song, and I betook myself to the wider and lonelier vistas of north London. Strangely enough, on the day the movers came, I was busy and buoyant. I watched as the piano was lifted from a trolley, then lowered on stout white straps to the floor of the van and wrapped in blankets, just as I had seen our nervy greyhound Lil before a race, covered in a tartan rug. Petrov's chandelier was placed in a tea chest and swaddled in asbestos. I even dug up a magnolia tree that flowered early, the white flowers cupped and neat like a bantam's egg.

In the new flat my friend and future neighbor, Robin Dalton, had brought a picnic, and we laid a cloth out on the floor and tacked black paper to the window, and there was no end to the resolutions that I was making.

But harmony would be short-lived. All the wallpaper, which I had barely noticed, was gloomy, a dark aubergine, and a dog, a Labrador, barked ceaselessly in the communal garden. Within twenty-four hours the magnolia tree that I planted had been dug up and left at the bottom of the outside stairs that ran down to the gardens. Later there was a letter from the secretary of the residents' association, informing me that no such liberties as the planting or spoliation of trees or shrubs were permitted.

It was at a dinner in the Gay Hussar restaurant in Soho, meeting with the other judges for the *Evening Standard*'s annual awards drama, that I admitted to my loss. These were volatile affairs, everybody at first marveling at how quickly the year had gone, looking forward to the roast duck and applesauce that was the specialty of the house, all affability until the judging started, and then it was acrimony and table-thumping.

According to one of the journalists, "rumor" had it that Lochinvar was seen carrying a fish pie, going into the cottage of a mistress in Dorset. I knew that he was telling it to puff himself up, and I also knew it was a lie. At that moment I believed more than ever that it was not over, that Lochinvar would be waiting for me, that our love had in it the lastingness of myth.

It was after midnight and bitterly cold when I came out. Without a thought, I asked the taxi driver to go to Carlyle Square and recognized my error only when I climbed the front steps and saw a milk bottle beside the foot scraper, with a note thrust into it. It was not my house anymore.

Each day, at my desk, I looked out at the communal gardens, at the hole from where the magnolia tree had been dug up, the steep flights of steps down from each of the tall houses, and heard the Labrador, who would be left outside by its owner, barking, barking, well nigh to dementedness. I had lost my Cherry Orchard, something I would rue for a long time, if not to say forever. I loved a man who did not know me as I really was.

It was a refrain that I would hear again and again from many a woman, but never did I hear it more poignantly put than at Christmas in King Edward VII Hospital in London, where I had gone for a hip operation. An alloy of metal and ceramic, five inches long, had been inserted in my hip bone, and on the bed was an open book, with exercises recommended for when I went home—leg swings, knee bends, and foot lifts.

Time and responsibility had been beautifully deferred. I thought of mothers in the shires, wrapping presents, stuffing birds, at near-breaking point when there was yet an elaborate dinner to be cooked, as I listened to the sweet chimes of the bells from various churches, extolling the festive day that it was. It had been snowing in the night, and the world outside was a veritable Christmas card, the side street and the slanted slates of the houses covered in a soft, powdery snow, with a bluish tint to it.

The atmosphere in the hospital was festive. A nurse wearing a huge red earring that flashed on and off like a traffic signal had brought me tea very early, and nailed to my door was a small wicker basket with chocolates, a miniature Christmas cake, and a miniature port wine, gifts from the hospital, wishing me a Happy Recovery. There was also a book of jokes in alphabetical order, and I read at random a Hollywood producer's verdict on Esther Williams as an actress: "Wet she's a star, dry she ain't."

The cocktail party, to which the assistant matron insisted I go, was at noon. She said that I might meet people I had not met for a long time, an old beau perhaps, "love's sweet refrain" once more. With this in mind, I had to get ready. Shoes were out of the question, but I had new striped angora socks, which a lovely friend called Therese had left downstairs for me, being too reticent to come up. Getting dressed was no mean feat. From a stick that had a flipper hook at one end, I had to negotiate donning the socks, then pulling the red silk kimono on over the hospital gown. Staff had gone to great lengths decorating the corridor. Stars of Bethlehem, swags of holly and lamé-crested cards all but concealed the various drawings of vertebrae, injured shoulders, and buckled knees. Most patients had gone home for Christmas, and the gathering was composed mainly of staff, who were off duty and in a high state of merriment, bedecked with paper hats and comparing the trinkets which they had acquired from their crackers. A house doctor looked absurdly forbidding in felt antlers, which were a gift from a "grateful patient" in Lapland. One of the anesthetists wore a white mask with a blood-red gash for lips and held a card which read, "Here comes the vampire." There were very few guests. A young Arab woman with long jet-black hair, sloe eyes, and a large emerald pendant was surrounded by her cohorts. They drank Coca-Cola. The other visitor, seated in the best armchair, was a stout Englishwoman, expounding on the deteriorated state of the country. She had fallen in her kitchen the day before, simply getting down that silly tin of sardines, and what with her maid gone and the floor slippery, she had come a cropper. More than an hour elapsed before the ambulance came, and she was brought to a hideous National Health hospital, kept waiting for hours in a room full of foreigners, a ghastly Babel. Worse, she had been kept there overnight, and with a missionary zeal she announced, "I now know what it is like to be in prison, having spent one night in a National Health hospital." She was now where she should have been in the first instance, in a hospital of which she was actually a trustee, and she was also on her second, if not to say third, glass of champagne. The conversation then turned to the Queen's Speech, one of the nurses saying that we would probably be on the plum pudding at that point, having had our first course, roast turkey and trimmings, and we would be in mellow mood. The battle-ax begged to differ. She would not be in mellow mood. She would not even listen to it—as a monarchist all her life, she could not bear to think that her beloved Queen had sold out to Europe. The doctor with the felt antlers tried to remonstrate with her, saying it was not the Queen's decision, whereupon she requested her crutches and rose like a general about to survey the troops.

I had hobbled back to my room when a visitor was announced. It was the writer Andrew O'Hagan, a new friend, who in a matter of two years had become a steadfast one. He brought the snow in with him; it was on his shoulders and on his eyelashes, so perfectly crested it might have been applied with curling tongs. He had walked miles in the snow, having earlier gone to Mass, where the singing of the choir brought him back to the scenes of his childhood, the family allowance book, his mother with four boys and a useless husband, an advertisement for Bell's whiskey on top of Central Station in Glasgow with the beguiling "Afore ye go." He had brought loads of presents: candles, gloves, a bottle of double malt, and a jigsaw puzzle with a picture of Emily Brontë in a tiled interior of pale brown and sepia, like a replica of the work of one of the Dutch masters. Emily Brontë, with her size-three shoes, said to have the mind of a navigator, instead remained in one place and navigated the perplexities of the crooked heart. He poured himself a little malt and discovered still another present in his Santa Claus bag. I asked him why it was that we, who had known hardship, were so profligate, and he thought about it and said that maybe it was because Saxon big brother made us Celts believe that we were "wee." I asked for a song, and he sang Robert Burns's "Where the Bonnie Lassie Lives," as various nurses put their heads through the door to nod their approval.

It was evening time, and after turning down my bed, Irina, a nurse from Eastern Europe, wondered if she might sit for a few minutes. She was lonely. She would have liked to have gone home, but home was five hours on the express train and cost much monies, which she could not afford. She was saving for the little house in her dream that was in her own country, and the other dream was of man, perfect man, coming to her. She had a boyfriend whom she loved, but he go live with other woman, but that other woman now tell him, "Go, go," because he fall for still other woman. She cried then and dried her eyes and apologized for crying and cried more, saying, "I have peace, but I have lonely." Seeing the books and notebooks and pens on my bedside table, she asked almost in invocation, "Madam, please write book for men about love, because they do not understand it as womans do."

I had not the heart to tell her that great love stories told of the pain and separateness between men and women.

I had left north London and moved back to a rented house in Chelsea, walking the back streets that I knew, past the small terraced houses with cottage gardens and enclaves of green, seed pods and pollen blowing all over the place, people sneezing, idlers exchanging the odd word. One pensioner from the nearby barracks would be in a wheelchair, while his companion went to get groceries, proud of his scarlet jacket, his tasseled hat, and a green paper swizzle, a bauble that he waved. He would say the same thing at intervals, "In Wales," giving Wales the mythic resonance of Troy.

PART THREE

The Blank Page

The words would not come, and I would remember when they had come and it had been so effortless, the rapid, handwritten pages of this story or that. I had brought Zig pens specially from America that were lucky and were also photo-safe, acid-free, waterproof, archival quality, light-fast, fadeproof, and nonbleeding. But they did not suffice. Henry James said that these lapses or intermissions or spirals of depression, or whatever they might be called, "were good for [his] genius," but I was more inclined to agree with Virginia Woolf, who in one of her shriven states had said that she should go to John Lewis and get a dress made, nearing madness. I reread the books that I loved, the old ones and a few of the new ones that had something of the timbre of the old ones. I kept a diary. I read with misgivings that only the very young and the very mad keep diaries. There were jangled entries—the "Poisoned Flower of the Borgias," "Pluto's Dark Door," Nietzsche's "We possess art, lest we perish of the truth." All very edifying and useless.

Sometimes I went to speak to students at universities or colleges where I was supposed to be imparting nuggets of wisdom. I brought Kafka to read to them and told them how Kafka had said a book must be the ax to the frozen seas inside us. In Hull the wind from the North Sea, with a wet spray to it, hurled against the windowpanes, which shook and shivered, naked to the world. In the almost empty dining room, the talk came round to the blank page and the places writers flee to in the belief that it will help them to write. One of the lecturers had just returned from Lapland, a Boadicea on her sled, driving four huskies through the snows, chopping her own wood, making her own fire, setting up her own tent. Each night, before settling down to sleep, she looked out at the silent, silver, blanketed night that became the substance of her dream, in which she conceived a fairy tale that was an astonishment to her, but that alas vanished at the very moment of her wakening.

I thought of the numerous futile journeys that I had made in desperation. Who in her right mind would go to a small house in the country of England, in bleak winter, for the ministrations of a guru who claimed to have gleaned the secrets of the libido from East and West? He wore white, white robes and a white turban and was waited upon by a bevy of ex-wives and current mistresses, who addressed him as "Guru This" and "Guru That." Taking his cue, perhaps, from Wilhelm Reich, he was clearly an advocate of the orgasm, insisting on nudity for massages, where he pressed his being on the various chakras for added intensity and panted more than was reasonable. All that was needed was an orgone box. I had years before sat in one under the supervision of a Norwegian doctor.

In that small country house we were three patients, a friendly woman who ran a restaurant, a woman who coughed, and myself. The walls were paper-thin. One could hear the coughing at night and the giggles from the more private quarters, where the guru and his harem lived.

We drank juice with a concoction of minerals and vitamins, which was supposed to dispel hunger, which indeed it did. Since it was raining, we spent most of our time in the sitting room, the smell of burning joss sticks wafting in from the hall, little to say to one another as we read our horoscopes in out-of-date magazines. After two listless nonwriting days, I decided to cut my stay short. This did not go down well. The female brigade warned how distressing it would be for their guru, and he himself tried to persuade me to stay, saying I had not given his methods their due respect. In the train I felt I had been let out of school, and ordered a quarter-bottle of Australian white wine that was lukewarm.

The spa in Austria was different, more austere. One went for the "cure" and everything revolved around that. The dining room looked out onto a lake, with hotels distinctive as castles ranged on the opposite side, and the steep mountain slope was covered with evergreens that ran all the way to the summit, where the mountain dipped and soared, shutting out the last bit of lilac sky. Patients were advised to chew their spelt bread forty times until it reached the consistency of a puree. We sat at tables of four, Austrians, Germans, English, and myself, chewing the bread and pondering, perhaps, our digestive systems, or whether to have the mild or strong Epsom salts before retiring. I looked up the German word for saliva and copied it into my notebook. Talking was discouraged, and so was reading. The girls who waited on us were dressed in Tyrol costumes and little half-aprons, were polite but stern about our regime, so that there was no question of an extra rice cake.

After the main lights had been turned out, knowing I wouldn't sleep, I simply sat and looked at fish in a tank, endlessly moving, the water rippling as they darted through it. They fought. Skirmishes of all kinds, then a brief truce as they landed on bits of bark or pebble, establishing their territory and regrouping for battle.

I gave them names. Saddam Hussein was striped and strutting. George Bush was a lackluster figure with his braggart cohorts. Vladimir Putin occupied a millionaire corner, with minions fencing around him. There was one angelic coral creature, its fins quivering, whom I called Emily Dickinson, trapped among the totalitarians.

Fasting led to lethargy and whiffs of hallucination. In the afternoons I would sit out of doors, my virgin notebooks on the bench beside me and a copy of Thomas Mann's *The Magic Mountain*. Some patients sat on folding chairs, others had retired after the frugal lunch of rice cake and savory spread to have a compress of warm chamomile flowers, while a few heroic ones set off on bicycles or cross-country skis. I sat before a fountain. From a stone gourd, a corolla of water rose, then plashed down the sides into a font that for a moment held the gift of melting moonstone rings. I was trying to meditate, to become one with the water, but instead I was hoarding a few impressions for some story or other that I might write.

Low borders of privet hedging enclosed squares of grass, and orange flowers, which I took to be dwarf marigolds, bloomed listlessly. There was one birch tree, onto which a whole forum of small brown birds would converge and linger, never once roused to song. The kitchen was to the rear of where I sat, and the smell of roast, of which I would not be partaking, was galling. Patients who remained on after the "cure" were given delicious meals, once the punishing regime had expired, but I could not wait to leave. Even Thomas Mann seemed ponderous.

One afternoon a young girl, whom I sat next to each morning at the sitz baths, was leaving for England and I waited with her outside until her taxi arrived. I inquired about the building across the street and learned to my mounting excitement that it was the bar and restaurant for members of the nearby golf club. My spirits rose. I would go there quietly at six-thirty and treat myself to one glass of wine, prior to the bowl of clear soup which that evening was being added to my diet. I confided my plot to her. She gripped my arm and said on no account must I risk it. A Russian oligarch and his party had been to the spa, had betaken themselves to the restaurant one evening, availing of steaks and champagne, only to find on their return that they were escorted to their rooms and made to pack immediately, since they had broken the rules of the clinic.

After she left, I looked at the flyleaf of my new notebook and saw where I had copied out a line of Joseph Brodsky's: "The discarding of the superfluous is in itself the first cry of poetry." By having written nothing at all, I was approaching poetry.

Some evenings a young man from the town came to see to the fish. He would clean the tank, scatter something in the water, and talk to them before covering them in for the night with a dark cloth. I would try to engage him. What did they eat? When did they mate? Did they sleep in the darkness? And he would simply smile and say, "My English no good."

Yet on the morning that I was leaving, he left a handwritten letter, with the title "My Fish Family":

Sex, food, war, that their life. Fish always watch for enemy. Every one watching for who is strongest. Striped one always on stone. Blue always on wood. Littlest fish born in this tank, his father the yellow born in Lake Malawi. His mother unknown. All fish, they cruising all day long. Hundreds, thousands of meters. Males fight. Females not fight as much. The more colorful the more the fighter. Easier to survive without color. Male sees female shivering and wants to be great man for her. Then dance. Male dig a hole in sand floor, then swim to female for her interest and she follow. Female lay eggs on sand and take in mouth for three and a half weeks. Eggs secure there. After four weeks baby fishes they swim. When lights go out all cruise less but never fully sleeping, never fully still. You ask if I have favorite. The lapis blue. She called Ahli. She very beautiful with blue body and white stripe on head. But all are beautiful and needing best care. Do not forget us. Caretaker Michael

My hopes buoyed when the invitation came to the villa in Mallorca. I had been to the island years before, in springtime, when the almond trees were in full flower, and my memory of it was of a flowering paradise, with windmills dotting the hilltops. A young girl from Ghana, whom I called Ophelia, had got me the invitation, since she had done the interior decorating for the owner. She would come with me, staying for the weekend, and then I would be alone for twelve days to write.

From Palma airport we took a taxi, and as it fell dark, she began to fret about the directions once we left the motorway. Side roads became narrower and narrower, the countryside unfamiliar, with here and there a light from a house set far back in a field, little bumpy bridges, then narrower roads, more tracks, and after almost two hours of mounting suspense, she said, "Eureka, eureka," as she sighted a hoarding with a huge picture of a wild cat.

"El gato, el gato," she said, and told the driver to make a left fork down a dirt road, which he did so hurriedly that we could hear the loose pebbles hopping off the bonnet. Then a third "Eureka" as we arrived at the green gates that led to the avenue and the *finca.*

There were two entrances, but because of our luggage, she decided we would go by the courtyard entrance, and as she turned the big key in the lock and still more slowly pushed in a wooden door with its iron beveling, I recalled the erotic interiors of Luis Buñuel. An anteroom with a metal sink in one corner led to the salon itself, which was shadowy, high arches following one upon the other and stretching to a wrought-iron staircase beyond. She groped for lights. There were leather chairs and sofas and illustrated books and a long wooden table, where I could spread out my notes and get down to work. It was cold as a mausoleum. In the huge fireplace that skirted one wall, the bole of a tree had been placed on a bed of white ash, numerous small saplings jutting from it.

To get to the boiler we groped our way through a series of rooms, some lit, some not, and there was a Ping-Pong table, tennis racquets, brand-new motorcycles, and a boiler that seemed to have expired. The pilot light was quenched. Beside it was a wooden olive press, the wrought-iron handle upright, like a compass without destination. Back in the living room, we rolled newspaper into balls and idiotically flung them on the top of the unbudgeable bole of wood, believing it would warm us. She found the wine cellar and returned, triumphant, with a bottle of vintage claret, which in a halfhearted manner we vowed to restore.

Before going up to bed I got out all my notebooks and glanced at the scattered things I had written, mere jottings that bore no relation whatsoever to the work I had come to do.

The bedroom was even icier than the downstairs. I kept saying "Ca'an D'Or" to myself as if it were a mantra and warming my hands on it. This was another villa belonging to the owner, where we could go the next day, as it had all the amenities: heat, light, and an electric stove that had actually been fitted. It took some doing to get the curtains to overlap, but enveloped in a white duvet, I got into bed and had a heart-to-heart talk with myself, debating whether or not I should leave with Ophelia on the Sunday.

A sort of milkiness gauzed the sky, and soon I got up and I went outside to survey my surroundings and watch the sun come up. Olive and lemon groves all around. The olive trees, bent and gnarled, warts and bulges on their limbs, yet their leaves, tapered and silvery, letting out little whispery rustles. The terraces that ran up the fields in tiers were perfectly husbanded, and beyond them the pine woods, dense and pathless, to the range of gray-white mountains, the sierras, whose summits glistened with snow. To the rear of the villa there were low stone walls, and crouched under one, as if it had just escaped from a Damien Hirst formaldehyde tank, was a sheep, stunned, silent, with not a bleat from it. This would be my companion.

Ophelia appeared, refreshed. She had rung the owner, who

was perfectly agreeable to my moving to Ca'an D'Or, and we would go to the estate office and get the keys. It turned out to be even more friendless. A square modern house, set down in the middle of a field, with no olive or lemon groves around it. The central heating did indeed come on at the press of a giant white switch, but the racket from several fans was such that it would preclude any possibility of writing. It was decided that I would stay in a *pensión* in the old town at night and each morning take a taxi back to the *finca* to work in solitude. In the one *pensión* that was open, the *patrón* gave us the keys to the two upstairs rooms, to choose which one I preferred. They were identical. One looked onto a square and the other onto a narrow street, which I settled for, thinking it would be quieter.

After Ophelia left to catch her plane, I saw crowds gather in the square and learned that the fiesta known as Calle di Calvari was happening that evening. It was for Sant Antoni, Saint Anthony, patron saint of farm animals, who had already been blessed in the farms earlier in the morning. There would be a pilgrimage, which entailed climbing 365 steps to a small chapel that nestled at the top. This was known as Calvary. Along the way there were beautiful homes, gardens, and even shops. I got halfway up to Calvary, but by then the first pilgrims were on the way down and breathless from the climb. I turned back with them down to the square. It was already lit with the lights of numerous paper lanterns, and loud drumbeats signaled the commencement of the revels. A witching night. A night of wine and wassail and a huge banner with black lettering that read EVERYTHING LICIT IN THIS NIGHT OF FIRE. Having done the penance of the climb, people were in high spirits as they trooped into the square for the bacchanalia. Harlequins and Columbines, their faces ghostly, danced about, and children danced with them and ran in mock horror from the devils, whose horns, fresh from the slaughterhouse, dripped with blood. Youths were dragging a huge tree across to the steps of the church to set fire to it, and a woman who was closing her stall sold me a knitted shawl for half price, a grudging expression on her face.

Marcel Proust has described bells as being "resilient and ferruginous," but in that small room in that *pensión,* on a narrow bed with the pale green band of light from the clock radio, they were bold and presumptuous, punctuating the wretched hours.

"Nobody sleeps at fiesta, madam," the daughter of the house said, as I came down very early to give back the keys. The deposit I had to forgo, since, as she said, her father had arranged the best terms possible for me, and moreover, they could have let the room to an honorable person. The square in the early morning was deserted, the yellow sandstone of the church of Nostra Senyora dels Àngels drained of sunshine, as an elderly woman with a soft green broom swept the debris away. The church door was closed, but I recalled its interior, so ornate, figures of the Virgin, angels, and saints caparisoned in gold, their arms bedecked with it, gold crowns on their heads.

In the bodega I bought things that did not need cooking, picturing as I did the electric stove still in its wrapping inside the kitchen door of the villa. Almonds, tins of sardines, salt biscuits, and stuffed olives. On the way down the steep passageway, in the window of a shut boutique, the female dummies in fawn bast, with their little turrety breasts, were huddled in a heap, as if someone had vacated the place in high dudgeon. At the side window was the name and telephone number of a gentleman who did shiatsu massage, and I copied it down carefully.

On my way back I kept asking the taxi driver to go slowly. *"Lento lento,"* I would say, so that I could note some landmarks in order to give directions to the masseur. There was a roundabout, then a left turning, then a sculpture of a rooster, red-brown and not very beautiful, then a belt of trees where the road got dark, a monastery on a hill, which he told me the name of, Puig de Santa Mar'a. He was in a hurry. The car bounced over the narrower roads and the bumpy stone bridges, and I barely had time to catch sight of the wild cat on the hoarding.

"El gato," I said.

"Salvaje," he said, and soon after swerved to the right, barely missing a tree, and onto the rough track that I saw in daylight to be sand-colored.

"Salvaje?"

He shrugged and said tourists were *"loco loco"* to go into the forest where the wild cats lived. He was annoyed at having to get out to open the green gates, and then it was on down past the olive groves and the vineyards to the villa, in which I was hostaged for eleven days.

There were heartening signs. The gardener had come. A fire blazed and crackled in the huge grate. The bole of wood had been pushed back and served as a sort of chimneypiece, and the tall logs had been placed pyramid-wise to allow for a draft. He had filled three wheelbarrows with wood, assuring me that I would have enough until he returned on the Thursday. *"Jueves. Jueves."* On that day also, oil would be delivered. I inquired about the solitary sheep under the ruin, and all he said was *"Estúpido, estúpido."* Seeing the books and the notebooks, he asked if I was a *"Profesora,"* and wanly I said I was not.

After he had gone, I decided to have the massage that very day, to arrive at the *"mucha calma"* state, a phrase that I had discovered in my phrase book. Everything depended on this Japanese man; his Zen-like touch would do wonders for my raveled, unslept state. A woman answered the telephone, and I could not tell whether she was Japanese or Mallorcan. She was the essence of courtesy. I communicated with the help of a dictionary: no sleep, nervous. *"Nerviosa,"* she repeated, and said that her husband would come immediately, as it was obligatory for him to help all people *nervioso.* Three o'clock. *"A las tres." "Es a la disposicion de usted."* He would be at my disposal. She wrote down the directions as I spoke them in English, with smatterings of Spanish. He must take the road out from Pollensa, past the roundabout, past the *esculpido,* cockerel, and then the *arco* of dark trees and the "Puig," where the monastery was. He will think, I told her, that he is going nowhere as the roads become narrow and narrower and bumpy, but he must persevere until he gets to the bridge, *el puente,* and the picture of the cat, *el gato.* He will go down an empty road until he comes to a green gate and then up the drive, the *camino,* to the *entrada,* where I would be waiting, waiting. *"A las tres."*

I carried the duvet down, along with towels and sheets, to be near the fire, believing that he would bring a massage table. Now and then I went out, just to see if his car was coming. I was not too concerned when by three-thirty he had not arrived. She assured me that he would stay as long as I wished, one hour, two hours, whatever my requirement. Several times I stood on the terrace flapping my arms idiotically so that he would see me as he turned the last loop of the private *camino.* Rushing to answer the ringing phone, I skidded on the stone floor, barely avoiding casualty. My agitation conveyed itself to the woman, who assured me that he was on his way, he had been doing so for two hours, but sadly he had mistaken the directions and was without a map. *"No carreteras,"* she said, no roads, but I must not trouble, as it was obligatory for him to help those in pain or *nervioso.* I repeated the directions, the roundabout, the *arco* of trees, the rooster, the bridge, the dirt track, and so on, as my faith in this expedition began to falter.

With each new phone call things became more misconstrued, her voice shriller as she repeated words I had unwisely spoken, very little light, getting more dark, narrow lane, it seem nothing, you feel you are nowhere, but you must persevere until you come to green gate. I decided that I would walk to the top of the avenue or even beyond and watch for his car, which was a red Honda.

The light began to fade, and I felt something soft on my cheeks, feathery, like a moth wing, except that it was snow, a thing almost unheard of on that island, snow that turned watery as it fell. I could hear sounds of motorcycles revving up and became convinced that local thugs had heard of my arrival, a *señora sola,* in a villa alone, and were setting out on a maraud. I ran the whole way back to the house, and the phone stopped its ringing just as I entered. I took this to be a good sign, that she was merely ringing to say he would be arriving presently. I thought this all the more, since she did not ring back again at once. I read the leaflets that I had taken from the church and the *pensión,* simply to pass the time. Saint Anthony was a Coptic saint from Egypt, a saint of the desert, and father of all monks who went into the wilderness. He was tempted by the devil with boredom, laziness, and phantoms of women, and when that did not break him, the phantoms of women converted to wild beasts, wolves, lions, snakes, and cats. A lifelong hermit, he wove mats of rushes. Next I read of the olive tree, cited in the *Iliad* and in the Bible, native to the coastal areas of the Mediterranean basin, western Asia, North Africa, and northern Iran, at the south end of the Caspian Sea, distantly related to lilac, jasmine, and true ash trees and more disposed to poorer soil. An olive leaf was what a dove brought back to Noah, when the flood had ended.

All seemed propitious.

Shadows were thickening under the high wooden arches, and I did not have to put my face to the window to know that daylight was gone, completely gone; it would be pitch-dark out there, partly snowing, the terrace, the olive trees, the orange garden, the tennis court, and poor *estúpido* Damien Hirst all swallowed up in it. I dare not step outside, as I might slip or miss a step. The telephone rang. Her equanimity had been sorely tried. Her husband had had to turn around and go home, as the obscurement became too great. There were *muchas puentes,* many bridges, but sadly not the bridge that would have led him to me.

I knew, as I know each time, that the entire journey—the extra canvas bag that I had to buy at Gatwick airport in order to remove some of the books from the overfilled suitcase, the notebooks with the references to the poisoned flowers of the Borgias, black Pluto's door, the *pensión,* and the aggravation of the ringing bells—had all been for one reason only, to postpone the terror of starting the book that I both did and did not want to write.

The only sound in that room was the hissing as water from the green wood that I had inadvertently thrown on the fire was sucked up by the gleeful flame.

The North

To write about the North was to enter troubled waters, wrath and accusation from some, fractured friendships, along with the sneering insinuation that I was "sleeping with Provos." Such was the accusation, in a restaurant in Dublin, the author Hugh Leonard called across to me, for all to hear.

I admired those who had written about war, especially Hemingway, Orwell, and Auden. But this was a different war, the "dirty war," as it has been named, fought openly and in shadows, death and devastation by the IRA, the four Protestant paramilitary organizations, the security forces, and the British army—street battles, curfews, terror and counterterror, car bombs, booby traps, honey traps, roadblocks, assassinations, ambushes, feud deaths, punishment beatings, and the murky world of agents and double agents, a war where courage and criminality overlapped, a war where ideals were shafted in the all-out hurrah of victory.

My mother, in her letters to me, would dwell on these atrocities as she read of them, pitying the living that had to go to the mortuaries to identify their own, often merely by a coat button, a buckle, or a shoe. She saw the pity of war; whereas, for many in the South, increasingly the IRA were the "mindless hooligans" who brought shame on their fellow Catholics and a stain on the altar of the nation. The "mindless hooligans" on the other side were not nearly so vehemently rebuked.

The first thing I would notice when I went to Belfast in 1974 was the light. A gray, rainy light, working-class Protestant and Catholic houses, identical, Lilliputian size, the presence of mountain and sea, and heaped clouds that cried out for poetry and not bloodshed.

Here were two sides who shared a language and a landscape, yet with an atavistic zeal, claiming it as their lawful birthright. I was amazed at how people went about their daily business, but there were always the sirens and the covert fear of worse havoc at any moment. No corner shop, no pub, no car park, no disco, no filling station, no lay-by was without the "miasma" (as Seamus Heaney called it) of spilled blood. There would be no *Guernica,* or no *Homage to Catalonia* for this; it was as Anna Akhmatova said of her years under Stalin, "My muse has been flogged to death." It bore no resemblance to the rebellions of yore, the ones I had learned about at school, rebellions crushed in a matter of days, the last being Easter 1916, of which Yeats wrote the beautiful cathartic poem of "sweet and daring" men. This was a war that reached epic magnitude, slaughter and counterslaughter, which on paper could be termed Jacobean but in life became a gruesome statistic of death and mutilation, so that, as in Hamlet's Elsinore, "carnal, bloody and unnatural acts" were committed by all sides.

It was not that there were no stories; it was that there were so many, barbaric and inchoate, often defying human comprehension. To take one week alone in the history of the province is to give an example of the madness, the mayhem. It was 1988, when three unarmed members of the IRA, in Gibraltar, who were probably intending to carry out an attack, were shot in the street by the SAS, and their bodies, flown home to Dublin, were met by thousands as the cortège headed for Belfast. At Milltown Cemetery in west Belfast there were thousands more mourners when a loyalist gunman launched an attack, firing a handgun and throwing hand grenades. He was chased and followed by dozens of Catholic men, three of whom he killed in the chase, and then out onto the motorway, where they caught him and beat him unconscious, until a police car arrived and he was carted away. A few days later, at the funeral for one of the three men whom he had killed, two British army corporals mistakenly drove their vehicle into the cemetery, and the nationalists, believing it was a repetition of the attack of a few days previous, pulled the two men from the car and shot them. It would need Dante, from down among the damned, to grasp the convolutions and repercussions of that week alone: cold murder, mad murders, hatred and revenge in all its sunken, telluric depths. Poison and fear and funerals.

Two buses left the city center twice a week for Long Kesh prison, one for Catholics and one for Protestants. I saw the faces of mothers and wives, wearied, stoic, lugging parcels, lugging children, faces that, if one were to see them in Dublin or London or New York, one could not say, This is a Catholic face or This is a Protestant face. Then unexpectedly, the needling bitterness. I boarded the Protestant bus by mistake, and on hearing my southern accent, a woman told me to get off and go with my own lot, "the Fenian scum." What I will never forget on that bus journey is a plucky little boy, aged about six, walking up and down the aisle, index finger pointed, saying to each person, or each pair of persons, the interrogative word "So?" I would write that, except that I couldn't. Did his mother teach him rebel songs? Would he grow up to be a gunman, or would the stalled peace initiatives eventually succeed?

> What price peace,
> Will it cost us all our lives?
> And when there's no one left to die
> Will peace come then?
> What price peace, is it coming, is it gone?

The Catholic youth Stephen McCann, who wrote that song, has a white cross bearing his name erected alongside thousands of other white crosses for innocent victims, in the grounds of City Hall, Belfast. He paid for it with his life. As he returned from a dance at Queen's University at two in the morning with his girlfriend, he was picked up by some Shankill Butchers, bundled into a car, and driven to a remote place, where he was shot in the head and his throat cut, something that happened on Saturday nights, when they went with knives and cleavers to get a "Taig."

Yet when their leader was shot by the IRA, hundreds of loving eulogies appeared in the columns of the *Belfast Telegraph,* including one from his aunt, which read, "Nothing could be more beautiful than the memories we have of you, to us you were very special and God must have thought so too."

Over the years I would hear the harrowing tales of the mothers robbed of their children in atrocities committed by one side or the other. There was the little revenant Julie Livingstone, killed by a plastic bullet in a police riot, who had written her name with a crayon in the airing cupboard, under the stove, and on the inside of the wallpaper, for her mother to find after her death. There was a Catholic mother who had gone to live with a man in a Protestant area whose house was bombed by loyalists, and though she managed to jump out of a window, calling to her children inside to go to the stairs, the stairs had already gone up in a sheet of flame and the three children taken. There was a Protestant mother who had lost a son when the IRA bombed a fish shop in Shankill Road, who chained herself to the exit turnstile of Long Kesh prison to confront his killer, who was due a ten-day Christmas parole. Anne Maguire was wheeling a pram on a road in west Belfast, her other two children along with her, when a car swerved out of control, up onto the pavement, and crushed them. It was a getaway car, driven by an IRA member, his comrade Danny Lennon beside him, having just been shot dead by a soldier in an armor-plated Land

Rover. She was unconscious for two weeks, but when she came to and had to learn the fate of her children, she could not believe it, as she had not seen them buried. The loss was too much, and eventually she cut her wrists with an electric carving knife and left a note asking to be forgiven.

When the IRA bombed England, the fear and apprehension were palpable, one woman asking me in dismay why the Irish would want to kill innocent people in Manchester or Birmingham or London. It was useless to cite history or the chain of deaths surrounding Anne Maguire. But reactions in Ireland were different, more personal, more heated, more challenging, and at times vacillating. When in 1974 loyalists set off three car bombs in Dublin and Monaghan one day, inflicting the greatest slaughter so far, dozens of people were killed in the rush hour, dozens more injured; it was said that the morgues were the grimmest places Ireland had seen in a long time. That grimness could hardly be mitigated when an Ulster Defence Association spokesman said, "I am very happy about the bombings in Dublin. There is a war with the Free State, and now we are laughing at them."

Knowing that I went often to the North and was hoping to write something, people at home would ask me how I could turn a blind eye to the criminality of the IRA, an army that brought death and devastation on its own people, an army that got guns and Semtex from Colonel Gadhafi, an army whose deed the Pope of Rome had denounced as "inhuman" when, at a dinner dance of the Irish Collie Club, a device attached to the grille of a window detonated and people were engulfed in a ball of fire, the room literally a furnace, as rescuers pulled the curtains off the rails, trying helplessly to crush the flames. I was not blind to any of it over the years, the escalating woes, allegations of the Royal Ulster Constabulary's withholding incriminating evidence that might be used against loyalist paramilitaries, the macabre and dehumanizing depths of hate, as for instance when Robert Hamill, a Catholic youth, was kicked to death by a loyalist group in Portadown, his sister would afterward be jeered at in the street, sympathizers of his killers jumping up and down asking, "Where is Robert? Where is Robert?" I asked myself then, and I ask myself now, how the province did not descend into anarchy and total madness. How, for instance, could a mother or a wife or a daughter contemplate the reality of one of their own in a solitary cell, sitting on a blanket soaked in urine, maggots on the floor, and with the walls smeared with excrement? This was when republicans, in order to be recognized as political prisoners, began the "Dirty Protest," while outside in the province prison officers and personnel were being targeted by the IRA.

Then came the hunger strike, ten men in phased exercise, led by Bobby Sands, an iconic and messianic figure who had been jailed for fourteen years for possession of a handgun. I read his writings, which were full of pity for his own and loathing of the enemy. "I Fought a Monster Today" was the title of one of his pieces, the monster being the inhuman system that put him there, the jailers who taunted and beat him, and his ever-engulfing hatred.

After sixty-six days of fasting, in May 1981, lying on a water bed in the prison hospital, with a large crucifix in sight, which the Pope's envoy had given him in a fruitless attempt to mediate with him, Bobby Sands died. I have heard that when the news circulated, one of his warders laughed and one cried. Fierce rioting erupted in the streets, police using plastic bullets, and several Catholics were killed. In north Belfast a Protestant milkman, Eric Guiney, and his son Desmond were stoned to death by a Catholic mob.

Across Europe there were marches of solidarity for Sands, streets named after him in Paris, Milan, Ghent, and Lisbon, while the Union Jack was burned in Oslo. In New York the Longshoremen's Association staged a twenty-four-hour boycott of British ships, and Irish bars were closed for two hours. Some papers fulminated at the triumph of terrorism, while the *New York Times* noted that the British had misjudged the depth of Irish nationalism. But there is no doubt that his death and those of the nine other martyrs who followed him changed forever the perception of the Troubles.

Some years later I wrote a verse for Bobby Sands:

In your pigsty with thousands
Of hours to fill.
Did you dream—
Bloodhounds
The prophet Sirah
And blackberries ripening in Rathcoole.
Your mouth a mutiny.
At the corner of Sebastopol Street,
You look out from a weatherbeaten mural
How beautiful it is,
Such radiance
Manna it says, fell from Heaven
Once.
Visitors catch you on camera
To take home—
Leaves blowing up around you
And rain—
That mural is sometimes sodden
History rinsed and rerinsed
But like you said—
"You were going the distance"
with the ghost of a smile.

It was at home in County Clare that I eventually chanced on the story I would write. I was at lunch in my sister's house, and the talk was of Tina, poor Tina, numb since the bank raid five days before, arriving early, as she always did, when, as she was having a cup of tea, two masked raiders, bypassing the alarm system and wielding guns, were telling her to hand over the cash bags and be quick. Four minutes in all. Although no one had claimed responsibility, everyone in that kitchen said it had all the hallmarks of the IRA. They cited the case at the post office up the mountain, a few months previously, on the morning when the social-security bags were being dropped off. An armed man with a balaclava surprised the postmistress, who, as she would later tell the guards, "roared like a jackass" so that the desperado fled. For her courage she would come to be named Annie Oakley. The desperado was later shot, just a few miles down the road, in a shoot-out with a local guard. After lunch I went to see the guard, and as it was still bright, he offered to drive me up there, so that I could get "the feel of the thing." This is how he recalled it, in an urgent, singsong Cork accent:

A fine sunny morning, I'd say 'twas one of the finest for May and the chaps had made their drops with the welfare money, when over the radio system I hear the sergeant tell me to go up the mountain fast. We are doing well over a hundred miles, belting up there, the siren on when we see their blue car coming toward us. We drive past them. I fire a warning shot to show we mean business. The fella in the passenger seat winds the window down, the balaclava on, holes for his eyes, shouting obscenities at us. We turn round, and the two cars, our white and their blue, face each other and the shootin' starts. My driver is flat down behind the two front seats when the two fellas let out bursts of fire. I return fire. It's war now. I hit their driver with three bursts, and I know I've got him, because I see him slump over the wheel and the balaclava hanging off. I've scored. The second fella is shouting wild feck talk, what he'll do to me, and he gets out of the car and I get out too. We're behind our cars, crouched, edging out to shoot, and then back again for the next rounds, bullets flying, and he having the advantage because he has a rifle and a revolver. We're less than thirty yards from one another and I think it's me or him, it's the moment of truth. What happens next, but a timber lorry comes suddenly around the corner, and seeing that he's boxed in, aiming the rifle, the fella walks across, says a few snappy words to the driver, and hops in, onto the spare seat. As I heard later, the driver was ordered to take him to a disused quarry, where a second car was hidden. His rifle and his paramilitary jacket were found there, and he set out on foot for a godforsaken mountain, ending up in a Gypsy encampment, with no idea of where he was.

For us at the scene, it was a different story. The guy slumped over the wheel is unconscious, but he's breathing. He's not dead. We pull him out and we make a pillow of a fluorescent jacket and lay him down. Shells everywhere. Beautiful morning, birds all gone, the shooting sent them away. The scene has to be preserved until the ambulance and the forensic people arrive. A man from a house not too far away, up an avenue, comes across a bit shaken, says he was giving his children cornflakes, but when it started, he put them down on the floor and they huddled together. He offers us a cup of tea. I'd have given anything for a whiskey. The priest and the doctor are the next to arrive. The priest administers the last sacrament and then reads us a sermon, asking was there a need for this and saying the country had gone pure mad.

"Oh, it was high profile, I tell you," he said, slightly abashed as he looked around and noticed that the birds were back.

"What did you feel?" I asked him.

"When you're shootin' it's fifty-fifty, but when you've shot him it's a different story, because we're all Irish under the skin." He said it with such gravity that it spoke more to me of the complexity and pathos of that war than all the reams and reams of newspaper invective and television coverage. It provided me with the first lines of my novel *House of Splendid Isolation: History is everywhere, it seeps into the soil, the subsoil, like rain or hail or snow or blood. A house remembers, an outhouse remembers, a people ruminate, the tale differs with the teller.* It was the story of an IRA man come South, who billeted himself in a big house where an older woman is bed-bound and disbelieving when he bursts through her door. Gradually, as they came to talk to one another and to argue, finding a sameness and a difference, it was clear that one or the other must inevitably be sacrificed.

In some quarters there was regret that the virtuosity of the language could not redeem the repugnance of the theme, while David Hare, whom I scarcely knew, wrote me a letter to say that, as an Englishman, it gave him some insight into that war. The crowning moment was the white card, embossed with the gold emblem of an eagle, an invitation from Hillary Clinton to dinner in the White House. When I saw her for the first time in that glittering gathering, as she came through a side door into the throng, she looked shy and tentative, as if she too were a visitor like us, being given a tour and standing to look at Lincoln's rosewood bed with its vast headboard and draped canopy, the bed which some say he never slept in. It was there I spotted Jack Nicholson, whom I had met in London with Anjelica Huston when he was filming *The Shining.* I asked if it would be possible for him to give me a lift home, a request which must have surprised him, as he regaled the group with the astounding fact that I had taken a taxi to the White House, something unheard of in those echelons.

At dinner I was seated with Jack and Hillary, and the talk came round to the delicate matter of when one should turn to the person on one's other side, however reluctantly. I told them a story, as Ralph Richardson had once told it to me, citing it as an example of social correctness. He was next to the Queen, who he believed was sedulously ignoring him, and was feeling somewhat quashed, when she turned, "mid-chop," and said, "Sir Ralph, how often have you played in Ibsen?" The words were as welcome as if she was ennobling him anew. "Mid-chop" was the word that Hillary would use in the few letters we exchanged after that.

Belfast and the "miasma" of blood seemed very far away.

After dinner we watched a movie in which Nicholson starred; there was popcorn and informality, and now and then, when the President was called out, I could not help but remember the moment in *Dr. Strangelove* when it was thought that a lunatic general had got his hands on the nuclear button.

No such cordiality followed upon my writing the profile of Gerry Adams for the *New York Times* in 1994. There were rumors of a whispered political breakthrough, and also the fact that he might be given a visa to attend a conference about the North of Ireland in New York.

He was something of a pariah, hated by many north and south of the border; the envoy, it would seem, of every single death, and by writing about him, I too would be implicated. For some years he had been holding secret talks in a monastery with John Hume, both men leaders of nationalist parties, committed men, with totally different ideologies, Hume making no secret of the fact that the IRA (with obvious reference to Nazis) saw themselves as the "master race." Yet despite their differences they persisted, and it is due to their courage and their perseverance that the first serious, albeit halting, steps toward peace were taken.

It was in the Sinn Féin press office on the Falls Road in Belfast that I met Adams. A small room, with half-empty tea mugs, bulging ashtrays, and a wedge of cardboard in the window that had not been repaired since the time, years before, when an RUC constable posing as a journalist got himself admitted and shot three people, before escaping through the window and soon after shooting himself.

There was something bafflingly calm about Adams, that and a lack of invective, which could hardly be said about his Protestant counterparts. Whereas Michael Collins was outgoing and swashbuckling, Adams was thoughtful and reserved, yet the shadow of Collins's fate cannot have been lost on him: Collins who, when signing the treaty that allowed the partition of Ireland, knew he was signing his own "death warrant," meeting his end soon after in his native County Cork, in a district tenderly called "The Mouth of the Flowers." Many in Adams's Catholic community, tired and battered from twenty-five years of bloodshed, were urging him "to settle, settle," while elsewhere there were fissures, still others suspecting him of a sellout, their displeasure made clear by the graffiti on a pebble-dashed wall, near the Catholic church.

He looked exhausted, his eyes dark and vulpine. His hero, as he said with passion, was Nelson Mandela, no doubt seeing the trajectory from the Armalite to the negotiating table. He was putting the finishing touches to a speech he would make that evening in Belfast, asking Prime Minister John Major for clarification of a document that Dublin and London were soon to issue and that was to be a framework for envisaged peace. But the obstacles were many. Major was insisting that the document "be free of the fingerprints of the IRA," while his Irish counterpart, Albert Reynolds, was imploring him to persevere with it. Meanwhile, in the streets, the killings from both sides escalated. Loyalists, fearing betrayal, became more and more virulent, so as to goad the IRA even further, and James Molyneaux, leader of the Ulster Unionist Party, predicted that there was nothing in the document for Catholics, while the UDA published their own document outlining a necessary scenario, which was the "ethnic cleansing of Ulster, an all-out war, using some Catholics as pawns and allowing for a nullification of others, to reduce demands on food supplies." The entire thing would be finished in one or two weeks, they reckoned. Reverend Ian Paisley was letting it be known that his party were not in the business of getting anyone "to talk to Gerry Adams about anything." Others proposed that he be put in quarantine, to be decontaminated. Despite all this, he was surprisingly optimistic, saying that the peace process was on an "irreversible thrust." Since Dr. Paisley, in trying to wreck the possibility of any peace or any joint assembly, was firing his "vintage assaults on the South, the Catholic Church, the IRA, and perfidious Albion," I asked Adams if, in the unlikely event of its coming about, would he shake hands with Paisley?

"Why not?" was the answer. It was not cynicism, it was not appeasement, it was the pragmatism of politics.

But peace, as Yeats said, "comes dropping slow," and hopes that had burgeoned turned to despair.

On the Shankill Road on a Saturday in October 1993, when streets were filled with hundreds of shoppers, a bomb exploded. Two IRA men, wearing white coats to give the impression that they were delivery men, carried it hidden under a cover on a plastic tray into a fish shop, where they believed the command staff of the UDA were to meet in a room upstairs. The dcvice detonated prematurely, killing the fishmonger and those inside the shop as the building collapsed, killing others who were passing in the street and were soon buried under it. Police, locals, and ambulance men all converged on the site, using axes, crowbars, and their bare hands to dig out the dead and survivors. As limbs were lifted out, rescuers listened for a groan or a breath, and a doctor, who later wrote about it in a British medical journal, described looking at a young woman whose eyes, when he opened them and shone a pen torch in, had dust on the glistening corneas that had the vague opacity of death. "I do not know if this is human," he wrote.

Reprisals were swift. The UDA leader whom they had hoped to kill let it be known that "John Hume, Gerry Adams, and the nationalist electorate will pay a heavy, heavy price for today's atrocity."

Loyalist gunmen went on a spree, killing six Catholics that week, and then in a lounge bar at Greysteel, where Catholics had gathered at Halloween for a country-and-western dance, catastrophe struck. "Trick or treat," two gunmen called out as they went in, people at first believing it was a Halloween prank, until the gunshots rang out. It was a young boy, Raymond, who had previously driven me on my visits to the North, and who was in that pub but miraculously escaped, who described the scene of carnage, the screams, walls with blood and bloodied limbs, a picture of gore. The doctor who looked into the dying girl's cornea on the Shankill Road and wondered if it was human would have to ask the same of this massacre.

It would be fourteen years later, in 2007, after numerous failed initiatives, avowals, and disavowals, that the two mavericks, putative men of cloth, the Reverend Ian Paisley and the Jesuitical Gerry Adams, came from their lairs of power to sit side by side at a diamond-shaped table and face the cameras to announce that they were ready to work together in a newly formed Irish assembly.

I was alone in my house in London and watched it with understandable emotion and incredulousness, watched, as David McKittrick put it, "the closest thing to a miracle that Belfast had ever seen." I remembered that, when my interview with Adams had ended, he had conveyed me downstairs to the bookshop, to give me a gift of a book of Belfast sayings in Belfast parlance. A lonely, iconoclastic figure, yet, despite everything, with that innate certainty which would eventually lead him to the grand staircase of power. I remembered, too, that by having written about him with an openness, for my "silly novelettish mentality," I would be described in an English newspaper as "the Barbara Cartland of long-distance Republicanism."

New York, New York

I was often invited by some or other American university to teach for a semester, and I welcomed it. It was a respite, a stimulus, and an escape from the doldrums. I taught several times at City College in New York, which is on the corner of 136th Street and Convent Avenue.

New York was always enlivening, it was as if the air itself had some strange elixir. I could barely contain myself in the customs queue, which was often at a standstill, officials behind desks bent over forms, and then, with a maddening sadism, wandering off, deciding to have us sweat it out and fuel the multiple fear and my own particular fear that my visa might not be in order.

Then the excitement of a taxi ride in from the airport, usually at dusk, passing the few remembered landmarks, the site of the World's Fair, with a huge globe of the world perched in a ring of steel, then on past some clapboard houses, all identical, and towering blocks of flats, gray and huddled together, before coming to the bridge and into the purlieu of Manhattan itself. The flutters of impatience became more urgent as we got nearer to my destination, willing the face of the traffic signal to go green, "Go green!" Along Fifth Avenue was a low building in the park set far back, like a keeper's cottage, that in its quiet and its quaintness seemed a relic of the old New York, the one my mother used to speak of and the one I saw in sepia advertisements for soaps and eau de cologne.

I used to stay at the Wyndham Hotel, where the welcome from Mrs. Mados was unfailing. Randy, the concierge, would be standing at the desk to present me with a single red rose in a flute of glassy paper. Then a bellman (one of whom was later to become a famous Hollywood agent and whom, years later, by chance, I would see escorting Nicole Kidman in a restaurant in Los Angeles) would bring me up to Suite 1006; there, waiting, were more flowers and telephone messages on slips of pink paper, with a tick on the sign that read YOU WERE CALLED. The whole world, like the Statue of Liberty itself, opening its arms to me, and England was a nunnery by comparison.

When I recall the many people I met there, it still comes as an amazement. Several introductions were through Milton Goldman, a theatrical agent whose parties in Sutton Place were legendary, as was his habit of strenuously introducing everyone to everyone else, including Arnold Weisberger, his companion of many years, to Arnold's own mother. It was with Milton that I met Stravinsky's second wife, Vera de Bosset, in her nineties, sitting totally composed, while we queued to exchange a few clichéd words with her. At a swish party given by the designer Halston, to which Milton brought me, I met Martha Graham. She was tall and commanding, and seemed to me to be the reincarnation of a tribal ancestress. I remember our conversation and the coincidence of the fact that we each had a title for a work yet to be done and that title was "Blood Memory," which she would use for her autobiography, in which she claimed life was dance and dance was life.

In the lobby of the Wyndham there were always celebrities, and once I was introduced to Coral Browne, who, with barbed glee, since she was going out to dinner with Mr. and Mrs. Mados, promised to bring me back a doggy bag. The rebuff was short-lived, because the next night, for a St. Patrick's Day celebration along with Gregory Peck, I would recite Irish poetry from the pulpit of St. Patrick's Cathedral to the accompaniment of Phil Coulter's music. To the rather deserted dining room, where the red color scheme owed a distinct debt to the Russian Tea Room on nearby Fifty-seventh Street, I invited people, Vincent, the operatic maître d', treating us to some of his favorite arias. My children wondered when I was coming home, and Carlo reminded me that the washing machine was broken. Sasha, however, was jubilant to report that, along with Laurence Sterne, Gene O'Neill, Oscar Wilde, and Samuel Beckett, I had been featured in a song by Dexy's Midnight Runners.

On an earlier visit, for the publication of *August Is a Wicked Month,* I had stayed at the Algonquin, and also by chance met a galaxy of people. There was a long session in the Blue Bar with Thornton Wilder, who next day was setting out on a Greyhound bus across America, admonishing me for my yearning heroines, enjoining me to follow the pluck and dauntless humor of Rosalind in *As You Like It.* I would receive a handwritten letter, which read, *Dear Edna O'Brien, Will you meet me in Blue Bar at seven o'clock this evening, and if we like each other after five minutes, we will go and eat big fish or other animal. Yours, Günter Grass. PS: This is my first letter in English.* When I came down the stairs a few minutes after seven, he was already on the house phone, presumably ringing my room. It was in those days that I was sometimes mistaken for Maureen O'Hara, and once in a taxi, irked with being asked yet again, I said, "Yes, yes, I am," to which the driver replied, "You're a goddamn liar, 'cos she was in this cab yesterday and you're not her."

So why had he asked me? Only because he thought I might be her sister or something.

Oh yes, there were other New Yorks, apart from these gilded haunts, the New York I had read of in many works of fiction. There was Saul Bellow's *Seize the Day,* a New York for which the celluloid *dream,* through aggrandizement and delusion, though different from that of Gatsby's, had also turned to a "valley of ashes." There was Isaac Bashevis Singer's New York, immigrants who met in old-fashioned cafés, without a groschen, but with rich memories of rabbis and matchmakers, imbuing life with improbable tales of love and riches. There were the bohemians of Anatole Broyard's down in Greenwich Village, and the junkies and hoodlums and hookers and transvestites in Hubert Selby's *Last Exit to Brooklyn*.

Brooklyn, just across the bridge, where my mother had lived for eight years and where I intended to go to research the novel I would write about her. For Brooklyn, New York, was the "vast Gomorrah across the water." I had read that. I had read also that Walt Whitman recited Shakespeare from the top of a stagecoach, drew inspiration from its people, and drew water from the street well. There, too, Henry Miller would chart his spiritual initiations from his time in the flophouses, and it was also where Norman Mailer was known to have stabbed a wife.

From Brooklyn my mother had brought a cache of memories that she kept locked, and only once, as she was confiding in another woman, did I overhear her talk of the man she loved, ah, the man she should have married, and how, strangely, as he walked her home one night and they passed a house of ill repute, he had suggested that they might go in. She had worked first as a maid in a house and then graduated to becoming a cutter in the tailor room of a big department store. She had brought back glamorous clothes, for which she found little wear—a black gauze fan, appliquéd with splashes of white rock rose, a georgette dance dress, and silver shoes. What I have is not those fal-lals but the scissors from the cutting room, half the size of a shears, rusted now and kept in a drawer, a prized possession, as if between us there is still something waiting to be cut.

The first thing I would do when I arrived in Suite 1006 at the

Wyndham, half-believing that it was mine, was to look under the papers that lined the drawers of bureaus, to see if notes I had left were still there, and sometimes they were and sometimes they were not. I would go out onto the terrace, where there was a terracotta tub, to see if the packets of seeds that I had sprinkled had flowered, and occasionally a few limp petals of pansies had braved the city clay. My visits were usually in December, the zesty time, when real snow was no match for the artificial pageantry in the windows on Fifth Avenue. I was constantly surprised that from the volumes of books in the glass-fronted bookcase nobody had stolen Tom Wolfe's *The Bonfire of the Vanities.*

Up the street from the Wyndham and two doors away from Sixth Avenue was my favorite restaurant, Jean Lafitte. At that corner a maniac drove by regularly with the window down, shouting obscenities at well-dressed women, believing they were prostitutes, and in my long green coat I too was the butt of his rage. In that stretch of street by a luggage shop three shamrocks had been beveled into the tarmac, and nearby was a delicatessen, the specialty being chicken soup with dumplings, which they were famous for.

I was with the film director Neil Jordan, and from a nearby table Miloš Forman carried on a lively conversation. I knew Miloš from Prague, remembering that first day I met him when I visited him in a tiny apartment in which the heat from the black iron stove was tepid. I had searched him out because of my admiration for his films *Black Peter* and *Loves of a Blonde,* and on that first visit he said, "How do I ask a woman to take her coat off, without taking her clothes off?" I said that, for some, there was not an appreciable difference. There in Jean Lafitte he scolded me again for preferring his friend, the director Ivan Passer, when they had stayed with me in Deodar Road in Putney, and he remembered a dinner I gave, where four people, including himself and Rita Tushingham, had been allergic to lobster.

My evenings were always full, thanks to my two stalwart friends Arthur and Alexandra Schlesinger, who had included me in nightly invitations. I can still see those gatherings and "that brooch of faces," as Philip Larkin once said, the sanctums that exuded rose-breath and privilege. The reception halls of the apartment buildings would be full of flowers, seas of red poinsettias on the chessboard marbled floors, and in the autumn one could be excused for thinking one had strayed into a forest, what with the cornucopias of leaves, fruits, branches, and berries. There would be a porter to escort one up in one of the waiting elevators that were padded in red leather, with a narrow velvet seat. Ah, the voices, the voices, as one was disgorged from the elevator into the penthouse suite. Famous faces, writers, actors, politicians, and a phalanx of jewels, enough to support a starving country. The hostesses always had such composure, like Thomas Dewing's *Lady with a Lute.* I recall a Magritte, a garden in blue dusk, with blue cedars that led up to a ghostly house. In a different salon there was a Picasso, in which, astonishingly for a bullring, he had chosen pale green colors and not the hot red blood of the corrida. The audacity of genius. In the Frick Collection, where I often went to sit, I was astonished that for *Saint Francis in the Desert,* Bellini had draped rock in whey green and added a donkey, bamboo trees, and a little lectern for homeliness.

The seating at those grand dinners would be carefully, sedulously, planned, and one was either above or below the salt. Often I was lucky enough to be next to Norman Mailer, who had mellowed with the years. I had known him in his swaggering days, the very first being at a party of George Plimpton's, when he called out to the author Bill Manville as he left, "Manville, tell Plimpton I said good night." Another time he suggested that we might have been married, since my voice reminded him of that of his former wife Jeanne Campbell, who was Scottish. There were many Mailers: Mailer the artist, Mailer the bruiser, Mailer the intellectual, forever trying to shrug it off with fights and confrontation, and Mailer the boyish man who shyly kissed me in Saint John the Evangelist Catholic church in Brooklyn, where we had gone to shelter from a shower of rain. He gave me a walking tour of the city, as I was researching the novel I was intending to write about my mother. When I told him the gist of it, he shook his head, said it was too interior, then repeated it, "You're too interior, that's your problem." He suggested that instead of that I should go with him and George Plimpton to Havana, where they were putting on the play he had written about Fitzgerald and Hemingway and their wives. Their Zelda had dropped out, and I could fill in for her, except that I was due to teach at Bard College. Truth to tell, I would gladly have swapped the sedate environs of Annandale-on-Hudson for the racy nights in Havana. His literary heroes were Dos Passos, Thomas Wolfe, Henry Miller, and, most of all, Hemingway, Hemingway, so great and so lamentably misunderstood. For a man who had gone on record as saying that he had less connection with the past than any writer, Norman's memories of Brooklyn that day were acute: the boardinghouse where he wrote his first book, the house where he lived with his first wife, his mother's house, and the famous house where during a party he had thrust a penknife in his second wife's chest. People recognized him in the street, men touched his arm as we went by, and in the various pubs to which we repaired for a quick shot, the owners and the bartenders were all beholden to him.

The grand dinners, on the Upper East Side, or Sutton Place, or Central Park West, always passed surprisingly quickly, since there was the ritual of speeches and especially the awaited speech of the guest of honor. A little bell would be tinkled, at which my heart invariably sank. Some pundit—it was always a male who had just returned from Beijing or Istanbul or Jerusalem—was about to disclose his findings, air his sagacities, put the world to rights, the world nevertheless going its mad, murderous, money-crazed way. One such night I escaped to the bathroom, and there, just sitting on the lavatory seat, was Mrs. John Kenneth Galbraith, simply passing the time. She had heard it all before. That bathroom, like all the bathrooms, was a temple of quiet: vials, glass-stoppered bottles and amphoras, balms and salves and perfumes that might have come from the apothecaries in Florence in the reign of the Medicis.

Having received so much hospitality, I was honor-bound to give a dinner. It was on a Sunday, when people would have returned from the Hamptons or Connecticut. It was a warm evening, and those at the bar at Jean Lafitte huddled by the opened window, with noises from the street drifting in. The first to arrive were the Schlesingers, who brought Yevtushenko and his wife, Masha, then Bill Walton, Marietta Tree, Carlos and Sylvia Fuentes, and Al Pacino, with his beautiful girlfriend Lyndall Hobbs. There were also several children and the friends of children, more people than I had bargained for, and a center leaf had to be added to the round table. Mayhem. Coke, Diet Coke, Stoli, Grey Goose, bourbon. No oysters. They never served oysters. No shellfish, as it was Sunday. Al Pacino, quite shy, wearing a bandanna and trying to be invisible, nevertheless created a stir. It was as if a bush telegram had gone round to say he was there, and the place filled up. The maitre d', Claude, erstwhile a paragon of tact, asked for a private word with me; his friend had appeared as an extra in a film with Mr. Pacino and would like to come over and say "Hi." I pleaded with him to wait. Yevtushenko stood, to have his wife take a picture of him with Al, then said that he had sent a play to Dustin Hoffman, and not having had an acknowledgment, he would now like to send it to Pacino. I began to feel embarrassed, especially as I barely knew him. We had met two nights before, backstage, when he and Suzanne Bertish had starred in Oscar Wilde's *Salome.* It had taken some coaxing to get him to come out to dinner with us, and I can still recall the little jugs of red and white wine, and flatbread, thin as communion wafer, with specks of rosemary. Whereas in Jean Lafitte he fell silent, in Orso's the conversation rippled—Oscar Wilde, his mother Speranza, John the Baptist, Herod—while at intervals Suzanne got up to have a smoke by the coat rack. There he had stories to tell. Maybe he had not been a janitor in the Bronx as a young man, but it was enough to hear it, to enter into it, marveling on how the future Michael Corleone, who knew nothing about boilers, was called one Christmas Eve to one of the apartments where a boiler had burst and, finding a ravishing woman answering the door, had insanely asked her if she would care to dance.

The place was packed, and the service understandably erratic. Someone got a steak tartare who hadn't ordered it, to which the overwrought waiter said, "You're down for it anyhow." Arthur was adamant about onions. "No onions," he kept saying loudly. A soufflé expired before my eyes, and children were having tantrums about their chips not having arrived. I swore I would never invite famous people to a restaurant again. Were it not for Arthur, the evening would have been a disaster. People were beholden to him. He was being asked about the Presidents he had known, their foibles, their greatness, their pluses and their minuses. He loved JFK with an uncritical love and made no secret of it, but he had to concede that no President of his acquaintance answered to Emerson's ideal—"The great leader suppresses himself." No Russian. Or Japanese. Or German. Or

Cambodian. Or Chinese. Drink pepped things up. I prayed that the Gypsy woman would not come around with red roses, as that would lead to more anarchy, but then remembered that she showed up in a different restaurant over on the West Side, where there were booths with colored glass paneling. I ate almost nothing. Our table, as they say, was the cynosure of all. Why did everything in New York have to be extreme, the good times and the bad times, the welcomes and the snubs? Why did Robert Mapplethorpe, whom I met in a loft down in the Village, look at me and look through me with such cold, compassionless eyes? Why did I receive so many roses all in one day? Why, when sitting aimlessly in a café on the Upper East Side, with a little bit of plastic trellis separating it from the adjoining café, was I accosted by a group of angry, vociferous men, who were handing out leaflets that poured shame on a scab employer on Ninety-third Street who hired nonunion contractors? Why, when I skittered along a parquet floor in Lindsay Duncan's rented apartment and broke my shoulder, was I too embarrassed to say so as the group watched the Oscars?

I paid the bill in Jean Lafitte after they had all left. Still sitting on the high stool was the large black man, who had been an extra on the film with Pacino and was chuckling at the fact that they had exchanged a few words.

Afterward I sat on a stone seat that circled a tree, halfway down to the Wyndham, exhaling, exhaling. I was alone now but still unnerved, as if it were an inquisition I had narrowly escaped from and not a dinner party. No Lady with a Lute, I. The skyscrapers came into their own, with the street almost deserted; they seemed to sway at their summits, up there in the languid heavens. Elderly couples from the various restaurants strolled by, and vendors were pushing their carts, their dark skins blended into the darkness, while in the carts, under cover, lay the handbags and scarves that on the morrow would be on display over at the corner on Fifth Avenue or up on Sixth Avenue, where the raving zealot cruised.

My play *Virginia* was in rehearsal at the Public Theatre, and Kate Nelligan was asking me to take her through Virginia Woolf 's last walk, across the fields in Sussex, before putting stones in her pockets to drown herself. A stagehand beckoned me aside to say there was a phone call from Jackie Onassis, but that most likely it was a hoax. It wasn't. There was Jackie at the other end of the phone, wondering if I had any time for her. I had, and so I was invited to dinner for the following evening. Her apartment was exquisite: there were modern paintings and sculptures, along with torsos and figurines from the ancient world. Jackie, feather-light, girlish, affectionate, capricious and willful, a Scheherazade who, instead of telling stories, encouraged them in others. That night, as she inquired into what I was writing and if the teaching curtailed it (which indeed it did), I remember her saying, "I want you to have a piece of the pie."

It amazed me that she would jog in Central Park, go to Morrissey's hair salon on Madison Avenue, walk all over without a bodyguard; but, as she said, sometimes people stopped her, though it was twenty years later, to tell her exactly what they were doing on that day in Dallas in November 1963. As I got to know her, I saw how she could do this, because of an instinctive gift to distance herself and, if necessary, to freeze someone out. In the ten years of our friendship, we had one rift that I regretted. Natasha Richardson invited me to a screening of *Suddenly, Last Summer,* in which she starred, and her heartfelt hope was that I could bring Jackie along. I mistook it to be a private screening, but instead there were hordes of photographers who swarmed on Jackie, asking her to look this way or that, and with a tartness she said, "Edna, this is *not* a private screening."

Next day, from a shop, she sent me a gift of a velvet drawstring purse with a note attached that read, "For a lock of your true-love's hair." She was not a romantic, but she held on to the shibboleths of it, to see her through the carnivore world of celebrity.

We are to meet at a cinema on Sixty-second Street, and it is pouring with rain. I get there early, only to discover there are no films showing, as a private screening had been booked that evening. Cars and taxis, bumper to bumper, sloshing rain, and presently an argument between a taxi driver and another driver, obscenities flying, *"Asshole, asshole,"* as they get into the street to fight it out. The woman passenger in the taxi has slunk out and is asking me to please hide her, as she does not want to be called by the police as a witness. Both men are staggering, and like wrestlers in a comic clip, even as they maul each other, they have to cling to one another for balance, but they are not abdicating the fray.

Jackie arrives, headscarf well down over her face and an umbrella with a spoke missing. Not that anyone notices, as all the attention is on the pugilists, cars hooting, traffic at a standstill, and the wailing sound of the sirens coming closer and closer. Jackie surveys the scene and says it is hardly one that will make it to the nice neat happenings in *The New Yorker*'s "Talk of the Town." She is sorry to be late. I outline the situation about there being no movie, and walking on, we look in vain for a taxi. She suggests we take a bus, but the bus queues are miles long, and then, without a word, she nods and I follow her to the entrance of Bloomingdale's on Third Avenue, where the chauffeurs sit. She taps on the window of the very first limousine, disturbing a driver in his nap, and in that inimitable voice, with its slight breathiness, asks, "Do you think you could take us to 1040 Fifth Avenue?" Then, with a beautiful dexterity, she pulls the headscarf back, fluffs her hair, so that, to his disbelief, he realizes he is being asked by Jackie Onassis to take her home to upper Fifth Avenue.

That evening in her apartment there was only us, as her companion, Maurice Tempelsman, believing that we were still at the cinema, had arranged to meet us later on in a restaurant. She spoke of the Kennedy men, the undoubted and inherited magnetism and their weakness, implicitly alluding to their infidelities, which she skimmed over. Mr. Kennedy Senior was not averse to touching her knee under the table, something her husband, even as President, was resentful of. The very first time she met Jack, she "fell," although she disguised the fact that she had fallen; she knew in her heart that by marrying him life would be a roller coaster, yet the alternative would be unthinkable. After the President's assassination, Robert Kennedy was the one to keep her from falling apart, calling on her in her widowhood each evening, so much so that many mornings she would find that his dog was outside her door, just like Argus, the dog in Homer, awaiting Odysseus, his master. She was at her most confiding and affectionate that particular evening. I was one of the three people on the planet whom she loved most. I said, how would it be, were she and I to fall in love with the same man, at which she remonstrated, said she would want me to have him, she would be my bridesmaid, but I did not believe her.

She had no dog then, but once upon a time she and Ari Onassis did have one. In most of the salons in New York small dogs presided, nestling on woven tapestry cushions that bore the exact likenesses of them. The film producer Tom Johnson was the one who told me the story about Ari's dog and Jackie's *froideur.* Late one night he was walking down Fifth Avenue with a very pretty young girl, when they chanced to meet Onassis walking the dog. They were invited up, and Jackie, who was preparing for bed, was none too cordial. To make matters worse, Ari flirted with the young girl, who was both dazzled and slightly tipsy, and the visit was cut short. The next day Jackie had a large bouquet of flowers sent to the girl, with a card bearing Onassis's signature. The girl subsequently made a fool of herself and rang Onassis, who did not even remember her. It told me something about Jackie and that inscrutable trait that is the essence both of power and of the handmaidens of power. She was different from the other women, at once more amenable, more indiscreet, and yet aloof. She might grace this or that gathering, arriving like the costumed fairy queen who would mingle for a short while and then vanish. She was a reader, she worked in a publishing house, and she loved literature. She wrote to me about my books and the books of others. Once, when I sent her Zbigniew Herbert's *Still Life with a Bridle* from Loeb's bookshop on Madison Avenue, that same night she penned a three-page letter, extolling this Polish poet she had never heard of. Her last letter to me, on notepaper the color of dark blue hyacinth, as she was dying, was full of hope, the spring, things we would do, life at full tilt again. It was not sentimentality; it was self-preservation. Long before she was a First Lady, she had the certainty of one who was cherished, and the little girl in her held on to that; it was her armor, and it saw her through varying nightmares with astonishing poise. Ironically, Marilyn Monroe, who in her sheath dress sang the birthday tribute for President Kennedy in 1962 (when Jackie was noticeably absent), had no sheath at all, the little girl in her had been cut to the core. Jackie was the opposite, she went through life veiled, and left it with her stardust intact.

New York friendships survived the long intervals, and each time I returned, it seemed that they were just waiting to be resumed. Roger Straus would come from his office in Union Square to take me to lunch at La Côte Basque, that bastion of civilization that had been the setting for Truman Capote's unfinished novel, *Answered Prayers.* Roger, so dapper in his white suit and silk handkerchief, with a zest for gossip and an uncanny instinct for literature. Of all his authors, and I counted myself fortunate to be one of them, his avowed favorite was Joseph Brodsky, and he would carry one of Joseph's books around, just to show it.

Brodsky was a brilliant, bristling man, with a cold scorn for "literary filibusters." It was a catchphrase of his, along with "cat's pajamas," sundry words that he had picked up. He had a liking for the ballad "The Night Before Larry Was Stretched," which Brendan Behan had sung to him. It was a droll song of Larry about to be executed, when his friends, a bunch of Dublin bowsies, pawned their clothes in order to buy enough drink to sit all night for the wake, to give him a good send-off with drink and snuff and cards and song, before the noose was tied.

Joseph had the generosity of a pharaoh, and often, with David Rieff, I would be invited to the Russian Samovar, where Roman, the owner, would welcome us. Once he gave me a gift of a blue china egg, which I wore for luck. Joseph and Roman might have just arrived in New York City, out of Russia—not totalitarian Russia, with its poisonings and its purges, but the great Mother Russia of the steppes and the tundras that had given birth to such complex and subversive geniuses as Pushkin, Gogol, Mandelstam, and Bulgakov, whom Joseph quoted with a plenary flourish. There was no mention of his enforced times in mental institutions or prison in the cold north or the fact that he stood trial as a "parasite" before being expelled. All his life he had fought for poetry, and he won. He made jokes: Comrade Gorbachev had a mustache, as had Comrade Stalin, the Kremlin mountaineer, whose name was also that of a Georgian boot polish. We sometimes sparred over Chekhov, because he agreed with his muse, Anna Akhmatova, who had included him in her *Rosary* cycle of poems, saying that Chekhov was "uniformly drab, a sea of mud, with absence of heroism and martyrdom, absence of depth and darkness and sublimity." Pasternak did not think that, as I would remind Joseph, but peace was restored by his acknowledgment of the fact that "Ward No. 6" was a great story. The vodka came in little cruets, which because of their bright colors were deceptively harmless, and I cannot say that we were totally sober when Roman would bring us to the inner room, to inscribe the visitors book, where Joseph had already written and deleted several lines in Russian. One night they walked me from West Fifty-fourth Street to West Fifty-eighth, two chanting dervishes, reciting Pushkin in their native tongue, their voices deep and sonorous, rolling their *r*'s, their sounds so alien, yet accruing an audience who, though they did not understand it, felt the passion of the words.

The streets of New York always seemed to me to have more life, more immediacy, than those soulless apartment buildings with their long, lonely corridors, dark brown carpets, newspapers several days old, and a deathly, suspenseful hush, like that in the great novels of Georges Simenon.

Whenever I could, I would be outdoors, and even in winter, I would choose a bench outside a café on Sixty-fourth Street and sit there to see the world go by. It was December, Christmas in full swing, Santa a block away, his shabby shoes in glaring contrast to the festive red and white, and in the side garden of the Catholic church snow had lodged on various bushes, making white floppy flowers the size of cauliflowers. There were the voices and the jingle bells, snatches of life stories, dissension on cell phones, the caterwauling of the horns, and birds scrabbling for crumbs. Many of the women who went by wore fur coats, and you could see the shiver on the thinner hairs of the collars where the wind ruffled them. People were hustling and jogging, mothers pushed strollers, two women paused to look at the price of cakes in the café and backed off, affronted, one saying, "You know what... I'll bake my own." A wife, who with her husband, Ted, had recently seen a very raunchy play, was telling her friend how, since then, life at home got "so degenerate." In the midst of all that medley, a young Asian boy passed along, carrying a white orchid in a box, snug in its bed of tissue, his pride in it as great as if he were carrying the Olympic torch. The woman sitting next to me on the narrow seat coughed repeatedly and said flowers always got to her. There were art galleries across the way, so rarefied that only a connoisseur would dare go in. But higher up on the same buildings were the makeshift showrooms, and air-conditioning boxes, black and sooted, hanging off the windows.

I made friends and acquaintances all over New York. I had often gone downtown to see quacks who were to lead me to my inner self, my combat zone, and my pleasure-seeking endorphins. An astrologer had me in her clutches, and before each session her elderly mother relieved me of two hundred dollars, the twenty obligatory red roses, and a piece of jewelry. It was there, too, one Sunday, at one of those apartments, that I was invited to meet the beautiful Japanese artist Kazuko. She was famous for her crystals, which were like so many thousand flowers—fobs, pendants, rings, and necklaces, little worlds that brimmed with light, the light of sunsets, the light of yellow muscatel, the light of pink roses and lapis and sapphire and rubies shimmering away on strips of white cloth. Later she moved to Fifty-seventh Street, to an apartment that looked out on the mists and sunrises and sunsets of Central Park. Whereas formerly she had worn black, she was now wearing white, as in bridal array for a groom. That groom would be the "Bobby Bird."

One morning on her windowsill there was a wounded bird, small and brownish and to all intents almost dead. She took it in, nursed it back to life, fed it glucose and honey from a pipette, and had its broken wing removed. Soon it flopped about, though bandaged, and Bobby Bird was almost ready to start his trills, which, alas, lacked the sweetness of music. She had read somewhere that birds, each night, dream the songs they will sing, and so she decided to enrich the dreams of her little charge by playing Mozart all the time. Her studio was filled with the sounds of Mozart, and after I had gone home, her letters would be filled with news of Bobby's prowess, singing to his heart's content, no interest or curiosity about the world beyond, no yen to escape to one of the trees in Central Park and the morning dews. She would dilate on Bobby's burgeoning genius with song, on how they had graduated to Bach's *Oratorio,* her pride in him like a mother's who sees her child excel at school, not forgetting to mention his tantrums and irrational jealousy when buyers came to look at her most recent collection.

Whenever I arrived at the Wyndham, there would be a gift from her waiting for me, a necklace or a ring, and a further account of Bobby's expanding repertoire. When I visited her, bringing white flowers now she wore only white, I would have to endure Bobby's tantrums, as he flicked the crystals that bedecked his cage, the very crystals that contained the special healing powers chosen for his highly strung temperament and that he was threatening to destroy.

Then one year I came and found no package at the Wyndham. In the hall of her apartment the elderly porter, recognizing me, came out from behind the desk, throwing his hands up helplessly. I did not have to be told it to know that the Bobby Bird and his owner were gone.

I would be driven to City College by a man called George, who kept a Sten gun under his seat. He was a fast talker, and on each journey I got a summary of the nightly murders, rapes, and robberies. Leaving Park Avenue and going north for several blocks into Harlem was like entering another country, the brownstones crumbling and dilapidated, the streets almost empty, the few children on the sidewalks and men, alone or in a group, staring out but looking inward, while George filled me in on the latest crime rate. It was before Harlem's second Renaissance, when tourists were lured by soul food and gospel music. I thought of Lorca, who had walked there in 1930, when he was a student at Columbia, seeing it as a place eclipsed, sensing what he called the "garnet violence" running in the blood.

Because I never went to university, I always found the environs of any campus forbidding, what with all those bicycles and lockers and gowns and anonymity. In the classroom itself, I was conscious of Vladimir Nabokov's unbending proprietorial judgment, berating the "buxom best-sellers." The other teacher that came to my mind was Joyce, with his dilatory methods, swerving from one subject to the next, the courtesans of ancient China and the pregnancy of the Virgin Mary.

I would read to my students at first, something stirring, the escalating glee of Iago's jealousy, or Faulkner's biblical parables of the Deep South, but they were more eager to have their own work read and did not take too fondly to my reminding them of Lorca's edict for the writer: "true poetry, true effort and renunciation." One of the students was Walter Mosley, who was eager to learn, whose tastes were eclectic, and who understood the tug and traction of a perfect short story. It intrigued me long after, when he had published his famous Easy Rawlins series of crime fiction books, that I had called him aside one day and said, "You're black, Jewish, with a poor upbringing, there are writing riches therein."

On the days when I did not teach, I corrected the students' work, wrote the reports, and then walked around New York as I had never done in any other city.

Sometimes it was as if I saw ghosts, or certainly saw things that other New Yorkers had not seen. Once, I was on my way to *Traveller* magazine, which at that time was on Madison Avenue near Thirtieth Street, when at a corner I saw a group of black men, wearing caps, silent, elderly, all with sticks, waiting, as I believed, for an appointed onslaught. There was something so apprehensive about them, standing there, like avenging figures from the Old Testament, waiting for their doom.

Often I would repair to the seventh floor of the Home Section of Bergdorf Goodman. It was filled with treasures: tables, coffee tables, tallboys, whatnots, exquisite plates, glasses, ivories, cranberry bells, a veritable palace that my mother would have reveled in. One day on the escalator I sighted an outfit in the fashion department and immediately jumped off at the next floor to have a look at it. Designed by Valentino, it was a beautiful green silk georgette with pale, embossed rosettes of gold. I went week after week, watching, waiting for the price to be marked down. Each time I returned, I was certain that it would be gone, but it wasn't, it was waiting for me. Then one week it reached a figure that, though still exorbitant, I could just afford. To my dismay, it was a two-piece, when what I wanted was a jacket without the matching, skimpy miniskirt. A manageress was called. She was Chinese and smiled bafflingly at my pathetic request. Eventually, for seven hundred dollars, the jacket was mine, and as I held it, in its folds of wrapping, I might have been holding my trousseau. On the seventh floor, I sometimes imagined what it would be like to be a wife, a wife of privilege, that is, with several packages, being escorted to the side door, where a chauffeur would be waiting to take her to a white house, upstate—the gravel nicely raked, the wide lawn bordered with cedar trees, onyx lamps at "his and her" sides of the enormous bed—but then I would remember the stories of John Cheever—rancid marriages, drink, infidelities—and my daydream would come to an abrupt end.

It was in a lamp shop that I had my next little adventure. For some time I had been admiring an orange lamp, the glass shade of which had the delicate droop of a toadstool and was dotted with brown speckled spots. It would not, I reckoned, be too awkward to carry home. Eventually I went in to inquire the price. I was greeted profusely. The young man, in a black suit and black suede shoes, moved with a stealthlike ease. He was Middle Eastern, and his voice was very quiet, saying what an honor it was to have me drop by.

Presently he was reeling off his credentials. He had been to Cornell and afterward to Harvard Business School, but his real interest was the esoteric. He ran the store only to please his old man. When he heard that I was a writer, his interest quickened. He had stories to tell, stories that would make my hair stand on end. Hinting at a racy past that might easily have slipped from the pages of *The Arabian Nights,* he said that if we got to know one another, he might share some of these adventures with me. We could collaborate: his vast experience, my craft, wow, man, we could have a movie deal. The lamp was mine. For nothing. He was no tomcat, no sir, he could have all the ditzy blondes he wished for, all the alimony junkies who hung around, except that he had taste, he had soul, and he had the esoteric. He was suggesting that he and I go across to the Plaza Hotel, where he kept a permanent suite, so there would be no hassle at the desk with passport or ID. The suite was massive, two bathrooms, and the color scheme was soothing. I began to envisage scenarios. I would be in a kimono, oyster silk, eating Turkish delight or sherbet off a wooden spoon. I would be the Emma Bovary that Woody Allen put into a short story, who, having got a taste of the high life, refused to go back into the novel and commit suicide. Then again I would be a corpse, zipped up in a black plastic bag and brought out by the servants' entrance. He saw that I was hesitating, and presently I was the proud possessor of two lamps, which he would have shipped to London. The second lamp was green, the green of a grotto, and I imagined them on a table or a desk at home, winter evening, gray London light, and those bewitching lamps with veins of color rippling through them.

Being as I was from the "old country," he listed the several blends of Irish whiskey in the Plaza cocktail cabinet, and how agreeably the time would pass, listening to music, sipping our cocktails, and getting to know one another. He was so close to me now that I could see the lettering engraved on the gold medallions that hung on his dark chest. The whole experience, he could promise, would be etched in my mind forever. It was on the word "etched" that I got shaky. I made for the door and he followed. We were now outside, his voice barely audible, because in the adjoining doorway a man with cats and a litter of kittens, whose station it was, was holding up a cardboard sign alerting passersby to his pitiful circumstances.

I was sometimes invited to do readings in different states across America.

In a revolving restaurant in Duluth, I saw that it was snowing outside, and I felt like someone trapped inside a paperweight. "I will never get out of Duluth," I said to myself, and I watched the traffic down below, seeming to go at a snail's pace, crawling, as it were, along the several lanes, the headlights so wan. Bob Dylan had left Duluth just as Scott Fitzgerald had left the wheaten steppes of Minnesota, though he modeled Gatsby on a local tycoon who built the railroads joining the Great Lakes with the Pacific Ocean.

I had been invited to give a reading in a college that was a few miles outside the town, the invitation so beguiling that I found it difficult to decline. Reality was different. Duluth and its big lakes were for oceangoing vessels and not for me. Earlier that day I had had a walk down Main Street, a main street with its sad, sullen aspect, like main streets all over the world. In the porch of a church, along with various flyers, there was an announcement for a song competition, the winning prize being a trip for two to New York to see the musical *Anything Goes.* There was the Red Bull Inn, from which not a single sound emitted, and, farther along, a queue of men waiting to give blood, for which they would receive a stipend of two dollars a pint. I pitied them, just as I knew that they would despise me for my pitying of them. They wore wadded jackets, quiet men, dour men, the kind of men Bob Dylan would write a great, lonely lyric about.

Something had happened after my reading that unnerved me.

I kept being told that it was "outstanding," and the word circulated in the room where a party was being held. It was very genial. The women wore long skirts and sensible shoes, and there was a selection of salads and dips, along with white wine and mulled red wine in a jug. I was drinking the red wine when an eager young student asked me why I had been so unforgiving of my mother in my fiction, and lo, the glass of red wine literally floated out of my hand and I no longer felt outstanding. I can still see the little crimson puddle on a white rug. A message from beyond.

Up there in that revolving room, I thought of all the writers who had written about snow: Nabokov's snow-smothered estates, Hemingway's evocation of the creaks that the skis made up in the Austrian ski slopes, John McGahern's drops of blood on a wounded owl, dragging a steel trap across snows, and Sylvia Plath's line "The snow has no voice," except that it had: it was telling me, as it castled beyond the several panes of window, that I would never get out of Duluth. Four days later I did.

It is true to say that on my trips away from New York I felt somewhat stranded. In Los Angeles, where I had gone to meet producers who had taken an option on my short story "Paradise," I was more or less confined to a bungalow at the Beverly Hills Hotel, taking the odd stroll in their tropical gardens. I received large bouquets of flowers, but met nobody, and in the adjoining bungalow a man with a loud voice would ring his stockbroker in New York very early each morning and give a bawling out to the person at the other end of the line.

My forays into the film world were intermittent. In 1963, after I had left my husband, I had worked with Desmond Davis on *Girl with Green Eyes* and found it so happy and congenial that I used to walk up Curzon Street in the evening, looking forward to the next day's collaboration. Sometime after, I was invited to do a brief stint of rewriting on a film in Rome, with the director Damiano Damiani. Our method of working was this: I would write each day, and each evening he would come to the Hassler Hotel, having read the previous day's work, and in a charming but resigned way, he would hand me back the pages and say, "I think it is an herror." Eventually, in that same lobby, the producer called me aside to say that my services were no longer required and my successor was being escorted to the table where I had just sat.

For the adaptation of Andrea Newman's *Three into Two,* directed by Peter Hall, in which Claire Bloom, with beautiful restraint, played the deceived wife, Frances, I worked with the

American producer Julian Blaustein. Each morning, when I arrived at his flat in Chesham Place in London, he would hold up a white card, always with the same perplexed question: *"What is the motivation of Frances's vagina?"* I didn't have an answer.

It was in London one bright, solitary Saturday evening that a surprise call came from John Huston, whom I had not seen or heard from for at least ten years. There he was, with that inimitable, persuasive voice, inviting me to Puerto Vallarta to work with him on a script. I was jubilant. It was a novel by A. E. Ellis called *The Rack,* and there, in the heat of Mexico, I would hope to construct love scenes set in a sanatorium in the deep snows of Switzerland. The script sessions went well, and Huston was full of praise at first for scenes that I had written. He would arrive each morning about eleven, like a high priest, in a long white tunic shirt, coughing on the stairs. He was followed by his dog Don Diego. From the maid, Lupa, I knew that Don Diego could tear a person to pieces. At the canine school to which he went, Don Diego had been taught certain key words, which when spoken were the cue to go for the jugular. It was not always easy to concentrate on script matters, seeing Don Diego's rhubarb gums and dark molars, knowing that if, by the merest fluke, I uttered one of those key words, I would be a goner. Not that I could mention it. Huston loved animals and only respected people who also loved animals. "Honey, I can't stand cowards" was a refrain I heard many times.

Things went well for the first month, although I almost expired in the heat and was covered with various creams and sprays to ward off the mosquitoes. I had been relieved of all my possessions, so that my wardrobe for the remaining ten weeks was scant, not that it mattered.

For his birthday that August I had managed, with what I might only call clairvoyance, to find the only two bottles of

Dom Pérignon in all of Puerto Vallarta. Huston came with his much younger girlfriend, Mariella, and it proved to be one of those enchanted nights. He was at his most expansive, as he talked and reminisced, recalling his affection for certain actors, but especially Bogey and his father, Walter Huston, calling him "Dad, Dad" with the sentiments of a young man. He talked too of the house in Ireland, St. Clarens, and the Galway hunts, the paintings of Juan Gris, and the first time he saw Bernini's *The Ecstasy of Saint Teresa.* Sometime later he began to reverse his opinion of the script, vehemently and relentlessly. Scenes that he had admired, he now hated. Dialogue that he had said was written "only by a spirit" was now useless. "What is this, honey, what is this half-baked rubbish?" he would ask, and I became so unsure, so certain of my own failure, that I could not tell if "Hello" was a good line or a disastrous line. After he left each day around lunchtime, I would indulge in a bit of weeping. Lupa asked why I was crying. In halting Spanish I said I was crying for home and for my children and for roses. It sounded somewhat pretentious, but my vocabulary was limited. The next morning she arrived with three roses that she had stolen from some garden on her way to work. Three roses, wilting in the heat. We put them in a tumbler of water, and when Huston came for yet another tense session, he noticed them, saw their depleted condition, and asked, "Which of these is you, honey?" I pointed to the most limp of the three, at which he chuckled and said, "Oh my my, you do yourself a disservice, I think you're that one." His voice was low and conducive as he picked another rose, only to see the petals fall one by one in his hand with the whiteness of milk. Four more blistering weeks to go.

The film was never made. I learned that the Hollywood moguls were livid when he showed them the script, and I felt ashamed that I had let him down. Yet the last time we talked he was magnanimous. Even though he was ill, he was filled with excitement, preparing to shoot Joyce's *The Dead,* for which his son Tony had written the script and which his daughter Anjelica would star in. No longer the White Hunter with the Black Heart, as Peter Viertel had called him, but a Prospero, who had chosen for his last work Joyce's tender elegy on death.

It was December 2009 when my play *Haunted* opened at the 59th Street Theatre in New York. Critics in England had been enthusiastic about it, and I somehow looked forward to the same reception. It was not to be. I had wakened very early in my hotel, waiting for the good news. By eight o'clock and feeling jittery, I rang my friend Marilyn Lownes, who was giving me a birthday party that evening. Upon hearing the first few disappointing and damning adjectives, I asked her to go no further. The newspaper, as I well knew, had been delivered around six, and was on the outside doorknob in a plastic folder, but I felt disinclined to open it. Having heard the verdict, I picked it up, went down the corridor to the quarters where the staff worked, and found the double doors ajar. In there was the hum of various fridges, large vacuum cleaners, and trolleys piled with breakfasts half-eaten that had big white napkins folded over them, as might a corpse. It contrasted lamentably with the neatness of the corridors, the plush carpeting, the tall flowers that had to live in a sort of twilight zone, and the unoffending soulless pictures along the walls. A young man, whom I recognized as the surly one who constantly checked the minibar, showed slight offense at my having barged in there and was at a loss when I handed him the folded newspaper, saying, "Burn this."

The street where Marilyn and Victor lived led from First Avenue toward Sutton Place and the East River, and still clung to its fond legends, Marilyn Monroe, Arthur Miller, Bobby Short, and Cy Coleman all having lived there. It was in fairy-tale mood, what with real snow and simulated snow, Christmas lights, Hanukkah candles, and doormen in tuxedos, running with a breezy alacrity to get taxis, their whistles shrill and rivalrous in the crisp cold air.

"It's Fellini... it's eclectic," Marilyn said of the party, which was in full swing when she met me in the front hall. She was wearing a gold brocade dress and gold lace shoes, drawing me into a room that was alive with chatter and Frank Sinatra striking the witchcraft keynote:

> Those fingers in my hair
> That sly come-hither stare
> That strips my conscience bare
> It's witchcraft

At a side table presents that I had been sent were stacked, and a bowl of chocolate roses, cream-colored, exactly resembled real roses, even down to a little brown sugared stamen in the center. Robert Downey was telling me that there was no God, no White Light, when one passed over. He could vouch for it, because after being given wrong prescriptions that were almost fatal due to his diabetes, he nearly passed away.

"You weren't dead enough, honey," his wife, Rosemary, said.

"No God and no White Light," he repeated.

"You weren't certified dead," Rosemary said, and everybody laughed, and more people arrived, including the three actors from *Haunted:* Brenda Blethyn, a powerhouse as Mrs. Berry; Niall Buggy, her dreaming deceiver; and Beth Cooke, the waif who unwittingly brings trouble into their threadbare abode in Blackheath, London.

Philip Roth is already there. Known to be a hermit, he sometimes comes out and is invariably the magus in any gathering. Unyieldingly scrupulous about the written word, and with a knife-edged intelligence, he is also, when in jocular mood, the funniest person on earth. I have seen him spin a story to such a dizzying height that it is like witnessing a mind in excess of itself. At his encouragement, Jake LaMotta is reenacting the fights he had fought and survived, the good fights, the great fights, the crummy fights, the besmirched fights, the bites, the close-in, the speed, the crouch, the combinations, the failures, the comebacks, building this narrative to the massacre in Chicago, on St. Valentine's Day, thirteen rounds with his nemesis Sugar Ray Robinson, when he was beaten to a pulp. To Philip, as he told me afterward, it was like a page out of fiction, to meet his boyhood hero, whose career he had assiduously followed by subscribing to *Ring* magazine. He said that, sitting opposite Jake in his twilight years, he could scarcely imagine the violence that body had taken and the violence it had inflicted.

"Thirteen rounds and he never got me down once," Jake is saying, and everyone applauds because it is well known and was often written that LaMotta's "courage in defeat had made the early Spartans seem cowardly."

A speaker was being set up in the hall, and we were ushered out for the surprise event. As guest of honor I was seated on the one high chair, the throne, men ranged at the back, women in front, the flicker of expectation in their eyes—Patricia Harty, Brenda Blethyn, Beth Cooke, Kim Cattrall, Alexandra Schlesinger, Rosemary Downey, Mary Downe, and many more. Marilyn and her tango teacher were gliding under the light of the dimmed chandelier, like two dreamers miraculously caught up in the yearning of the tango music, close and yet strangely detached, all the while their feet, as it were, painting pictures on the floor, and now and then, as he turned her round and round, the pictures were peeled off with a kick, then a second, higher, triumphant kick, as she separated from him, only to merge with him again. The young man who operated the lift was so spellbound that he kept coming up and down, drawing back the gates, just to look, to fill his eyes.

"Either it grabs you or it doesn't," Marilyn said, suddenly detaching herself from her teacher's arms, and shy now as we filed back into the room, she saying there was no way in this world that she would make a speech. Women surrounded the tango teacher, all wanting lessons, wanting his secret, to which he replied with enigmatic courtesy, "The tango is a beautiful excuse for living."

It was my turn to sit with Jake LaMotta. He was wearing a brown Stetson hat, identical to the one his young wife was wearing, which Victor had just presented her with. He watched his wife's movements with a keen interest, calling across to say she was spending too much time with that barman. His face bore no mark of the bashings it had had, except for a small clod of flesh above the nose, and his hands were smooth and white and pampered.

"You have the hands of a concert pianist," I heard myself idiotically say, to which he said, "When you break bones, they come back stronger." We had nothing in common, so that a stony silence ensued. Marilyn came and knelt by us, telling him about *Haunted* and the injustice done, and he looked from her to me and back again and asked, "Is she able to hit the spot?"

"She's able to hit the spot," Marilyn said, and he gave me a look, a little grin of acknowledgment.

It was time for music, and it was mainly left to Niall Buggy to draw on his great repertoire of Irish songs, giving them such a heft of emotion that the mood in the room changed, the faces looked softer, and eyes welled up with tears. Soon it would be the parting glass. Already I had arrived at my hotel, and walking down the long corridor and hearing the sound of the wind from the lift shaft, replicating the winds that blew in from the Atlantic, I thought of travelers who, when they hear those winds, far out at sea, know them to be a hearkening toward home.

PART FOUR

Donegal

It was to Donegal, in the most northwestern tip of Ireland, that in the 1990s I headed, in order to build a house. The very place-names so rough and musical, the country dotted with lakes and hemmed in by the mountains of Errigal, Muckish, Blue Stack, Doonish West, and Snaght.

Stephen Rea and his wife, Dolours, were the ones who led me there, Stephen in his wry Belfast way saying, "It's the best of the north and the best of the south without the fuck-up of either." In this he was gloriously mistaken.

The venture would have its excitements and its obstacles, dramas and melodramas, and the getting of a site at all necessitated a wiliness to interpret that no might possibly mean yes and that any yes was equivocal. Overnight a site that might have been promised would next day be withdrawn, because of a phone call to a son or a daughter or a brother or a sister, in England or America or Australia, who opposed it.

In my ongoing search my solicitor Paddy Sweeney and the contractor Phil Ward trudged with me, often sinking into mire and quagmire, only to arrive on a spit of land that might, just might, be for sale. In Bloody Foreland, the gales were such that we were literally flung together and torn apart, like flaps of old newspaper. On another occasion Sasha, as future architect, was directed from the airport to where we stood on another bit of isolated barony, the waves hammering the headland across the way and more waves rolling ponderously around our feet. He pointed out to me that it was not only the shifting sands that were an obstacle but the hidden channels of water under the sands, so that, as in "Kublai Khan," I would end up with a house that first floated and then literally was carried out to sea.

I had almost given up.

Then one morning, in London, my friend Manus Lunny telephoned me to say that as his plane took off from Carrickfinn, he noticed a FOR SALE sign on a post down below. It was in a quiet cove, which the locals called Point, and already I saw myself there, availing of the "peace that passeth understanding."

That evening I boarded the selfsame plane, on its return journey up to Carrickfinn, and had my first spectacular view of the county. It was like a moonscape, rock and water, and the vast basin of sea scarcely stirring. The houses, all white, were like dovecotes, set so snugly down in this seemingly washy tender archipelago. I would see those houses more distinctly as Paddy, Phil, and I drove along the sea road, the small houses with hall doors varnished red and loads of washing on every clothesline. Postcard picturesqueness. The evening was balmy, and down on the shore, fawn cows ambled about, the scene, in its simplicity and timelessness, recalling the paintings of Constable. Admittedly the Church of Ireland, a stone building on a hilltop, did look forlorn, and the glass door of the public telephone, swinging open, was the last word in desolation.

There it was, at the end of the road, the FOR SALE sign, no gate, a small overgrown drive, willows clinging to each other, and the little ruin of a cottage facing the Atlantic. There were two dwellings nearby, a cottage and a larger house on a hill, with sloping front gardens. Mount Errigal towered above the sea, streaked with whitish marble, like veins of new snow. They called her "she." They said, "She's shimmering for you," and she was, the crystallized lava from millions of years before there to greet us. It was a secret corner where families had lived for decades, with the ingrained memories of a suspicion of the stranger, which I was.

What did I envisage as I stood there? Nice neighbors, getting to know the many facets of the sea, the seabirds, and perhaps a last sustained love.

Across from us the lights of Gweedore came on in twinkling succession, linking to the lights of the long low hotel, so that the effect was of looking toward a metropolis. Remembering that Maud Gonne had ridden on horseback among the peasants of Gweedore, as their cabins were being razed to the ground, I thought I would name my future house after her, except that in the end and accidentally it came to be called the Pink House.

Since I had left London that morning, two other parties had put in a bid, so that, as Paddy informed me, the sale would proceed by auction. I was on tenterhooks all next day, as I lay on a single bed in the small hotel, awaiting calls, which came regularly, as the price escalated. Rain slid down the narrow window with such swiftness that I thought I was in a car, with the windscreen being endlessly washed, and I questioned the common sense of my adventure.

By four o'clock the site was mine, and that evening Paddy, Phil, and I drove up there. A rainbow looped from Errigal across the estuary, bending its last painted toe exactly above the ruin. All three of us saw it and smiled. It faded slowly, with such cadence, getting fainter and fainter, the orange tint being the last to fade, a rind of tangerine. The men undid the padlock, pushed the door in, and we were in a small kitchen with a steep stairs to an upper floor. Everything smelled of damp and mold, since the place had been vacant for almost twenty years, and in one corner, on the mortar wall, there was a fresco that seemed to be a likeness of Christ, the Good Shepherd, in red raiment, holding a wand. I made Phil swear that no matter what alterations we would make to the place, the Good Shepherd would stay.

The site was thirty feet above sea level, and rather than have the rocks dynamited, Sasha decided that our "dacha" would be built on different levels. Many distressing meetings with the planning officer were to follow. We did not always see eye to eye, baffled at the insistence of "classic contemporary," which was the vernacular of the moment. The house, we were told, must not veer too far from the existing tradition, so that the big rooms I wanted (more sprees) had to be housed inside a series of small buildings that ran on one from another, like a series of cottages. After we abided by all these stipulations, it was finally built, and would in fact be painted in three different shades of pink, as the local paint shop had only a given number of cans of each shade and we bought them all. Just before building began, I returned one night to Donegal on a hunch, suspecting there was foul play. When I stepped into the kitchen, even before I turned on the torch, the first thing I smelled was the aftermath of a recent fire; the walls were sooted and the Good Shepherd so charred as to be unrecognizable. I went across to my neighbor, an elderly woman to whom I had once spoken and in a spirit of camaraderie had given a patch of ground for her oil tank, which by rights was within our boundary. Her lights were out, her curtains drawn, and so I sat on one of the big rocks and wrote a distraught note, wondering if she had noticed the fire. Her letter to London, a week later, could not have been more reassuring. She painted a hypothetical picture, that since it was Halloween some youths from Dungloe (nine miles away) must have cycled up, seen the FOR SALE sign that was thrown on the ground, broken in out of curiosity, and decided, as a prank, to make a fire, one that unfortunately got out of hand. I both believed it and didn't believe it. In the very next post, I got a letter from Birmingham which read, "We, the six sisters, intend to contest our late father's home-made will." This led me to fear that the purchase might be invalid. Other writers had moved into strange places and were warmly received. J. M. Synge, an author whom I love, had men and boys walking at his heels, telling him stories, girls giving him maidenhair fern that they pulled from between the rocks, and by fires at night he had heard stories of such imaginative pulse that they informed his great works. Lesser writers also wrote enviable accounts of settling in Provence or Tuscany or the Greek Islands, whereas I was in jeopardy. The fire and the warning letter were mere preludes to sinister occurrences. Gorse bushes on a hillock in front of my house were also set fire to, and I received an incensed call from the elderly woman's daughter, who lived in the house on the hill, ringing to tell me that our intended house was too large, it spoiled her view, it was out of keeping with the surroundings, and it must go.

Then one night in London, a man who did not give his name, but had a Donegal accent, rang to tell me that my house would fall, block by block and, moreover, that the cement that was being used was rotten. It was only then I learned from my builder that each evening, after they left the site, the cement blocks they had put up were being removed, before they had hardened, and thrown down in defiance. Phil, being a local, kept telling me not to lose heart and that bad feelings would blow over. They didn't. A blue boat appeared in the mooring of our house, and letters to remove it were ignored. Eventually, a letter from my solicitor was answered by one of the many members of the clan, saying that if I were a decent countrywoman, I would cut out all this "bull" and hop along to my aged neighbor and put her mind at rest. It was impossible to know who was most instrumental in all the trouble, whether from this house or that, or a house in the hills that I hadn't even seen, an entire community perhaps colluding with one another. My visit to the local Garda station was met with some coolness. Here was I, an outsider, building a big house and incurring spleen with neighbors whom they knew well and might even be distantly related to, since they all had the same surname. Only with the threat of the court in Letterkenny, and the High Court in Dublin, if necessary, did the aggravations stop, but the hostilities simmered on.

The move came in December, and the sound of the big removal vans trundling up the narrow road was thrilling after four years of setbacks and stalled hopes. The list from the auction room where I bought furniture is testament to the extravagances that I went to. There was, for instance, a Chinese red lacquer cabinet, painted with pagodas and a garden landscape, on a gilt-caned timber stand, Chinese panels of parcel-gilt and polychrome, giltwood armchairs with two-seater canapé en suite, hand-carved ornate dining table and chairs, in mango and mahogany hues, along with suites of metal garden chairs and pear-shaped mirrors, etched and surmounted in Venetian style, with leafy cresting and foliate apron. The beautiful Gothic fireplace, made of sandstone, suffered a gash along its forehead as the movers dropped it in the short descent down the three balcony steps into the salon, but irrepressible as I was, I heard myself say it merely added an authentic touch.

I, who crave silence, had the quietest bedroom in the world, and all I could hear was the sheep as they nipped the thin pickings, between the boulders, in the field next to me and the whirr of the little airplane as it set out early each morning.

"Tara's Halls" was how my friend David McKittrick christened it when he came with his wife, Pat, for a little housewarming. Carlo's children, Georgia and Euan, eight and five respectively, were putting on a play. The preparations all that day were intensive: apart from penning the epic, there was the printing of the programs, which were then decorated in watercolor, the choosing of costume and props, and deciding in which wing of the balcony to stage the performance. It was to be after dinner, and we were made to stay at the "mango and mahogany" table, since surprise was imperative. We stayed a long time. Eventually Georgia came in, woebegone. Her brother had stage fright. He had taken off his war paint and his costume, which he had stamped on, and had locked himself in the Rock room, declaring that he was the most useless boy ever born.

It took endless coaxing. His mother and father pleaded with him; so did I. Sasha vowed to get in by the window and, what with that and the promise of double the asking price for the programs, Euan finally emerged wearing a man's hat and a silk kimono with a buckle that with its magic propensities would be a significant part of the unfolding drama. Georgia was in white like a vestal. The performance, considering the buildup, was remarkably short, and the dialogue, insofar as we could interpret it, was a mishmash of English, Teutonic, and Elven.

"There... there" were his first words, as with much puckering and collusion, he pointed to the foeman dragon, who was represented by a fallen chair behind a curtain. The curtain, I should add, was a beautiful bale of lemon-colored tulle that I had intended for several windows, but that evening it was "All for Hecuba and Hecuba for me."

The ensuing acoustic consisted of a lot of Naa Naa and Raa Raa, and the repetition of the word "Longsaddle," which presumably meant an imminent escape on horseback. The dragon behind the curtain must be put to sleep, by a sorcery from a certain object. The object was a clock, one of the three clocks that had stopped since I moved in, obviously disliking the salt sea air. The clock, when put to the head, could stun a person. This we learned as it was put to Georgia's head and she obligingly fell into a swoon. The idea was that she would creep in under the curtain and stun the dragon. Here she spoke her first line of dialogue, which had been dutifully translated in the program. She said nervously, "*Sut an?*," which meant "How long?" Euan tried to reassure her, said his heart sang to her, then circled her face and forehead with the buckle as protection, and off she went. The parley with the dragon was mute, except for the ringing of a little Druid bell which had also been filched from my bedside drawer. Slipping out of character, Euan used the occasion to tie his bootlace, and then resorted to Naa Naa and Raa Raa until she emerged smiling, carrying two important things, a scroll tied with red ribbon and a white lace mantilla.

"Getting married," she said, in a sweet, scarcely audible voice, while her brother, having read the scroll, formally placed the veil on her head, and then, hands joined, they stepped down off the balcony and out by a set of double doors onto Longsaddle and into the proverbial sunshine. The applause was astounding. There were five curtain calls, in which the porter's armchair, chosen no doubt for its claw feet, represented the dragon. Everyone, including the protagonists, shed tears of pride and joy, the promised sums of money were handed over, and glasses, large and small, brimmed with champagne.

On that same balcony, Stephen Rea and Marie Mullen read from Yeats and Joyce for a program I was preparing for the BBC. One sunny Sunday, Stephen rounded up some gifted musicians, among them Neil Martin, who played on the cello his song cycle of the Oileán na Marbh, the Island of the Dead. It was music that he had written for poems by Cathal Ó Searcaigh, in which a mother of one of the many unbaptized children speaks of her sorrows and rage at the Catholic Church, which would not allow such children to lie in Christian grounds. In one of the accidents of history, some soldiers who had been torpedoed by German U-boats during the Second World War were washed in by the tide on that Donegal coast and were buried next to the children in unmarked graves. The loneliness of the music, coupled with the loneliness of the place and the sob of the sea, gave me the feeling that all was right and that I had settled in, yet the certainty could be undone by a night of storm when I was alone.

The storm had no regard for seasons, came any time, bawling its rage.

Waves powered by winds and crosswinds came roaring in, cresting, then toppling on the foam, as the next and the next onslaught came crashing in the same confused and angry froth. I went around checking the hasps on the windows, all twenty of them, and tucked towels in the jambs of the front and back doors. In the yard outside, the security lights crazily kept coming on and off, and through the kitchen window I saw that the willows had succumbed and lay in a heap. Birds dropped down into the floe, flung this way and that, and one, maybe a cormorant, was a mere tatter up there, a plaything spinning out of control, like a stringless kite. Rain sluiced over the ledges of rock in the yard, oozing into the Pink House and its foundations. I blessed myself and prayed for morning.

Mornings: clear as crystal, the sea silken, with every color to it, the pale blue and pale pink of the matinee coats that I'd seen in the souvenir shop in Dungloe, alongside the ubiquitous green marble Cross of Cong, and a miniature Belleek lavatory bowl with the sign that read FOR BUTTS ONLY. But there was no capturing these colors for long, as there would always be a bit of a downpour, nicely called "sun showers," and the sheets on my neighbor's clothesline would get a second dousing. I lived for those mornings, that primordial calm that comes after storm,

Trip to the Lake District in England with Sasha, late 1970s.

the world, as it were, being put to rights again. I would go outside, the sands dove-white with the mimicry of the waves on them and scarves of mustard-colored seaweed drying on the rocks. Yet, storm or sunshine, there was the gnawing realization that I wasn't writing that much. I would joke and say that the rooms Sasha had designed were too big, too palatial, and did not make for concentration, but I could have hidden, and indeed did, in the porter's chair to keep distractions out. Places are at the heart of writing, and I was no match for that rugged world of crag and granite and scree. I inclined toward softer, leafier places, ditches choked with wildflowers, weeds, and convolvulus, small rivers where the brown and speckled trout ran. I could not imagine myself into it, its dictions too gnarled for me.

The back of an ambulance is a big place to be in alone. One Easter Saturday I was diagnosed with a strangulated hernia, and were it not for the fact that Sasha and a girl called Shoba were there, I would have gone "among the shades." So remote was the Pink House that the ambulance, which the doctor had called, couldn't find us. Sasha was standing outside the gate, waving for all his worth, only to see it turn around when it came to a bend where the road seemed to jut out into the sea. He ran with all his might and caught up with them, still searching, at another fork in a road, so that by the time I was lifted into it and covered with a red blanket, I was woozy from the injection the doctor had given me. We would have driven past Errigal and on through the Poisoned Glen, except that I was oblivious to it, hurtling back and forth in what I can only call a quasi-world. It was with great difficulty, on being admitted to the hospital, that I could remember my name and my mother's maiden name, and I felt that the barrage of questions was too much. Then it was a big ward, with televisions blaring, and after what seemed too long a time, I was being wheeled in a trolley by two young men, who were eagerly discussing the tos and fros of the hurling match the following day, Easter Sunday. It was bumpsy-daisy as we careened along corridors, up one floor and then down another, and then up again to the operating theater, where so many strange figures in white coats, white hats, and white masks waited, as for some ritual.

I wakened with my mouth full of tubes, gasping for water. A youth came to take blood, but was unable to raise any vein, telling me—as I begged him to cease—that it was a "learning curve" for him, too. Later he was replaced by a Sri Lankan nurse who was like a jeweler with the needle, the blood happily bubbling into the glass vial.

The woman in the bed next to me was dying, as I could tell by her moaning and by the many relatives that kept arriving. Then the screen was put around her, and not long after, the priest came, carrying the oils in a wooden box, to give her viaticum. A nurse followed, with a tall, lit wax candle in one hand and a white cloth in the other. The quiet droning of their voices as they recited the Rosary, the smell of the lit candle, and the warm oils made for a happy scene, and it was not like death at all; it was as if she was merely passing from one chapter of her life into another. I longed to follow her, as the thirst was well nigh unbearable and the machine inside my mouth felt like a forklift. She was carried out in the bed, and after the screen was removed, I saw my two pink earplugs that had fallen off my bedside table and lay forlornly on the floor. It was sheer luck that I had found them in my purse after being admitted to the hospital, and they had been a buttress against the constant noise and blare of television. They were retrieved and washed, and that night, sounds were once again muffled.

The day the tubes were taken out and I could feel my swallow and then taste the first drops of water that were like nectar, I felt a great gratitude to be alive.

Yet it was when I got home I began to weigh things up, as I sat and read the get-well cards and looked out the window at the daffodils on one side and the sea on the other. I had to concede that as a nondriver I had picked a lonely outpost indeed. No seafarer I. Yet it was a year before I put the house on the market.

And so the day came when I was wrapping the glasses and the several ornaments, hanging torn sheets over the mirrors, emptying drawers, finding leaflets about caring for one's carpet and novel ideas for cocktail recipes. Great stacks of cardboard boxes were already packed, and the sitting room had a sacked appearance to it. I jumped at hearing a light tap on the door. It was a young woman, one of the "six sisters," who had built a small house on a hill above mine. She wore a long calico skirt and a white drawstring blouse with blown poppies on it. Her shyness was evident from the way she hesitated. I had often seen her in the years that I lived there, deft as a mountain goat, moving from rock to rock, and one Christmas Day, when she thought there was nobody about, she peeled off all her clothes and literally ran into the ice-cold water. She emerged a few minutes later, a verdant Eve, slathered with seaweed, which clung to her, the weed they called sea lettuce. What impulse had made her do that? I would see her often in the evenings, with her tin can, searching the undersides of the rocks for mussels for her dinner, but we had never spoken, neither of us had dared to break the ice.

She came in, wondering if I needed any help, and before I could answer she had already begun to pack things. There was something I had always wanted to ask her. Had she resented my being there, those ten years? "Yes. Twice." The first was when she saw a second chimney put in the gable wall that was the stone wall of the house she had grown up in. The second was the night we moved in, lights in every room, so that to her, a few hundred yards up the hill, it was a fairy castle from which she had been banished. There was one other small thing I had to ask. What had made her plunge into the cold sea that Christmas Day? "Ah now" was the evasive answer.

Piling the books, she asked if I had read them all, and mentioned the only one she had read in years, *The Bridges of Madison County*. Then her eye fell on an open page of one of the books and she read aloud: "The sea, and Homer... it's Love that moves all things." She liked it, copied it on the back of one of the cocktail recipes, and put it in the pocket of her long skirt. He was a tall man, a stranger from the Land of the White Nights and the Cloudberries, and the previous Christmas he had docked his boat over in Gweedore harbor and she'd left a daft note in an empty beer bottle that was on the deck of his boat, which was named after a Norse goddess. No, she did not dream of sailing the high seas with him, she would never leave that coastline, she was married to it, the way one cannot be married to a man.

Pointing to the low window, she said, "That's where they laid my mother out, the night she died." She was a child at the time. Her mother had given birth to eleven children in that tiny house, and she belonged to it, in a way I never could.

Under the stairs I found a last bottle of champagne, and we sat on the edge of the long table that the movers would soon dismantle, looking out to sea, not saying a word.

It was still dark when I left the following morning and put the back-door key through the letterbox of the big ceremonial oak door with its iron rivets. I had also left a letter for the auctioneer marked "Urgent." He was coming later to look at a damp patch which had been discovered and was causing concern for the purchasers, so that the sale was in danger of falling through. A copy of it is in my book of memorabilia:

Dear Brendan, I have talked to my builder and he says the damp patch is nothing to worry about and is not spreading into the hall. It is caused by the fact that a corner of the house was built on rock (not unlike St Peter's!). What they intend to do is put electrodes under it then a waterproof plaster which will be painted over, so that no damp will flow further along. The outside is being repainted as requested.

The minicab driver was not the young man I had expected, he was older and seemed peeved in some way, maybe the early hour.

In that pale light we came upon a strange and ghostlike spectacle. A field full of hares, dozens of them, peculiarly still, their ears cocked. There was something eerie about it, a suggestion of madness and menace. I asked the driver to slow down, and as he did, some, obviously the females, scattered to one side, to allow for what would be the tournaments. Standing on their hind legs, grouped in pairs, the males began to box one another. They did it expertly and with a formality, as if it had been rehearsed, which it couldn't have been—this hooking and jabbing they knew by some innate instinct, the battle that had to be waged to win the hand of a lady love.

Fearing I would miss the plane, the driver started the engine up and, apropos of nothing, said, "I had a good marriage," his cue to tell me how suddenly his wife died, had been given the all-clear when she went for a checkup, and he was called in from the waiting room to find her, the doctor and two nurses, one male, all in floods of tears, as she had only a week to live. He could not remember what he had done in the two years after her death, could not remember which daughter he had gone to for the Christmas dinner. He drifted through life in a haze and was given counseling that couldn't help. Eventually, he decided to take up the taxi work, to meet people, and then, late one evening, he was called to drive a lady home. When she got out of the car, she suggested they might have a walk sometime. Already they had taken a run in the car over to Letterkenny to look at the shops and another on a windy headland above Gortahork, where they were nearly blown away. He wasn't saying anything, but maybe if I came back on a visit, I might see a change in him, he might be a family man again.

The plane always took off in one of two directions, depending on the wind, and as I had hoped, it cruised above the Pink House, so happy down below, an odalisque, her soft contours opening to the elements.

The Night of Time

The cry of a fox at night is a baneful thing. I mistook it at first for that of an infant. It had bitten into a dream, a dream I did not wish bitten into, though I forget what it was. The fox was a vixen, a putative mother, making preliminary reconnaissance for a place to burrow, and the garden, smothered with bushes, fig trees, and shrubs that have seeded themselves, was ideal cover.

It was snowing. Thick pilings of it, on the flowerbeds and hedging, snow falling, snow flurrying, snow settling, and snow waiting, in the sulky fleeces of the sky.

She started to come in daylight, would arrive suddenly, stand her ground, a burnished apparition juxtaposed against the white of the snow, the chin so pert and pointed and a strange kind of desolation in the expression that was curiously human. Having sized me up, she would sally over to the fig trees and the high back wall, such a taunt in the swish of the brown tail, and sometimes, when she turned to look back, there would be a rush of blood that boded terror in two recesses behind my earlobes.

January 2011, and according to the weather reports, the worst winter since 1963, when Wimbledon Common was completely blanketed with snow and in their virgin whiteness you could not count the steps up to the grand houses across the way.

That was the winter after I left my husband and had rented a room on the Common, when Sasha wrote "Help" in the condensation of the windowpane, being too embarrassed to admit that he wanted to go back to his father's house, because it was the place he knew, even though he was wretched in it. He and his brother were to be separated for that one night, and since I was allowed to have only one or the other, they tossed a coin for it and Sasha won the toss.

We were in the new flat, bare, except for a mattress on the floor, a kitchen chair, some mugs, and a gas ring. I had put the kettle on to make cocoa, when on the condensation, from the steam of the kettle, the word HELP, in large capitals, showed on the window.

We had had a bit of a humiliation earlier on in the steak house on the Ridgeway. I had sufficient money for one dinner, one order of steak and chips, and asked if we could share it. The befuddled waiter called the manager, who, with a smug superiority, said all tables were already fully booked, and we had to make a shaming retreat.

I suggested to Sasha that perhaps he wanted to go home, and he nodded "Yes," and we put on our Wellingtons and our coats and went out to the pay phone. After I had dialed the number and his father answered, Sasha spoke haltingly to him, and it was agreed that his father would collect him in half an hour. We waited downstairs in the porch of the house, and for those interminable thirty minutes we didn't say much. The path of snow under the streetlight had a pink flush to it and was slippery.

Next morning I left that flat, and a young assistant in a shop in Wimbledon, after some pleading, agreed to take the mattress back, since I explained that I had not taken off the plastic covering and had not slept on it. I moved to a room in Putney that was on the river and not far from the woman who had allowed me in on the night of the drifting fog. This rented room was my futile and lamentable attempt to make a nest. I would think, irrationally, that if we could go down, down, into a deep snowdrift and hide there, our troubles would be solved, I would get custody of them, their father would be reconciled to it, and life would have a normal hum to it again. In the new digs, I was often alone, as the owner went to a house in Cornwall, and I brought the children for visits. They were intrigued by a collection of maps and compasses in her father's study, a nautical museum that he was not likely to see again, as he was an invalid in his house in Cornwall, which overlooked the sea.

I received a commission, Francis Wyndham, who was an editor at *Queen* magazine, asking me to write a descriptive piece about horses.

The check for one hundred pounds called for an outing, and the following Saturday I took them to the Strand, to a stamp shop. Sasha, having developed a precocious interest in stamps, saw himself as a putative stamp collector. Afterward we went to the Savoy for lunch. There were loaned ties, the waiter holding an array of them on his arm for them to choose from, and then he conducted us into the opulence of the dining room, where we sat at a round center table. Such suavity, such attentiveness, waiters flying to meet every command, and soon after, as a trolley was wheeled to our table and half a silver salver lifted back, he inquired as to the preference of the "young gentlemen."

"It's pukka... it's pukka," Carlo said, appropriating the English phrases that they had overheard, forgetting the ones they knew from Ireland, and even their accents were slightly changed.

Afterward, a little tipsy from dessert wine, in an anteroom with a beautiful blond writing desk, they helped themselves to engraved notepaper to pen a letter to my mother, of whom they were inordinately fond. From Sasha she received a treatise on stamps, followed by a long account of the Siege of Khartoum in 1884, where General Charles Gordon held out for ten months against a Sudanese army but eventually was beaten, having been outflanked by an enemy who took advantage of the low level of the Nile, rushed the walls, and broke down the gates.

He hoped one day in some box in a junk shop that he would find a stamp from that era, with its Egyptian franking and, most marvelous of all, tucked inside the envelope, a soldier's account of the hungers and afflictions that they endured. Carlo, determined to write an equally long letter, recalled a prayer, the "Desiderata," which railed against life's "vexatious" trials. I too availed myself of the engraved notepaper, stuffing sheets of it into my handbag, believing it would be lucky for the novel I had started to write. I wrote in every free moment, on buses, in railway stations, at the school gates, and the novel *Girls in Their Married Bliss,* written in that frenzied time, was deemed a departure from my earlier, lambent, lyrical tone.

That was the winter I met the film director Jack Garfield, who sent me a hamper from Fortnum & Mason, delicacies such as I had never tasted, hams in aspic, foie gras, quince jelly, cheeses, and truffles filled with cherry brandy and kirsch. That was the winter I was invited by T. P. McKenna to a party given by Sam Peckinpah, but never actually met my host, which was not unusual for parties in the sixties, since guests brought friends who then encouraged other friends, and gate-crashers made nothing of walking into a house where a front door might be ajar and "I'll send all my lovin' to you" full blast.

That was the winter I bought a Cossack astrakhan hat in the palest gray and one or two men kissed me, but I was not ready to kiss anyone, I was still frozen.

That was the winter Sylvia Plath took her own life, having written poetry of such searing and murderous truth. Her husband, Ted Hughes, in a book dedicated to her, had written a poem in which Husband is the shadow to the Lady, but shadows swap places in life, just as they can in courtly verse. I had met Sylvia Plath once, after a poetry reading in the Queen Elizabeth Hall, when Robert Graves introduced us, and I felt something inimical and harsh in her. Yet in time, and with my mounting adversities, her poems, filled as they are with the presence of death and the presence of children, were bulletins to my soul. I felt I could bear things just by reading them, the words so perfectly placed, so perfectly honed, the beautiful imagery, the gravity: "Lilies. Lilies."

"The moon... staring from her hood of bone."

In the rented room, with the river beyond, the shutters did not meet, and cold moonlight ambled along the floor, picking up the acorns on a silver-backed mirror and the rosettes on a pink cloth slipper. I was afraid to sleep in case something drastic happened, in case my husband stole a march and took them to New Zealand, as he had threatened to do, since he had a sister there. In dreams I was constantly trying to reach them, racing up a flight of steps at Wimbledon station, only to arrive at the platform just as the train moved away and they were waving wanly. In another dream I was ironing, and suddenly the smell of scorched cloth changed to that of burning flesh, as their skins came off, sizzling on the bottom of the iron, and I wakened to a catastrophe of my own making. An Irish girl who once worked for us, and who was training to be a children's nurse, came occasionally to help their father, and on the Saturday morning when she could not come, they had been instructed to vacuum and, on the stroke of one, deliver their father's breakfast—Earl Grey tea and brown gluten toast, faintly burned and sprinkled with olive oil. I knew the Irish girl, with her proneness to blush in his presence, would take their father's side, and I feared that she would undermine me, which she did, when the black day came that I appeared in court. When she handed them over at the railway station, she never addressed a word to me, just whispered fondnesses in their ears, and then delivered the ultimatums from my husband about prompt bedtime, their brushing their teeth properly, and the necessity of regular bowel movements. So as to establish my waning powers over them, I asked that she bring a change of clothes and underclothes, which in some way brought me nearer to them, simply by seeing their vests, their socks, and their Fair Isle jumpers thrown on chairs.

In late February that year, it started to thaw.

Snow fell from the roofs in small avalanches, water pipes burst, the streets and the towpaths were all slush, and yet a few snowdrops had pushed their way through the dank, leaden earth.

The vixen came more frequently, her crying at night so eerie, like the banshee, a summons to the living and the dead. Two burrows had been made, but I did not know that there was an adjoining tunnel between them. I began to get nervous and consulted various organizations as to what I might do. From one I learned that foxes were nocturnal mammals, spent the hours of darkness hunting and scavenging, and that their life expectancy could be twelve to fifteen years. Attacks by foxes, it said, were rare, and it would only be a last-ditch measure for a fox to attack. But this was a last-ditch measure. The next organization that I rang was equally unhelpful. Did I know that foxes first colonized London in 1930? I didn't. The "urban" fox, which mine was termed to be, had reached a stage of equilibrium in the city, and shooting was not acceptable, nor was snaring. Foxes felt happier in a corner of the garden with a wall on both sides, where they would feel well guarded. I was to resist the urge to make them tame, though many householders derived pleasure by feeding them from their hand. Putting foul-smelling chemicals into burrows was illegal under the Food and Environment Protection Act of 1985, and it was a misconception to assume that one could move a wild animal to a new area, where it would not settle down and would not know the best feeding sites. By doing this, I would be committing another offense that might lead to imprisonment. A pest-control bureau that I located recommended a repellent that mimicked a rival fox's smell, the only drawback being that it was not to be found in any hardware shop, garden center, or DIY store, as the demand had been excessive.

One night the sensor light kept going on and off, ceaselessly, and when I got out of bed and looked out the window, I saw what I did not believe possible. Down below were eight or nine foxes, the young cubs, with the mad antics of squirrels, racing about, romping in and out of the flowerbeds, stirring the evergreen bushes, off which snow fell becomingly onto their furry coats, which were a darker brown than that of the parents. Down there, evincing, I have to say, a happiness unbounded, the mother stood, utterly still and slightly crouched, as they suckled from time to time, then darted about in a mad maelstrom.

I vacated the bedroom.

The room next to it used to be for entertaining, but there is less of that with the years. It is the hour, as I knew from one of Mr. W. G. Sebald's novels (that uncanny literary ghost), which Sir Thomas Browne called "the night of time that surpasseth day." It is the hour when Scott Fitzgerald contemplated his "crack-up" and lived it. The hour of the wolf and the urban foxes. Books everywhere. On the shelves and on the small space above the rows of books and all along the floor and under chairs, books that I have read, books that I have not read; for instance, I have never read *The Rise and Fall of Athens* by Plutarch, of which I possess three copies. Leaflets everywhere. Vedic sutras. A newspaper clipping with the heading "A Line to the Lord," by which Catholics were being given a chance to dial a confession for fifty pence a minute. A letter sent to my address by mistake is confirming my appointment with a coordinator for breast enhancement. Oh, sweet Jesus. There are the exercise manuals that I consulted in my halcyon times, the Tummy Toner, the B I Press-Mono, the Hip-Hop, along with idealized pictures of the hourglass waist. A pamphlet from the local council is offering advice for the over-sixty-fives. "Are you prepared?" the headline asks, to which I answer a spirited no.

It was while traveling in Singapore that I realized I had hit a nadir. Love had gone underground. As a writer I was deemed wanton and irrational, my range was thought to be narrow and obsessional, a mere concoction of clichés aimed at foreigners.

I could not, according to my critics, get any experience into perspective; the story was forever the same. An English lady journalist, obviously of Irish extraction, found my prose *"stifling"* and, with the sensibility of a small-town hussy, said that I had done well enough out of Ireland.

Singapore airport was spick-and-span.

I knew at least three people who had committed suicide. A man who once casually asked me to marry him and who in fact was due to marry someone else had gone into a wood, en route to London, with a loaded pistol in his overnight bag. In the bag, found subsequently, there was a pair of pajamas and a half-bottle of Bollinger champagne, should the pull of life have proven stronger than that of nonlife. A young boy in Geneva, bidding good night to his friends outside a crowded café, called, "I'll sleep sound tonight," and did not waken from the overdose he had taken.

One morning in a hotel on the Atlantic Ocean in France, a young woman offered to walk me across to the casino, to cash money, as the machine in the hotel was broken. She was the last word in chic, different outfits each day and very high heels as she tended to the multiple needs of the clientele. She was due to be married later in the year and was considering various cities that they might or might not go to on their honeymoon. It was winter. The sea was in a right old tether, disgorging waves of such gorgeous brightness, only to be swallowed up and annihilated in troughs of black and indigo. The carousel, on the other hand, was utterly still, the white china horses with golden manes and tilted forelegs, riderless and pearled in dew. After I had cashed the money, we sat to have coffee in the gaming room and she told me her story. Why she needed to tell me, I would never know. It may have been that the room, empty of croupiers and tables, with quenched lamps hanging low over the green baize tables, seemed, in its solemnity, a sort of confessional.

She had lived with her future husband for almost ten years, then had begun to notice a difference, a cooling. He was a traveling salesman, and she believed, and indeed later found proof, that he was having an affair in Deauville. She never mentioned it to him, though she discovered the name of the woman in question, the pharmacy where the woman worked, and the restaurants they had eaten in. One day, while he was still away, she decided to drown herself. She was a strong swimmer and swam far out to sea, so far that nobody walking on that shore could have sighted that ash-blond head bobbing up and down. Out there in that lonely vastness, she lost her will to die and began to turn back, but equally she lost most of her strength to swim. How she stayed up in that water, how after many hours she had crawled her way back through it and lay on the shore, she could not tell, but knew that she was found, lying in a wet bathing suit, freezing and her speech gone. A couple who found her talked to her, stood her up, tried to get her to talk, and eventually brought her to the hospital, where she was put in the psychiatric wing. It was weeks before her husband-to-be was contacted. When he did visit, he was like a mortician, formal and remote; he did not ask her why she had done it, but simply said that she could be a guest in his house for the period of her recuperation. Now, as she told me that morning in the empty casino, they were due to marry, but what she did not tell me was the changed nature of love, the metamorphosis that had taken place.

The hotel in Singapore, which my publishers had arranged for me, was in its own grounds, the gardens so beautifully tended, grasses, shrubs, trees, and wide rhubarby leaves in fan-like and carefree sway. It was October.

The "Business and Shopping District," as I learned when I looked through the brochure in my bedroom, was a mere seven-minute walk away, and though intending to take my own life, I still persisted with the niceties of the living. I was on my way to Australia on a book tour, expected in three cities, Melbourne, Adelaide, and Sydney. I would bring gifts to the people who were going to meet me there. The department store where I found myself was on many floors, all glassy and heartlessly bright, inane music throughout. At a cosmetics counter my face, in a standing magnifying glass, looked bleached and grotesque. Two young girls were showing off. They wore identical linen pinafores with tiny, braided straps decorated with flat cloth rosebuds. They were trying various lipsticks from a giant display, letting out hoots of laughter. They daubed their lips with layer upon layer of it, and soon their hands and cheeks were scored with bright tattoos. Then they clowned, doing glissades from counter to counter, proclaiming their happiness, their youth, and their blithe spirits. I hated them. I hated their giggles, their exuberance, their ponytails bouncing off their thin, dusky collarbones. What did they know of love, what did they know of despair? It occurred to me that if I were to say to them, "Excuse me, I am going to kill myself at eight-thirty this evening," the laughter in that department store would become infectious. I then permitted myself the fleeting vision of a man I was in love with, then withdrew without even a knowing gesture. By such sad associations love withers.

I bought silk scarves and silk ties for strangers in Australia whom I was supposed to meet but would not be meeting.

Back at the hotel the floodlit garden was like a setting for an outdoor theater, the various greens even more startlingly alive, tree trunks with little golden granules of light scaling them, the shrubbery lit from above and below, and the cropped, round crowns of box hedging, like cupolas, on fire. How beautiful life could be. Couples were on the terrace, having their cocktails, the men in cream and white jackets, the women with pearls and fur stoles. There was dance music, some distance away, and from hidden hoses water trickled quietly, faithfully, unnervingly.

In my room the bedcover had been turned down, Singapore orchids of pale purple on the pillow, a small square of dark chocolate, and a breakfast menu. The pills were in a handkerchief from long, long ago. It was yellow silk with a white lace border and a touching motto—"Love the Giver." I had emptied bottles of pills from down the years into it that I had accrued from various doctors, for jet lag, for journeys to America and elsewhere. I do not like the taste of whiskey, so I began with a glass of champagne. Then I sat by the window with the curtains open, hearing the voices down below, the waltz music and the incessant sound of the water, which somehow suggested my being flushed out, and that was something I recoiled from thinking about. Things were getting scarier. Only an hour to go.

I was on my second glass of champagne when there came a light knock on my door. Who could it be? There were three knocks in all, and then an envelope was slipped under the door with *Facsimile* printed on the outside. The message was from Sasha, in his familiar Cyrillic handwriting. It said, "Guess what, you are having lunch with Polly White tomorrow Sunday. She will collect you at one o'clock." She had been a friend of his at Bedales, and his first real love was her sister Lucy. I reckoned that he had bumped into her in Notting Hill Gate in London, just as she was returning to Singapore, where she now lived, and it was there and then that the rendezvous with me had been agreed. I walked around the room and kept repeating it, "Guess what, you are having lunch with Polly White tomorrow Sunday."

I could not imagine the lunatic self of moments before. I decided to go downstairs and talk to someone, anyone, in order to rejoin life. Looking down at the handwriting that I loved, the message hurried and breezy, yet secure in the knowledge and in the certainty that I would be having lunch with Polly White on the morrow, and so I would.

From time to time I go back to the bedroom in the irrational hope that the foxes have gone. They are still there, merry and frolicking. I wished William Faulkner would walk in. Lily Cushing, whom I met in America, described a visit she and her husband, Anthony West, had from Faulkner, who for one whole afternoon stared out the window at two foxes as in a frieze, the apotheosis of stillness, the Vladimir and Estragon of the animal kingdom. But William Faulkner is not in my sitting room, though all his books are in the glass-fronted cabinet among those books that I love most.

Flaubert's mother said that his love of words had hardened his heart. Could that be true? Could that be true?

In a pile of letters there is one from Carlo enclosing a letter that he has plucked for me from the vast memorabilia of his father. My husband's handwriting so faded and yet so familiar. It is a letter addressed to me and one that I have never received, or maybe one that he wrote merely for the sake of writing it. It was written about five years before his death. "My darling," it begins. The "My darling" bewilders me. It had been true once and for a time, its trueness most felt when in the evenings in Lake Park, I would sit in his study with the overhead light not on but maybe the Tilley lamp on the desk, where he placed it, having just come in from the toolshed, where he pottered during the day. In those early months together he said that he did not want to write, he was too happy to write. He would encourage me to tell him stories about home, dock and nettle, drunk men going home on a fair day, relieving themselves against the piers of our gate, and smells, dung and wild woodbine, and what for me was the most lingering smell of all, custard powder of the palest, airiest pink. He liked hearing these anecdotes, and he was not jealous then. The evening that stayed longest with me was when, in a tentative and yet emotional way, I told him that I might be having a baby. I had morning sickness for a few weeks and would go into the woods to vomit. A strange man in a coat made of various skins, a hunter perhaps, came upon me once accidentally and said that the best cure for my condition was to suck on a raw tomato. Another evening up there I caught sight of a herd of deer that were already moving, in mazed and weightless flight, scaling the barbed wire that was flecked with shivery bits of yellow-white sheep's wool, and I knew for certain that I was having a child, and the sensation was strange and startling.

In the letter that began "My darling," this estranged husband was suggesting that we live together again, because, though mindful of my innumerable failings, he had come to the conclusion that I would never be happy without him. I had loved him once, or thought I had, and there were three or possibly four other loves, one who had the makings of a poet and another who chose the path of power, and still another, who had fended me off as if I were a Dido, tempting him away from conquest, back to Carthage and to love.

It was in a beautiful garden in Dorset, with the smell of roses and lilac and fresh grass, croquet mallets on the steps, and an open book facedown on a wooden table, that it happened. Siesta time. I was biding my moments to go down to the swimming pool. It was in the garden of a house that Harold Pinter and Antonia Fraser rented each summer, and Francis Wyndham and I, like two excitable country cousins, would meet at Waterloo station, setting sail for our four-day vacation. I can still recall that intake of breath, our mutual exclamations at the first sight of the sea, like a spill of mercury, the light from it so dazzling, glimpsed and then lost as the train wound its way inward and ceremoniously from Bournemouth toward the fields and hedges and shales and coppices of Dorset. Four happy days in which conversation never flagged and Harold told stories that he had often told before, but like old wine (of which there was also an abundance) they were richer with age and not without the presence of death. Adopting the Scottish burr of the professor who had treated him in his illness, Harold would say, "But you're our star pupil, Mr. Pinter." Often he would recite for me lines of Yeats, though neither of us could name the poem, for Constance Gore-Booth, whom the poet saw ride out to the meet under bare Ben Bulben, "The beauty of her countryside/With all youth's lonely wildness" about her.

On a particular visit, word came that Jude Law and a producer would come to lunch in order to talk to Harold about a screenplay. It was still not confirmed, and I hoped they wouldn't come, since our rhythms now were so nicely established. I was in the bedroom overlooking the long avenue, with its echoes of *Last Year at Marienbad,* when I saw their car come over the cattle grid, saw the two men get out and collect their belongings, including swimming togs, from the boot.

It is afternoon in the garden, with hundred-year-old trees and a shaded walk and, underneath, tiny speckled flowers that I did not know the name of but that obviously preferred shade.

Signing books in Kennys Bookshop, Galway city, 1978.

Everything so quiet and slumberous. There was Jude Law, Adonis, fast asleep. I retraced my steps, as this constituted a setback to my intended swim. As a nonswimmer, I wore armbands for my dip, armbands which, when blown up, had in capital letters NIVEA CREAM prominently displayed. Moreover, I had a kitchen chair, turned on its side, to serve as a prop that I could grip before venturing in. Each day I had chosen this time, when the garden was deserted, but now there was Adonis, who might waken at any moment and wander across. I went back to sit at the bottom of the steps and keep vigil. He was walking toward me, golden-haired, lit by soft August sunshine, when unexpectedly he came over and without a word bent down and kissed me. Like fiction. I knew the story that it reminded me of, a Chekhov story, inevitably called "The Kiss." In it a group of officers had been invited to tea on the estate of Lieutenant von Rabbek, where there was also the smell of roses and lilac and fresh grass. One of them, not confident enough to play billiards or join in the mazurka, took a stroll throughout the large house, blundering into corridors and little anterooms, then, seeing a gleam of light from a doorway, the officer stopped, heard footsteps and the rustling of a dress, the light being turned out and a breathless, feminine voice whispering, "At last." Two soft, fragrant, unmistakably feminine arms are clasped around his neck, a warm cheek pressed to his cheek, and the sweet impact of a kiss. The bestower of the kiss, realizing that she had kissed the wrong officer, uttered a faint shriek and stepped back. But that did not happen in the garden in Dorset, with its roses and smell of cut grass. Like the narrator in Chekhov's story, who for hours afterward gave himself up to the sensation of it, I recollected the fact that Jude Law had kissed me, had not said a word, and then had disappeared inside the house. Yet by nightfall, when they had left, I thought how glad I was to be old, heaving a sigh of relief that it was not the beginning of something, of getting on the love trampoline—more intensities, more fervor, more hope, more desolation, more everything.

After weeks of bedlam in the garden, with foxes coming and going, I at long last located a company willing to take them to the country. Two men came to survey the scene. They looked shifty as they walked around, sniffing and following the tracks.

They called me by my first name all the time. They would bring cages, they said, and they did, or rather, one of them did. Big cages for the parents and littler cages for the cubs.

The bait was chicken wing, slightly bloodied, and suspended on a metal hook at the far end; the ruse being that, when a fox reached it, a spring snapped and the trapdoor was shut. The view in the garden was grim: ugly, squat cages, seven in all, and the bloodied chicken bait, which would get more rank by the day. I foresaw what was to come. Foxes in cages and those who had been crafty enough to avoid incarceration coming in sympathy to bay. There would be ongoing laments out there. Except that it did not turn out like that at all. Everything became weirdly quiet. At what hour of night, I asked myself, did the unsuspecting fox, perhaps the mother who had often outstared me, walk into her doom? Because next morning, treading my way, I saw a haunch—mahogany-brown and weirdly still. I froze, then hurried back to ring the man, asking him to come at once, except there was no answer from either phone line. When at last he came and picked up the cage, the fox was delirious, jumping back and forth, letting out mewling cries, which he answered with soft aspirations, the almost *o*'s and the almost *a*'s, as he put the cage in the back of the van for the long drive to the somewhere in the country.

Each morning after that, I went out to find trapdoors closed but no fox inside. They had twigged. When I rang, he said it could be gusts of wind, but I did not believe that, because several foxes had returned, treading in and out between cages, and I both feared them and waited for them. Then, about five mornings later, there was another fox, much younger, though not a cub, in a cage, under the fig trees, silent and seething. It kept looking at me, the gaze so fixed, so remorseless, that it brought to mind something I had put away, the gaze of the father to whom I was not reconciled.

We were in the nursing home, a friend called Agatha and myself, with my father. Our visit was just coming to an end, and he sensed it. It had not gone badly, but it had not gone well either. Questions and answers: "Why won't you eat in the refectory with the other patients?" "I told you I won't and I told you why. Mohawks, nothing but Mohawks. When are you going back?" I said I would be returning to England in a day or two, but hoped to be back by Christmas. "Christmas Day, the loneliest day of my life." "But you wouldn't eat with the others and pull crackers and things." "I told you I wouldn't and I told you why. The loneliest day of my life." We edged out of that small room somehow, Agatha and I standing and he now standing in furious silhouette. We went down the corridor, and I knew that he followed. He caught up with us in a big room that was the concert room, as I imagined, as there was a baby piano, a guitar, and a mural of ballerinas in the sickliest purples. Dipping from a low white cord were birthday cards, all with the word "Grandpa" in every conceivable lettering and color. There was even one that twinkled on and off. How many hours' twinkling did it have left in it? I wondered. He had caught up with us, and he dragged one of the many chairs along the floor, scraping the stone slabs. He sat down and started to sing "Danny Boy." "The pipes, the pipes are calling..." He sang it right through, and there were tears in his eyes, and when he had finished, he looked up with a desperate, imploring expression. I knew that he wanted me to go across and throw my arms around him, and I wanted to, but I couldn't, and the solitude closed in around him in that cavernous room.

The foxes had left by June.

Wild Horses

Connemara had the worst frost and snows in many years. The gardener in the hotel said that the frost would burn the spring grass and "do" for the fuchsia bushes and the weed on the river. The river was glassy and frozen, except under the narrow bridge where the water squeezed its way with a whoosh and then fanned out into a dark, supple flow. From the overhanging fir trees the melting snow hung like panels of frayed lace, the little saplings a dainty gossamer. Connemara ponies were rolling and reveling in the snowed-on mountain grass.

Connemara is one of my favorite places, where the epithets of "wild, picturesque, and rugged" are still true and where visitors went to get a glimpse of both the "natives" and the leprechauns alighting on tufts of bog.

I had spent the previous night in Ballynahinch Hotel, where I found a small, leather-bound book with a vivid account, by the author Maria Edgeworth, of her visit there in 1834. Her companions were Sir Culling Smith, baronet and philanthropist, and his young wife, Isabella. They set out from Galway city, ignorant of the perils on the road ahead. They traveled in a fine barouche in which there were wells for holding writing-boxes, dressing boxes, and maps, except that the maps proved useless, as the roads stopped and there were no signs to guide them onward. Before long the rugged beauty ceased to impress them, and Sir Culling, though full of schemes and improvements for the Irish peasants, had to appeal to some of them, since the horses he had hired in Galway would go no farther. Out of nowhere men and young boys, "bog trotters," appeared, wild and excitable, speaking in a tongue that the visitors did not understand. With bare arms they seized the carriage, standing, then jumping from stone to stone, a giant of a man called Ulick lifting the ladies as he might a doll, then the men in their frieze coats, and lastly the horses, and setting them down on terra firma. Sir Culling's philanthropy did not, however, extend to meeting the bog trotters' demands of a shilling each for their labors. He thought sixpence was reasonable. They screamed, they cursed, they scolded, while the women, understandably unnerved, threw coins in their way, so that they could be safely escorted to Ballynahinch Castle.

At that time the castle was privately owned by Thomas Martin, and the visitors were somewhat surprised to find a stonework, barely whitewashed, a pigsty, and a dung heap adjoining the premises, rooms sparsely furnished, windows without curtains, windowpanes that rattled, and yet, as Miss Edgeworth said, the supper was such that the bon vivants of London would have blessed themselves with surprise—venison, salmon, lobster, oysters, and game, along with champagne and the finest wines from France.

I arrived late at night, the taxi going slowly up the winding avenue, where stones painted a stark white bordered the grassy verge. The castle was faintly lit, its walls and turrets taller than the tall trees that surrounded it. As I pushed the hall door in, I found a young man in his shirtsleeves, on a ladder, reciting to himself. It was Hamlet's soliloquy, with the "too, too solid flesh" and the "little month, or ere those shoes were old/With which [Gertrude] follow'd" his poor father's body. Turning, he saw me, suddenly stopped, got down, pulled his tie from inside his shirt, and pointing to the blue bucket and the wet, stringy mop, he said, somewhat abashed, "This is what I do," and introduced himself as the night watchman. I was led from the hall to the Hunt Room, where the fire that was laid for the morrow was soon crackling and wine and fruitcake set down before me. I was being entertained with more flowing passages, rapturous and melodramatic, so that it was not simply a room in Connemara with a picture of a boar hunt on the wall but a pavilion in France where Constance, wife of Geoffrey, is claiming that she is not mad but wishes to heaven she were, or with Margaret of Anjou, the she-wolf of France, leading her army in the Battle of Tewkesbury, or Thomas Jefferson's dialogue between head and heart. Soliloquies that he had memorized kept him company, as he mopped floors, cleaned teapots, polished shoes, and prepared the breakfast trays. He had, as he put it, his own little theater to while away the worst of the night.

Later we stood at the open door to look out. A navy-blue sky spanned the snowy fields, and the mountain peaks gleamed with a heavenly, an other-world splendor.

Now that Ireland had lost its mojo, what would become of her?

"Poetry," he said, with the crazed fervor of a mystic, poetry that Ireland had been the cradle of.

"'Tis there...'tis still there," he said, pointing to such staggering beauty, and it was difficult in those transcending moments to doubt him.

His name was John.

It was morning and I was setting out with the artist Dorothy Cross, who had agreed to come and photograph Drewsboro, enticed by my description of it. Mother Nature, according to my nephew Michael, was now supreme, briar, dock, ivy, nettle, and even little, scutty ash trees with tiny shoots making their way in the crevices of the mortar and the rotting window frames.

It was still vacant.

Dorothy was an artist who sometimes took photographs, and the one of her dog Louis was the loveliest and loneliest image of isolation and indecision that I had ever seen. Louis was on an empty track, under a blue sky, with bluer mountain behind, the pebbled seashore covered in a net of ragged green weed. Louis's head was turned sideways; he was unable to make up his mind whether to go backward or forward.

She had traveled the world, the Andes, Antarctica, Tahiti, where she worked with pearl farmers, and in Papua New Guinea she had heard the shark callers, the sorcerers of the sea. Her sculpture *Virgin Shroud* was the one that had made her known, a virgin covered with the skins of Friesian cows, their teats like the Crown of Thorns, sunk in the uddered head. In contrast, the virgin might have been setting out for a ball, draped as she was in satin and veiling that Dorothy had found in her grandmother's trunk. It was both primitive and ethereal. As a young girl in County Cork she had read something in the *Farmers Journal* that haunted her — *The darkest place in the world is the inside of a cow.* Her work sometimes drew criticism, but she laughed it off. One farmer was reported as saying that the silvered glass goblets she had affixed to some male apostles for a convent in Madrid were a ladylike version of a "fella's hard-on." Yet she was the one who had come back to live in Ireland and I was the one who had stayed away.

Now she was queen of five acres of land, which she had acquired through pure luck, having lost the lease on her studio in Dublin to one of the property sharks. She was driving along this isolated road in Connemara when she saw a handwritten sign that said FOR SALE and got out of the car. From the boot, filled with junk and scrap that she collected for her artworks, she took her lucky horseshoe and buried it in that ground, while an inquisitive cow looked on at her. The five acres circled a bay that opened into the rolling reaches of the Atlantic, stretching to the New World beyond, with small islands off the coasts of Galway and Clare, glimpsed through mist, like floating basins of meshed green.

For the first six months, while she waited for the planning permission to restore the house, she slept in a little tin hut by the water's edge, her protectors being her seventeenth-century Burmese Buddha, an otter who drank from a spring each morning, and the cow that had first stared at her and whom she named "Hairdo," because of the crown of its head being so frizzy. She had saved Hairdo many times from the slaughterhouse by doing favors for the local farmer, who naturally believed that good grass could be put to better use. Her one friend, after she moved there, was a man called Mickey, an old man whose hedges she clipped, Mickey holding the ladder, calling her "Mrs. Darlin," boasting that his cottage garden would surpass the Gardens of Babylon. She would visit him in the evenings, alone in his cottage by the fire, his long, thin fingers, as she said, like pincers on the crook of his stick, not lonely, not waiting for anything, not lamenting either, a hardy Connemara man who had traveled the world and had come back to settle on the western rim of it.

Because of the frost, the drive was hair-raising, the swerves sudden, as we skittered off the road many times, almost landing in one of the big Connaught lakes, whose waters, cold and choppy, swished over the edge. Dorothy talking, talking. Admittedly the view was beautiful, the snow on the mountain slopes shone with mineral brightness and their summits pinkish-gold, the way heaven is always depicted in holy pictures.

She was telling me the story of New Year's Eve in her mother's house in Cork, fireworks from one end of the city to the other, Louis going berserk, chewing her mother's duvet, then a bed jacket, then cloth slippers, and, finally, the cord that connected the telephone to the wall, mistakenly setting off the fire alarm, so that they saw in the new year in the company of six able, full-blooded Cork firemen.

The little towns that we drove through were coming awake: an upstairs blind being drawn; a woman hurrying along the towpath, carrying two mugs and a teapot; barrels of beer being rolled from the pavement down into a cellar.

I had known some of those places since my gallivanting days, towns with a river, a stone bridge, a church spire, and raincoats on hangers outside, draper's windows. Oughterard, with its waterfall, where on a day outing Carlo and Sasha, aged about twelve and thirteen, in some arcane ritual of courtship, had pelted their cousin Marian with stones and Sasha had left his new anorak on the riverbank. Galway city, where sixty-odd years ago I had gone with my sister Patsy to the annual races, wearing a hat so striking that it featured in the following day's newspaper. Although chronically short of money, I had bought a hat designed by a Signor Forte, a black organza that was to be worn affixed to the side of the head, like a flying saucer. It also caught the attention of some gallants who invited us to the crush bar, one becoming so enamored of my sister that he proposed to her, but next morning in the dining room, sullen and hung over, he had said, "Are you a nurse? Your face is familiar." Then it was Clarinbridge, famous for its oysters and where I had attended an oyster festival during my ostracized days. The bishop of Galway, Bishop Browne, so objected to my presence that at the gala dinner in the hotel in Eyre Square that night, I was put to sit alone at a side table, the young hotel manager mortified at having to do it.

But all was "changed, utterly changed."

The sway of the bishops and their clerics was no more. Two reports, the Ryan Report and the Murphy Report, had just been published, documenting in all their dark and mordant detail the systematic abuse over fifty years of children by priests,

Christian brothers, and nuns, in orphanages, laundries, novitiates, and schools. The countless revelations of beatings, hunger, chastisement, and ongoing sexual abuse were all the worse because they had been so sedulously denied with the collusion of Church and state. The anger was scalding and heartbreaking. At Easter Sunday, outside the Pro-Cathedral in Dublin, railings were draped with infants' shoes, tied in black ribbon, for all the lost childhoods, and messages on various placards revealed bitter life stories. One, referring to the millstone in Saint Luke's Gospel, read "Some Millstone. Some Neck. Jesus Wept." Another maintained that the Catholic religion was "A Nazi Religion." In the grounds of the Archbishop's House in Drumcondra, a man who had been on hunger strike for weeks carried what might have been his own obituary: "Beaten every day to make me a Catholic."

As the Rock of Rome foundered, so too did the fabled Celtic Tiger, going from boom to bust overnight, as it were, and now known as the Celtic Carcass. A debt-saddened landscape, the never-to-be-finished houses and housing estates, rain seeping into the concrete, were livid specters and reminders of the boastful years and the ignominious fall. Ireland was in belligerent mood. In a brazen orgy of greed, graft, recklessness, and perhaps defiance for being so long the sons of a race associated with hunger and privation, there had been a gargantuan spree of borrowing and more borrowing and building. The highfliers, with the tacit approval of politicians, had robbed the country, so that when the "financial haircut" happened, trillions were written off and millions more written down to one-tenth of their former fortune.

"'Tis karma, 'tis karma" was the current phrase, except that no one knew exactly what karma meant, just as no one knew why Ireland would have been saved if, as one pundit insisted, she had followed the fiscal policies of Maynard Keynes.

A contractor had driven his cement mixer up to the gates of Parliament, taken the keys, and then disappeared, while someone had hit on the novel idea of auctioning a BMW which had belonged to one of the banking ventriloquists, the stipulation being that it be crushed, which it was, with "a smash and a bash," in front of the television cameras and a baying crowd.

Ministers had to go with a begging bowl to Brussels, to be bailed out by the financial heavyweights known as the Troika, who were now hated and accused of injecting "poisons of austerity" into Irish life. Politicians were "affrighted," an election was called, and in letters to the paper people were urged to vote with revenge on the tips of their pens. One maverick candidate, who said he was "pure of all pastiche" and grew his own cannabis, swore that he would free Ireland from the contagion and rot of money.

On a bridge on our way, I had read a sign that told it all, GREED IS THE KNIFE—THE SCARS RUN DEEP.

We had gone from County Galway into County Clare. This was home. Instead of walls of loose stone, the briars, the bushes, and the hazels nuzzled together to make boundaries between fields, and roads that would have been grassy in summertime were untrodden and pearled over. Suddenly a scalding memory, as I recalled the previous morning in a bookshop in Dublin, where I read in *Saints, Scholars and Schizophrenics* by Nancy Scheper-Hughes about a sheep farmer in An Clochán who railed against my writing and said, with evident satisfaction, "They ran that woman out of County Clare."

Cattle stared from gateways, as they always had done, lonely figures waiting as if at the Gates of Purgatory, and the trees and the woods that had their equivalent in some or other of Yeats's poetry, still beautiful, still storm-struck, the light a palish gold, with a watery shimmer to it and Dorothy hoping it would stay like that, because she did not want Drewsboro to resemble Connecticut.

Michael was waiting for us at the gate, and for a moment, it seemed to me, I was hallucinating. In his enthusiasm for our arrival, he had removed the very things—the bramble, the ivy, the ash trees, the whole lyrical paraphernalia—which had made the idea of photographing the house so appealing to Dorothy. All the poetry had been forked away.

"I can pitch it all back," he said, a little crestfallen by my dismay, as I stared at the hall door, no longer bowered, its red paint chipped and faded, the house a little old hag, buckled and sinking back into the foundations.

Nothing for it but to go inside. Proudly he led us through the back door, which all these years he had believed to be locked, as once, on a previous visit, he had had to wedge me under the narrow gap of a window, calling as I wriggled through, "Are you in, are you in?" The kitchen had a weird, inhabited quality, dirty Delft on the table as if highwaymen had just passed through and had had a feed, and the little radio on the windowsill was still stuttering, its battery having expired long before. Then into the dining room, where indeed the walnut cabinet, scummed in dust, housed still another dead radio, which in times past was a matter of great pride to my parents, sitting in front of it, as they might sit in front of a blazing fire. There was one half of an orange curtain, like a theater prop, and some dead crows had fallen down the chimney. The presence of my mother was still weirdly in everything: in the crinkles of the orange curtain, in the coal scuttle where she hid bars of chocolate, and on the cushions of bawneen where she had embroidered old Celtic designs, thinking they would impress me. How hard she had fought to keep it all together.

Upstairs, a wardrobe door creaked open and shut, and propped against the wall in my father's old room was the oak headboard with the uneven patch, whitish from the graze of his head, from where again and again he would call down repeatedly, to be brought more tea. In a jumble of clothing, there were silk lampshades, a scroll with a papal blessing, consecrating the marriage of my brother and his wife, and a jovial jockey on high stilts, wearing a black hard hat.

The ivy, the mad ivy, had come in through the windows, and in some rooms the beds with their damp covers seemed to house corpses. More crows, but this was not Chekhov's *Seagull,* this was Drewsboro, in its dying throes.

I looked in the press where my brother had kept a tin of peaches that he had won in a music competition, only to find a mohair jumper crawling with moths. Across the landing, in my mother's room, the holy water font had a residue of dried salt which was bitter on the tongue. I sat on the edge of the bed. The wallpaper, painted over, was now a pale magnolia, yet I could just discern the dipping branches on which tiny pink rosebuds hung, so lifelike on their thin stalks that I used to believe they would bloom, like real roses on the briars.

Drewsboro House, winter 2012.

It was in that room that I slept with my mother and that each night we pressed the cold metal crucifix along our bodies and to our lips, reciting the prayer of Christ at Calvary; "They have pierced my hands and feet, they have numbered all my bones." We were all lonely in that house, lonely and sometimes at loggerheads. In an adjoining room, where my father slept, one night I heard the loud crackle of fire, the leaping gusts of flames, and running across, I saw a bamboo side table on fire and the blankets that were over him as he slept, oblivious of everything, also on fire. Without thinking, I opened the window and threw things out, and my mother, in her last reminiscing days, surprisingly told the nun in the hospital about this and other tribulations that had befallen us, as if there was nothing to be ashamed of anymore. All the time Dorothy moved around taking snaps, marveling at coming on so many strange and evocative things. The room was so cold that my breath sent a cloud of bluish vapor over the lens of her little camera, adding to the ghostliness that she was determined to capture. Suddenly a wren, busy and spry, a taunt to the dead crows, flew into that room and fluttered among the sad debris, delighting in its new surrounds. When it dashed its forehead against the windowpane, its little yellow legs crawling hither and thither, we tried in vain to catch it, but it eluded us. In the end, with the spikes of a broken umbrella that was on the heap, we steered it out into the hall, above the stairwell, then down to the lower hall, where curiosity—it can hardly have been instinct—caused it to alight on an old wedding bouquet of artificial white flowers that had rusted at the edges.

Since the fields were empty, Michael took advantage to drive his own horses in, a roan, a brown, and a dun that stood under the chestnut tree, its boughs a plump black suede in the winter light. From the youngest age, Michael loved horses, the feel of them, the smell of them, that and the company of horsemen, riding sidesaddle with his father, as he was brought all over the country on Sunday hunts. He recalled the tally-ho, the farmers in their scarlet jackets, the hounds baying to get going, the sound of the hunting horn so merry, Sundays like Christmas mornings. He went on to be a champion rider and took the world record for bareback jumping, so that their sideboard was stacked with cups, medals, and ribbons.

Before saying goodbye to Drewsboro and its ghosts, he decided that for Dorothy's benefit he should once again relate the story of Paddy's Gold, the horse, whose bizarre adventures had been the talk of the country.

My nephew Michael Blake competing at the Dublin Horse Show, 1981.

Paddy's Gold, sixteen hands in height, a gelding, with a white stripe on his face, belonged to Jack Malone, who lived up the mountains. Jack had Paddy well schooled in gymnastic tricks, taught him the many steps to take so as to get off the ground and the exact spring for a clear jump. It was for the Lunging Competition held in Ballinasloe each October. There, each horse was brought separately into a pen, held on a long rope, and had to clear a succession of jumps, which were a series of oil drums laid on a plinth of porter barrels, and raised higher and higher for the final round of ten horses.

Paddy's Gold had excelled himself, and though by rights he was the winner, the two judges, man and wife, deprived him of his laurels, as they intended to buy him. By coming third, his price had dropped. They believed they had a "superstar" in him and that the investment of three thousand eight hundred pounds would convert to a twenty-thousand-pound bonanza in a short time. He was to be collected from Michael's riding center in a matter of days.

The couple arrived, along with their cousin, a priest, and with the niceties over, lo and behold, they found that they had forgotten to bring their checkbook. The priest, much to their chagrin, offered to pay, saying they could refund him. Jack took the check and then brought out the obligatory luck penny of twenty pounds from the inside of his cap, which he spat on, before handing it over.

In less than a week, Michael had a phone call. They had been diddled. Paddy's Gold was being returned. Paddy's Gold was not playing ball, was not the "superstar" they had envisaged. Instead of clearing poles and barrels, he was knocking them down. Michael said it was doubtful that Jack would take the horse back, since it was, after all, a commercial venture and business was business. Jack was adamant. He did not want the horse back. "Paddly-Waddly" were his code words when any bit of contention arose. He was not for turning. It fell to Michael to ring the purchaser and suggest that they coax the horse, teach him a few tricks, and give him the impulsion to get off the ground.

"He's a no-good pup of a horse," the man said.

"He's evinced a dislike, has he, for the pair of ye?" Michael said.

"Evinced, my arse" was what he was told, with the blunt reminder that the horse was coming back.

As they did not know where Jack lived, neighbors were alerted and warned not to give Jack's whereabouts if a strange couple arrived, and not to take the horse in. Soon, a horse box attached to a jeep was to be seen making its several and unavailing journeys, as the owners tried to navigate narrow laneways and byways, called on farmers in fields and in hay sheds, only to be received gruffly and set upon with dogs. Often they had to drive backward, since the lanes were too narrow to turn the horse box around, and from behind ditches children jeered them.

Yet that same winter evening, when Michael returned from the chipboard factory where he worked, "dark night," as he put it, "and pouring rain," what does he hear but Paddy's snorting, and long breaths, game as ever. Paddy was installed. His face with the white stripe, bent over the half-door, waiting for his oats. Next morning, the check bounced. Jack was bucking, said they took him for a fool and had never meant to pay him at all. Stasis. Jack did not want the horse, the new owners did not want the horse, and the guards did not want to know. Michael rang the couple, repeating Jack's demand for a check to be reissued, and reminding them that he would be charging them the given weekly rate for the keep of the horse. Your man at the other end said, "Tough," and hung up. Proceedings began, and the letters between solicitors became more bilious by the week. Meanwhile, Paddy's Gold roams the fields happily, nuzzles and noses the other horses, consumes his half-bucket of crushed oats twice daily, and ruminates in his cushy stable at night.

The case took six months to reach the District Court in Birr, and the judge, citing it as "most bizarre," ruled that the couple must take back the horse and pay the three thousand eight hundred pounds that was owing. However, no allowance was made for the several hundred pounds it had cost Michael in the interim, and so began the second chapter of the saga.

"Lock up that horse" was the advice a guard gave him as they left the court, and both he and Jack began their offensive. Michael bought a

padlock so that Paddy's Gold could be locked in, as he worked during the day in the factory. Returning home again, in the proverbial dark night and pouring rain, he saw the new padlock was thrown over the cobbles and Paddy was gone. Jack and himself, as he put it, decided on the "physical route," the knuckle-dusters. They reckoned that in the coming October, Paddy's Gold would be entered in the Lunging Competition and they would get their pound of flesh.

There, on the fair green, on the sandy grass, exactly as they had envisaged it, among a hundred horses, was Paddy's Gold, now completely indifferent toward them, being led into the pen, head in the air, whence he sallied over all the hurdles in marveling leaps. When the time came for the last round, the crowd pressed against the wire mesh of the pen, watching every sensational second of it, Paddy's acumen, front legs tucked up to his belly, head and shoulders well down, flicking his back legs for the perfect scale of the jumps.

The climax then moves to the hubbub of the saloon, with all the necessary embellishments, cheers, swillings, sloshed porter, as the proud owner is held aloft on the shoulders of the ebullient well-wishers and made to drink from the silver cup that is filled with whiskey, little knowing that his nemesis lies in wait. His nemesis is a Serbian, nicknamed Doctor Zhivago, six foot six inches in height, who works in haulage and is hired for the occasion. Michael is nowhere to be seen, he is sitting in the getaway van. Jack, apparently meek, is on his own, drinking a lonely pint, regretful at having let Paddy go. And so the tension mounts, until the pivotal moment when the owner stumbles into the Gents. As he goes in, Doctor Zhivago follows, and Jack crosses to man the door and stop others from entering. The Gents was a small cubicle with a square sink and the one lavatory. In there the two men come face to face, like the protagonists in "Dangerous Dan McGrew."

"You owe somebody money—pay up," the owner was told, at which he drew a blank, and followed it with a compound of effings, and then started to roll his sleeves up for a fight, but instead he was seized and held upside down, his face immersed in a sink of cold water, while also being relieved of the wallet from his inside pocket. Loose change rolled along the tiled floor.

"We left town fast," Michael said, with bravado, reliving his enjoyment of the scene in the saloon, men bucking mad, vowing retribution, while they, the three buccaneers, fled with the booty.

We strolled over to where the horses stood, near-motionless, like circus apparitions. They started then to come toward us, lifting their high haughty heads in curiosity, and as we got nearer, the bay, sensing that I was a stranger, flicked and reflicked her mane, then reared up in the air, Michael following with a "Whoa . . . whoa" to bring her down. Her flanks glistened, her teeth were bared, and she exuded a warm, jerky breath, her eyes slithering in every direction. He said to stroke her, to make friends with her, but I balked.

"Go on," he said, and he took my hand and laid it on the nape of her neck, and I could feel her nerviness as I ran my fingers over the knob of bone and down along the face that was almost fleshless, down to the wide crater of the nostrils and the wet pink blubber of her mouth.

"You're doing great," he said, but my heart was going pitter-patter as I remembered horses of long ago, in the stables at night, crashing against their wooden partitions and whinnying to be let free, their pent-up energy so great, so wild, it was as if they would break the door down. The fear they instilled in my mother and me, inseparable from the fear of my father.

That evening, when we had dinner in a hotel in Galway, the large dining room was not nearly so full as it would have been a year or two before. A few young couples, out for the Friday

ke in somewhat muted tones, and the gusts of so
dle flames gave the impression of being in some
silica. As she looked down at the purplish sediment
eglass, Dorothy began to cry.

"When I cry, I have to cry three times," she said, and attempted a laugh to hide her embarrassment.

It had something to do with going back, forever the need to go back, the way animals do, the way elephants trudge thousands of miles to return to where the elephant whisperer has lived.

"We go back for the whisper," she said, the dreamed-of reconciliation.

Banquet

I went to see my first 3-D film. I donned the goggles, which were cumbersome on the bridge of the nose, and sat not knowing what to expect. Suddenly, after the credits, a grassy track is coming through my head and I almost scream. I try to avoid it, shrinking back into the seat, ducking down, but it keeps coming, it loops and forks just as in back roads long ago — memory and reality overlapping. Then there are pillars of jutting stone, a vast cave — as this is Werner Herzog's *Cave of Forgotten Dreams.* Pillars, carved beasts, horses, bison, rhinoceros are coming through me, into my eyes, into my mouth, and into my mind, just as in childhood, when nothing could be shut out. The figure of a man, Werner Herzog himself, literally appears to walk just above my shoulder, though not touching it, and then he steps onto a platform, wearing a helmet and holding a torch. Appearing in succession are nine or ten others similarly dressed. I want to leave, but these figures and jutting rock bar the way.

I think if I move to a different seat I could escape them, but to move at all is too alarming. I decide that the only thing to do is to stick it out, and gradually I tell myself to look, to see the wonders on the walls, crystal stalagmites that almost bristle and figures of man and beast, staring out from a distance of thirty thousand years. A woman walks out of a bulge in the stone wall, murmuring, murmuring — a crazed Cassandra or one of the mothers with the Doomsday tidings. It is in fact one of Werner's team of archaeologists at the edge of the screen, and she is about to fall off. I put my hand out to catch her.

Ovington Street garden, 2004.

Blessedly, there is a remission, and the film has moved to the outside of a cave somewhere in Germany. A man dressed in reindeer skins and reindeer fur stands on an incline, when suddenly his right boot aims all the way up to my forehead. He bends and picks up a wooden flute, plays a few notes of "The Star-Spangled Banner," and it is beautiful, more than beautiful to me who knows so little about music, and it allays the fears, long buried but just accidentally brought to life. I think that all I ever wanted was someone to whom I could tell my fears, and from it an imprisoned music would flow.

Soon after, we are in another cave, and Werner, in that soporific voice of his, which I know from having met him a few times, is telling a story. He points to two footprints on the floor, those of a man and a woman, and asks if the one is following the other in friendship or in assail. He then throws in the thought that since the interior of those caves has changed with time, the footprints may have occurred thousands of years apart from one another. A gasp escapes me. I don't want them to be thousands of years apart, this man and this woman, I want them to be together.

It was dusk when I came out onto the King's Road, the welter of evening time, the violet hour of *The Waste Land,* except that the sky was pewter and people were rushing in or out from the nearby supermarket. My mind was still full of those caves, unable to imagine the lives lived in them, no more than, when looking at a few stars, I could imagine the black reaches of space beyond. I took to the back streets that, after fifty years of living in London, I was beginning to be familiar with. I passed a terrace of small houses that in daylight I know to be pink and green and blue, the colors of confectionery, and then into a more secluded street, houses set back, some with louvered shutters. Once, on one of those streets, I had written a verse about looking through windows into rooms at evening, lamps, sofas, ottomans, books, and how I had wished to go inside those rooms, inside those lives, forgetting that someone might pass my window and see my red room and have an identical wish to be in it—but I did not allow for that, being "inextricably, caught up in my House of Blindness."

I passed the triangular green, with the bench where drunks sometimes sat and sometimes vomited. The windowsill of the pantry where I often bought cakes and fudge to send to a friend in New York was completely bare, except for a small teddy bear placed on a rack in the center.

Farther along, a woman stopped me and said she hoped I

wouldn't mind, but as we were fellow countrywomen, she would like to shake my hand. She was a retired nurse who also lived locally. In order to get out and about and not mope, as she put it, she had subscribed to walking tours all over London; they cost next to nothing and she met people, all sorts, including widowers who were slow to come to terms with their grief.

For no particular reason she began to tell me of a rich aunt she had in Dublin, her Aunt Geraldine, who lived in Foxrock. Every spring, faithfully, Aunt Geraldine invited her on a journey to the Burren to see the wildflowers that sprang up between the flags of limestone, the whole place pickled, yes, pickled, with flowers on thin stalks, white, speckled, and blue, the blue of the gentian the most fetching of all. She said what a marvel it was to set out in a pony and trap from a hotel in Lisdoonvarna, to be driven around, and then at intervals to get out and just look at that feast of color. "That blue," she said, as if it had melted into her. It was also the blue that I had seen in the interior of a mosque in Istanbul and the blue for the Reckitt's dye that our mothers and our grandmothers put in the tub of rinsing water to freshen the linen and give it a little tint. She said that the thing about those journeys in the pony and trap with Aunt Geraldine was that they stayed with one — the blue flowers, the seats cut into the rocks from the wild Atlantic waves, and always, along the shore a dog chasing a ball.

She remarked then on how often, in the sixties, she had seen me on those London streets, glamorous, long earrings, a patchwork suede coat, and what a life I must have lived. There were so many "me's": the me she had seen; the me that sat on a cushion in Antiquarius market with Isabella, the highland seer, her crystal ball wrapped in layer upon layer of cloth, like a mummy, waiting as I might before the oracle at Delphi; the me that never conquered the fear of swimming, though I had taken lessons in the public baths nearby, from a man who stood on a ledge holding a piece of rope to which I clung, him believing that we were winning even when we were not.

Before taking my leave of her, I mentioned that I had just seen *Cave of Forgotten Dreams.* "Aren't they fabulous?" she said. She had seen the film only yesterday. I said I felt sorry at hearing of footsteps, two humans, perhaps a thousand years apart from one another, never to meet. "It was not two humans, it was not a man and a woman, it was a wolf and a child," she said quietly, as if she did not want to offend me. Her words struck, like an arrow, and I realized that in there, in that dark chamber, the separate footprints of man and woman had revived in me a love so strong that, though it had not flourished, it had not died either, and so it lived on and on, in that dark suck of secrecy.

We were about to part, she saying that no doubt our paths would cross again and I saying I hoped so.

"But we live here now," she said.

"We do," I said, and it was as if the two countries warred and jostled and made friends, inside me, like the two halves of my warring self.

At home, I turned on all the lights, including the red lamp in the upstairs room, and it did not seem empty at all, it was full of light, like a room readying itself for a last banquet.

Acknowledgments

I was reluctant to write a memoir, but my agent, Ed Victor, was greatly enthusiastic and eventually managed to persuade me that I should do it. I mistakenly believed that it was going to be an easy journey. Andrew O'Hagan brought me to the house of Faber and the introduction to my editor, Lee Brackstone, who, with my American editor, Pat Strachan, ingeniously helped and encouraged me throughout. Help came from many and often unexpected quarters, including Sister Reparata, Ian McKellen, Louise Hardy, Graca Marquez, Nadia Proudian, Monique Henry, Carrie-Anne Brackstone, Emma Couper, Mary Morris, David McKittrick, John Horgan, Albert Kelly, Patsy McGarry, Des Lally, Patrick O'Flaherty, Dorothy Cross, and Roxy Beaujolais. While writing it, I read numerous memoirs, and the ones that spring to mind now are *Childhood, Boyhood, Youth* by Tolstoy; *Moments of Being* by Virginia Woolf; *Speak, Memory* by Vladimir Nabokov; *Germs* by Richard Wollheim; *Patrimony* by Philip Roth; *Chronicles* by Bob Dylan; *Father & I* by Carlo Gébler; *Memoirs from Beyond the Grave* by Chateaubriand; *Sleepless Nights* by Elizabeth Hardwick; *John Charles McQuaid* by John Cooney; *Remembering How We Stood* by John Ryan; *Head or Harp* by Lionel Fleming; *The Best of Patrick Campbell,* edited by Ulick O'Connor; *Downstart* by Brian Inglis; *The Magic Lantern* by Ingmar Bergman; *Making Sense of the Troubles* by David McKittrick; *Letters Home* by Sylvia Plath; *A Self-Portrait in Letters* by Anne Sexton; *Conversations with Elizabeth Bishop,* edited by George Monteiro; *A Memoir* by John McGahern; *Stepping Stones—Interviews with Seamus Heaney* by Dennis O'Driscoll; and *Bowen's Court* by Elizabeth Bowen. I fear that in the years of immersion I have forgotten some of the people and some of the books that were an inspiration to me. I should also add that the dramatis personae of my childhood provided the richest material of all, and so I owe a huge thanks both to the living and the dead.

Copyright Acknowledgments

Illustration Credits

About the Author

EDNA O'BRIEN, author of *The Country Girls Trilogy, A Fanatic Heart, The Light of Evening, Saints and Sinners,* and other widely acclaimed books, is a recipient of the Ulysses Medal, the 2011 Frank O'Connor Short Story Award, the *Los Angeles Times* Book Prize, the National Arts Club Gold Medal, and the Irish PEN Lifetime Achievement Award, and is an honorary member of the American Academy of Arts and Letters. *Country Girl* received the Argosy Irish Nonfiction Book of the Year from the Irish Book Awards. Born and raised in the west of Ireland, O'Brien has lived in London for many years.